MEDIUMISTIC NOVEL

THE DEATH OF THE PLANET

DICTATED BY THE SPIRIT

JOHN WILMONT EARL OF ROCHESTER

VERA KRYZHANOVSKAIA

Adapted to English language by
Nadya Soto –Lima, Peru
December 2023

Translated from the Portuguese versión.
Title in Portuguese:
"A morte do planeta"
© Vera Kryzhanovskaia

World Spiritist Institute
Houston, Texas, USA
E–mail: contact@worldspiritistinstitute.org

About the Medium

Vera Ivanovna Kryzhanovskaia, (Warsaw, July 14, 1861 - Tallinn, December 29, 1924), was a Russian psychographer medium. Between 1885 and 1917 she psychographed a hundred novels and short stories signed by the spirit of Rochester, believed by some to be John Wilmot, second Earl of Rochester. Among the best known are "The Pharaoh Mernephtah" and "The Iron Chancellor."

In addition to historical novels, in parallel the medium psychographed works with "occult-cosmological themes." E. V. Kharitonov, in his research essay, considered her the first woman representative of science fiction literature. During the fashion for occultism and esotericism, with the recent scientific discoveries and psychic experiences of European spiritualist circles, she attracted readers from the Russian "Silver Age" high society and the middle class in newspapers and press. Although he began along spiritualist lines, organizing séances in St. Petersburg, he later gravitated toward theosophical doctrines.

Her father died when Vera was just ten years old, which left the family in a difficult situation. In 1872 Vera was taken in by an educational charity for noble girls in St. Petersburg as a scholar, St. Catherine's School. However, the young girl's frail health and financial difficulties prevented her from completing the course. In 1877 she was discharged and completed her education at home.

During this period, the spirit of the English poet JW Rochester (1647-1680), taking advantage of the young woman's mediumistic gifts, materialized, and proposed that she dedicate herself body and soul to the service of the Good and write under his direction. After this contact with the person who became her spiritual guide, Vera was cured of chronic tuberculosis, a serious illness at the time, without medical interference.

At the age of 18, he began to work in psychography. In 1880, on a trip to France, he successfully participated in a mediumistic séance. At that time, his contemporaries were surprised by his productivity, despite his poor health. His séances were attended at that time by famous European mediums, as well as by Prince Nicholas, the future Tsar Nicholas II of Russia.

In 1886, in Paris, her first work was made public, the historical novel "Episode of the life of Tiberius", published in French, (as well as her first works), in which the tendency for mystical themes was already noticeable. It is believed that the medium was influenced by the Spiritist Doctrine of Allan Kardec, the Theosophy of Helena Blavatsky, and the Occultism of Papus.

During this period of temporary residence in Paris, Vera psychographed a series of historical novels, such as "The Pharaoh Mernephtah", "The Abbey of the Benedictines", "The Romance of a Queen", "The Iron Chancellor of Ancient Egypt", "Herculaneum", "The Sign of Victory", "The Night of Saint Bartholomew", among others, which attracted public attention not only for the captivating themes, but also for the exciting plots. For the novel "The Iron Chancellor of Ancient Egypt," the French Academy of Sciences awarded him the title of "Officer of the French Academy," and in 1907, the Russian Academy of Sciences awarded him the "Honorable Mention" for the novel "Czech Luminaries."

About the Spiritual Author

John Wilmot, Earl of Rochester was born on April 1 or 10, 1647 (there is no record of the exact date). The son of Henry Wilmot and Anne (widow of Sir. Francis Henry Lee), Rochester resembled his father in physique and temperament, domineering and proud. Henry Wilmot had received the title of Earl because of his efforts to raise money in Germany to help King Charles I regain the throne after he was forced to leave England.

When his father died, Rochester was 11 years old and inherited the title of Earl, little inheritance, and honors.

Young J.W. Rochester grew up in Ditchley among drunkenness, theatrical intrigues, artificial friendships with professional poets, lust, brothels in Whetstone Park and the friendship of the king, whom he despised.

He had a vast culture, for the time: he mastered Latin and Greek, knew the classics, French and Italian, was the author of satirical poetry, highly appreciated in his time.

In 1661, at the age of 14, he left Wadham College, Oxford, with the degree of Master of Arts. He then left for the continent (France and Italy) and became an interesting figure: tall, slim, attractive, intelligent, charming, brilliant, subtle, educated, and modest, ideal characteristics to conquer the frivolous society of his time.

When he was not yet 20 years old, in January 1667, he married Elizabeth Mallet. Ten months later, drinking began to affect his character. He had four sons with Elizabeth and a daughter, in 1677, with the actress Elizabeth Barry.

Living the most different experiences, from fighting the Dutch navy on the high seas to being involved in crimes of death, Rochester's life followed paths of madness, sexual abuse, alcoholics, and charlatanism, in a period in which he acted as a "physician."

When Rochester was 30 years old, he writes to a former fellow adventurer that he was nearly blind, lame, and with little chance of ever seeing London again.

Quickly recovering, Rochester returns to London. Shortly thereafter, in agony, he set out on his last adventure: he called the curate Gilbert Burnet and dictated his recollections to him. In his last reflections, Rochester acknowledged having lived a wicked life, the end of which came slowly and painfully to him because of the venereal diseases that dominated him.

Earl of Rochester died on July 26, 1680. In the state of spirit, Rochester received the mission to work for the propagation of Spiritualism. After 200 years, through the medium Vera Kryzhanovskaia, the automatism that characterized her made her hand trace words with dizzying speed and total unconsciousness of ideas. The narratives that were dictated to her denote a wide knowledge of ancestral life and customs and provide in their details such a local stamp and historical truth that the reader finds it hard not to recognize their authenticity. Rochester proves to dictate his historical-literary production, testifying that life unfolds to infinity in his indelible marks of spiritual memory, towards the light and the way of God. It seems impossible for a historian, however erudite, to study, simultaneously and in depth, times and environments as different as the Assyrian, Egyptian, Greek and Roman civilizations; as well as customs as dissimilar as those of the France of Louis XI to those of the Renaissance.

The subject matter of Rochester's work begins in Pharaonic Egypt, passes through Greco-Roman antiquity and the Middle Ages, and continues into the 19th century. In his novels, reality navigates in a fantastic current, in which the imaginary surpasses the limits of verisimilitude, making natural phenomena that oral tradition has taken care to perpetuate as supernatural.

Rochester's referential is full of content about customs, laws, ancestral mysteries and unfathomable facts of History, under a novelistic layer, where social and psychological aspects pass through the sensitive filter of his great imagination. Rochester's genre classification is hampered by his expansion into several categories: gothic horror with romance, family sagas, adventure and forays into the fantastic.

The number of editions of Rochester's works, spread over countless countries, is so large that it is not possible to have an idea of their magnitude, especially considering that, according to researchers, many of these works are unknown to the general public.

Several lovers of Rochester's novels carried out (and perhaps do carry out) searches in libraries in various countries, especially in Russia, to locate still unknown works. This can be seen in the prefaces transcribed in several works. Many of these works are finally available in English thanks to the *World Spiritist Institute.*

Contents

CHAPTER I 9

CHAPTER II 25

CHAPTER III 40

CHAPTER IV 61

CHAPTER V 81

CHAPTER VI 99

CHAPTER VII 123

CHAPTER VIII 148

CHAPTER IX 171

CHAPTER X 193

CHAPTER XI 209

CHAPTER XII 225

CHAPTER XIII 239

CHAPTER XIV 257

CHAPTER XV 276

CHAPTER XVI 293

CHAPTER XVII 309

CHAPTER XVIII 324

CHAPTER XIX 351

CHAPTER XX 370

CHAPTER I

Beneath the rocky massif of the ancient pyramid of consecration, lies the unknown, and forever inaccessible to ordinary mortals, underground world. There survives what remains of Ancient Egypt, hiding there the treasures of its mighty science, which remains involved in mystery, protected from the curious eyes, just as it was in those times when the people of Kemi still revered their Hierophants, while the Pharaohs went out in ostentation to war against their neighbors. The Hierophants and the Pharaohs gradually rested in their underground tombs; time, which destroys everything, continued to dethrone and transform the ancient civilization. Other people and other beliefs began to emerge in Egypt and no one has ever suspected that a whole phalanx of mysterious people - who lived many centuries before, when the marvelous works, whose ruins provoke admiration, began to appear - continue to live in the fantastic shelter, faithfully preserving their costumes, traditions, and rites of the faith in which they were born.

Along a long underground canal, which extended from the Giza sphinx to the pyramid, glided silently a boat with a golden bow, adorned with lotus flowers, A dark complexioned Egyptian who looked as if he had just descended alive from an ancient fresco, rowed slowly, Two men, dressed in robes of Grail knights, stood on the boat, contemplated the wide open halls on both sides of the canal, where mysterious sages could be seen leaning over work tables.

When the boat docked next to stairs of only a few steps, the adventurers were met by a venerable old man dressed in a long white robe and Klafta, bearing an insignia on his chest and having three flashes of bright light under his forehead, indicating the importance of the magician's ancestry.

"Supramati! Dakhir! My dear brothers, welcome to our shelter. After so many earthly trials, come and recover your strength in a new work! Invigorate yourselves with new discoveries in the boundless field of absolute wisdom." And he added affectionately: "Let me embrace you all fraternally and introduce you to new friends." Some Hierophants approached and kissed the newcomers again. After a friendly conversation, the old magician said:

"Go, brothers, wash yourselves and rest before you are shown the places of your activities. And as soon as the first rays of Rá illuminate the horizon, we'll be waiting for you in the temple for the Divine Office, which will be performed, as you know, according to the rituals of our ancestors."

At the hierophant's signal, two young adepts who had been keeping to that moment a discreet distance from Aldo, approached and went to accompany the visitors. First crossing a long and narrow corridor, they went down a steep and cramped staircase that led to a door decorated with the head of the sphinx with blue bulbs in place of eyes. The door led to a round room with scientific and magical apparatus and instruments, in short, everything a laboratory of the initiated magician might need.

In this room, there were three doors, one of which led to a small room with a crystal bathtub, filled with clear blue water that was running down the wall. On the stools, the linen and striped robes were already ready. Two other doors led to completely identical rooms, with beds and furniture of carved wood and silk pillows; the furniture in the rooms, due to its unusual and unfamiliar style reproduced, apparently, the atmosphere of a legendary antique.

Next to the window, closed by a heavy curtain of blue fabric with designs and bangs, was a circular table and two chairs. A large carved chest next to the wall was, of course, intended to store clothing. On the wall shelves piled up rolls of ancient papyri.

First of all, Dakhir and Supramati took a bath. With the help of young adepts, they put on new linen robes with belts decorated with magic stones and put on the Klaftas and insignia, obtained by virtue of their rank. Then, in ancient garments, they became contemporary to that strange environment in which they found themselves.

"Come and call me, brother, whenever you need me," Supramati said to the adept, sitting down in the armchair by the window. Dakhir retired to his room, since they both felt an uncontrollable need to be alone. Their spirits were still oppressed by the weight of the last period of their lives on earth, but the longing for that, even if they had triumphed, invariably dragged them to one thought: their children and wives.

Letting out a sad sigh, Supramati leaned over the table; the young adept, before leaving, pulled back the curtain that hid the window. Supramati stood up, impressed by the extraordinary beauty and austerity of the spectacle: he had never seen something like that.

Before his eyes stretched the surface of a lake, smooth as a mirror; the still waters, sleepy and blue as sapphire, were crystal clear; and in the distance, he could see the white portico of a small temple, surrounded by trees with dark foliage that made it look black without being stirred by even the slightest breath of wind.

In front of the temple's entrance, over the stone altar, a great fire was burning, which, like a moonlight, diffused its lights far away, enveloping, like a silvery mist, the dormant nature, attenuating its contrasts of outline.

But where is the firmament of this fantastic picture of nature? Supramati raised his eyes and saw that somewhere nearby, above, lost in the gray darkness, a violet cupule opened. Supramati's amazement was interrupted by Dakhir, who had admired the same picture from his window and had come to share his discovery with his friend, not knowing that he was already enjoying the fascinating sight.

"How wonderful! placidly asleep! How many new and as yet unimagined mysteries to study," Dakhir remarked as he sat down.

Supramati didn't have time to reply, surprised by a new phenomenon that had occurred, both of them let out an expression of admiration. From the dome shone a great beam of golden and brilliant light, illuminating everything around... Sunlight without the sun? They had no idea where this golden light came from, and how it entered there.

A few moments later, his ears picked up the sounds of a remote, powerful, and harmonic chant.

"It must not be a chant of the spheres, but of human voices," remarked Dakhir. "Look there are our companions. They are coming for us in a boat. Didn't you notice that in your room there is an exit to the lake?" he added, getting up and going with the other to the exit door.

Like an arrow, the boat glided across the lake, coming to a stop at the steps of a miniature Egyptian temple. A mysterious community was gathered there; men in ancient costumes, with austere and concentrated countenances; women, dressed in white, with golden hoops on their heads, were singing to the accompaniment of harps.

The strange and powerful melodies resounded under the vaults and the air was impregnated with a soft aroma. The scene deeply impressed Supramati and his friend.

Here, time was also shifted by a thousand years; it was a live vision of the past, a gift that was given to them to participate in it by virtue of a strange event in their extraordinary existence.

As soon as the last sound of the sacrificial hymn was silenced, the people present formed two rows and, together with the superior, headed through an arched gallery to the room where the morning breakfast was already waiting for them.

It was simple but very substantial for the initiated. It consisted of dark rolls that melted in the mouth, vegetables, honey, wine, and a white, thick, and sparkling drink, which was not heavy cream but seemed like a lot.

Dakhir and Supramati were hungry and honored the food. Noticing that the supreme hierophant, next to whom they were both seated, was looking at them, Dakhir remarked somewhat uncomfortably:

"Isn't it a shame, master, that magicians have such an appetite?" The old man smiled.

"Eat, eat my children! Your bodies are exhausted due to the contact with the human mass that has sucked all the vital force out of you. Here, in the peace of our retreat, this will be overcome. The food we take from the atmosphere is pure and fortifying; its components are suitable for our way of life. Eating is no sin, because the body, despite being the body of an immortal, needs nourishment."

After breakfast, the supreme hierophant introduced the visitors to all the members of the community.

"First of all, take a rest, my friends," he remarked as he said goodbye. "For about two weeks you'll devote your time to getting to know our shelter, filled with historical and scientific treasures; besides this, you'll meet many interesting people among us, with whom you'll be delighted to talk. Later, together we'll plan your tasks: not those concerning Ebramar, but others with which you'll have to familiarize yourselves."

After thanking the supreme hierophant, Supramati and Dakhir went to their new friends and had a lively conversation with them. Shorty afterwards, the members of the community dispersed, each one going about their matters until the next breakfast hour.

Only one of the magicians remained, and he proposed to the visitors to show them the place and some of the collections of antiquities stored there. Walking around the place and the examination of the collections aroused a deep interest in Supramati and Dakhir. The guide's account of the origin of the pyramid, the Sphinx, and the temple, buried beneath the earth in the time of the first dynasties, opened to them the far horizons of the origin of Humanity.

And when some valuable object of 20-30 thousand years or a sheet of metal with inscriptions illustrating the narration, they were involuntarily overcome by a respectful tremor of admiration, even though they had long been gifted with knowledge of antiquity.

After dinner, Supramati and Dakhir retired to their rooms, each feeling the need to be alone. Their spirits were still suffering the consequences of the rupture of the carnal bonds that had bound them for a few years to life as mortal humans.

Sitting up, with his head lowered in his hands, Dakhir was sad and thoughtful. He could feel the thought coming to him of Edith, and the longing tormented him. Until then he had not been aware of how much he had attached himself to those two beings, who passed quickly through his long, strange, laborious, and lonely existence, in the resemblance of warm rays and the life giving sun.

This bond proved to be very strong and couldn't be broken at will. He had touched the heartstrings, and they now vibrated in two directions like an electrified wire. So, the exchange of thoughts and feelings didn't cease. Just as waves crash against the shore, reciprocal thoughts resonate on both sides.

Dakhir felt Edith's pain; and Edith, even if she wanted to, couldn't master the powerful feeling that invaded her entire being and stifled the excruciating pain of separation from her beloved.

Ebramar, who could study the human heart - and even that of a magician - so well, when he said goodbye to Dakhir said that, although time and busyness couldn't calm the painful longing of the spirit, he could see Edith with the child in the magic mirror and talk to his wife. Now, remembering those words. He hurried off to the laboratory.

Approaching a large magic mirror, Dakhir pronounced the formulas and drew kabbalistic signs. What was expected occurred: the surface of the instrument shuffled, sparks filled, the mist dissipated, and as if through a large window he saw before him the interior of one of the rooms of the Himalayan palace, where the sisters of the sisterhood lived.

It was a large and luxuriously decorated room; at the back, next to the bed with muslin curtains, could be seen two cribs finished in silk and lace. In front of the niche, at the bottom of which was a cross, topped by a golden chalice of the knights of the grail, was Edith in a genuflected position. She was wearing a long white robe - a sisters' garment - and her wonderful loose hair wrapped around her like a silk cloak.

Edith's beautiful features were pale and covered with tears: before her spiritual vision hovered over the image of Dakhir. Nevertheless, it was clear that she was fighting against this weakness, looking to prayer for support to fill the void that had formed with the left of her loved one.

Love filled her whole being; however, this feeling was pure, as pure was Edith's soul; there wasn't the slightest shadow of lust in her, only the desire to see, even once in a while, the beloved, to hear in the silence of the night his voice and to know what he thought of her and the child.

A deep rush of affection and compassion came over Dakhir:

"Edith," he whispered,

As faint as this whisper was, the young woman's spiritual hearing had received it; she shuddered and stood up, feeling the presence of her loved one.

At the same instant, she saw a band of light formed by the magic mirror that she already knew, and in it, the image of Dakhir, smiling at her and greeting her with his hand.

Letting out a scream. Edith ran up and held out her hand, but suddenly blushed and stopped in embarrassment.

"My thoughts have attracted you, Dakhir, I may have interrupted your important business. Oh, forgive my dear, my incurable weakness. During the day, I work and still manage, somehow, to face the tearful longing for you. I miss you like the air I breathe and I have the distinct impression that with you a part of my being has remained, and I suffer because of this open wound. Everyone here is kind to me. I'm studying a new science that reveals wonders to me, but nothing makes me happier. Forgive me for being weak and unworthy of you."

"I have nothing to forgive you, my good and gentle Edith. Like you, I suffer because of our separation, but we must obey the immutable law of our strange destiny, which obliges us to move forward... In time, the tension of this nostalgia will pass and you'll end up thinking of me with a peaceful feeling until our ultimate reunification. Today I came to your presence to give you good news. Ebramar has let me see you once a day; and at these quiet hours, I will visit you and the child. We'll talk, and I'll guide you, teach you and calm you, knowing that I'm at your side, you'll suffer less because of separation."

As he spoke, Edith's charming face changed completely. Her thin cheeks became flushed, her big eyes radiated happiness, and her voice denoted joy.

"Oh, Ebramar's goodness is infinite! How can I express my gratitude to him for this grace that brings back cheerfulness and happiness? Now I will always be able to live from one meeting to the next, and these moments will be the reward for my daily work. You'll explain to me that which I have difficulty understanding and your fluid explanations will calm my rebellious heart..."

Suddenly she became silent and ran towards one of the nurseries, and taking a little girl out of it, she showed her to Dakhir.

"Look how beautiful she's becoming and how much she looks like you, she has your eyes and your smile. What would I do without this treasure? - she added happily, clapsing the child passionately to her chest."

The little girl woke up, without crying afterward, and, smiling as she recognized her father, held out her arms to him. Dakhir sent her a kiss through the air.

"This little girl turns out to be a magician," Dakhir said, smiling. "You say she looks like me? She's your portrait."

When Edith laid the child down, who soon fell asleep, Dakhir asked:

"How is Airavala? I think that tomorrow Supramati will want to visit his son."

"That will be great because he's very sad and only cheers up once in a while when he sees his mother; he even calls her by name and extends his arms. Poor little magician!"

After talking for about an hour, Dakhir remarked:

"It's time for you to lie down and sleep, dear Edith. Now that you have seen me and know that we'll meet again soon, I'm sure you'll calm down and the sleep will strengthen you."

"Ah, how quickly time has passed!" sighed Edith. "I'm going to bed," she added, going obediently to the bed, "but don't leave before I fall asleep."

Dakhir burst out laughing and stood by her magic window; when she lay down, he raised his hand, and through his fingers streamed an azure light that enveped Edith like a radiant veil.

When the light went out and the mist had dissipated, the young girl was sleeping a deep and sound sleep.

While this was going on in Dakhir's room, Supramati was lying in bed, reflecting on the past. It had been a long time since his spirit had been so troubled by the weight of the fateful destiny that allowed him to love something and then take it away from him.

Standing up, he sat down at the table and began to put in order old sheets of papyrus, to be examined later, given to him in the morning by his companion as extremely interesting documents. As usual, he wanted to dispel his unpleasant thoughts with this work.

As soon as he had started to read the first few lines, he suddenly shuddered and twitched: his sharp hearing detected a faint noise like the rustling of wings beating against something. Then, he heard a trembling sound, poignant and pitiful, like a restrained cry.

Olga, she's looking for me! thought Supramati, standing up. Poor thing! Affliction is blinding her and imperfection puts a wall between us!

He took his magic stick and spun it around for about a minute in the air, and then drew a circle of igneous lines on the ground; then he made a gesture as if he were dispelling the atmosphere with the stick, and above the circle, a shaft of light formed; the transparent blue space that could be seen in it seemed to be surrounded by a gelatinous gas, which trembled and crackled.

Now, in the middle of the circle, hovered a gray human shadow that was rapidly becoming more embodied and acquiring a determined shape and color.

It was Olga. On her lovely face, the expression of melancholy and misfortune seemed to have frozen, and her eyes, expressing fear and, at the same time, clear happiness, aimed at the one who for her was an earthly god. Beaming from Supramati, great streams of light and heat were absorbed by the transparent body of the vision, giving it a living form and exuberant beauty. The blazing flame above the forehead illuminated the features of the face and the vast golden hair. At last, the vision took on the aspect of a living woman, and Olga, looking beseeching, held out her clasped hands to Supramati, who looked at her with affectionate and tenderness.

"Olga, Olga! Where are your promises to be brave and strong, to work and improve yourself through earthly trials? You're wandering sadly in space like a suffering spirit, filling the air with your moans. You're a magician's wife! Don't forget, my poor Olga, you still have a lot of work ahead of you. You will have to enrich your intellect and develop your forces and spiritual capacities so that I receive the right to take you to the new world, where destiny is dragging me."

Her tone of voice was slightly stern and Olga's face took on the frightened and embarrassed expression of a child who has done something wrong.

"Forgive my weakness, Supramati; it's so hard to stay away from you, aware of the obstacles that prevent me from getting closer."

"As you perfect yourself, the obstacles will diminish until they disappear completely. I have already told you that you'll have to purify yourself and work in space. In the earthly atmosphere, full of suffering and crime. There will always be plenty of work for a well-meaning spirit."

"Oh, I'm full of good intentions. Send me to earth in a new body for any trial, no matter how painful, and I'll submissively endure all sufferings and any privations because I want to be worthy to follow you; and finally, you'll be able to forget, at least for a while, that happiness I was able to enjoy."

Her lips trembled and tears choked her. Supramati stooped down and said affectionately:

"Don't be upset, my dear! I have not the least intention of reproaching you for the infinite love you have for me, because it is extremely dear to me and I love you: but you can't let it overpower you. Be sure that I will never lose sight of you and will watch over you during your earthly trials, but you must take advantage of and perfect your moral and intellectual powers, and you have plenty of these because you are my disciple. Use the powers and the knowledge which I have transmitted to you to help people; find among them those whom you can guide towards the good and try to prove to them the immortality of the soul and the responsibility of each one for his or her aros; study the fluidic laws which will allow you to protect and help your mortal brothers."

Then Supramati opened a box, took out a piece of some kind of phosphorescent mass, made a little ball out of it, and gave it to the spirit.

"And now, look at me. I'm here, you haven't lost me. Our spirits are communicating, and with the help of this little ball, you can reach me: but only if you use your time with dignity for work and study, and not for senseless whining."

Denoting joy and candor, Olga took the little ball. Raising her big and radiant eyes to Supramati, with a bewildered smile, she whispered timidly:

"I will fulfill everything you said; I will find a medium to work with and not complain; just give me a kiss so I can be sure you aren't angry that the magician's wife is wandering around like a beggar, around the lost paradise."

Supramati, unable to contain a laugh, pulled her to himself and kissed her lips and her head of blond hair.

"And now, my incorrigible troublemaker, go and keep your promises. I bless you. And if you need my help, call me in thought, and my answer will be in the form of a warm, life-giving current."

He made a few passes and the spirit quickly disembodied, became transparent, and like a mist, disappeared into the ether.

Supramati sat down pushing the pages aside and leaning over the table began to think. A hand on his shoulder brought him out of his thoughts, and raising his head he met Dakhir's affectionate gaze.

"Olga was here. Poor thing! The separation is too heavy for her: but I think her strong love will help her in her trials, lifting her up to you."

Then he told about his meeting with Edith and added:

"Come tomorrow when I go to talk to Edith. Airavala is very sad according to her; he will be very happy to see you.

The poor child was suddenly taken away from his father and mother."

They both sighed. Who knows if they will not awaken in the depths of the mages' spirits the feelings that afflict ordinary mortals?

CHAPTER II

They used the time of their relaxation to learn more about the extraordinary place where they were and to appreciate the impressive collections stored there.

At night, when the enigmatic window to Edith's room opened in Dakhir's room, Supramati also went to talk to the young woman and take a look at his son. The joy of the child, who impatiently held out his arms to him, and his frustration at not being able to reach his father, produced feelings of happiness and bitterness in Supramati's heart.

Among the new acquaintances, they became particulary fond of two. The first was a magician, carrying a single torch, a handsome young man with a thoughtful face and in the glow of his years. His name was Cleofas.

During the examination of ancient collections, among which were maquettes of monuments, known or not, but outstanding for their architecture and ornamentation, a magnificent work of a temple in Greek style caught Supramati's attention.

"It's the Temple of Serapis in Alexandria and the model is of my authorship," Cleofas explained, and, with a heavy sigh, he added: "I was a priest of Serapis and witness to the savage destruction of that architectural work, sanctified by the prayers of thousands of people."

Dakhir and Supramati restricted themselves to shaking hands with him sympathetically, and in the evening, when the three of them gathered in Cleofas' room to talk, Supramati asked if it wasn't painful to tell about the past.

"On the contrary," answered Cleofas, smiling. "It gives me pleasure to relive with my friends that remote past that no longer afflicts me."

And after a moment's reflection, he began to speak:

"I was born just at the time of the decline of our old religion. The new faith of the Great Prophet of Nazareth dominated the world. However, the eternal truth of light and love, propagated by the God-man, was already distorted, having acquired such ferocity and brutal fanaticism that even the Son of God, in his humility and mercy, would have severely censured it.

But I, in that confusing time of conflict, didn't realize it, being an ardent adherent of Serapis, just as the others were of Christ. I hated the Christians as much as they hated us.

Yes, my friends, the story of Osiris, killed by Typhon, who then scattered the bloody remains of the god of light over the face of the Earth, is as old as the world and will remain alive until the end of time. Don't men dispute among themselves the unacknowledged Creator of the Universe and the unique truth that comes from Him, innocently imagining that they can enclose Him exclusively in their belief, and to the detriment of all others? Their fratricidal hatred and the religious wars - is this not the spreading of the bloody remains of Divinity? Nevertheless, I will tell you about myself.

Being the son of the High Priest, I grew up in the temple and from childhood served God. Those were difficult times. We, the so-called pagan priests, were already despised, hated, and persecuted. Just the thought that our sanctuaries were being destroyed - and this would also be the fate of the temple of Serapis, drove me insane with despair. And the terrible day arrived..."

Cleofas was silent for a moment and then pointed to an ivory statuette that rested on a small column next to the bed:

"Contemplate, my friends, the miniature statue of God. It may give you a rough idea of the ideal beauty and truly divine expression that a brilliant artist will achieve to give to these features. Of course, you can understand what I felt when the sacrilegious hand of a fanatic raised the axe to break this incomparable work of art as if he were going to cut a cheap piece of wood.

Many of our priests were murdered that day, while I escaped by some miracle or fate. Seriously wounded, I was taken by my companions to the house of a friend of my father, a wise man, who lived retired on the outskirts of the city.

There I recovered and healed, and in time I became aware of the terrible reality: the temple of Serapis, razed to the ground, no longer existed. I won't try to describe to you the despair that fell over me.

At first, I was making plans for revenge; but later, realizing the impracticality, I fell into a deep depression and decided to commit suicide. One night I went to my protector and begged him to give me poison.

"Now that I can't serve God...except to watch the insults and humiliations of all that I loved, I prefer to die"

The old man listened to me in silence. Then he took a cup from the cupboard and poured into it a few drops of a burning liquid. Then he extended the cup to me and, with an enigmatic smile, and said: "Drink and die for all that has already been destroyed; reborn to venerate and serve the Divinity of your faith..."

"I drank it and fell down dead. When I came to myself, I was already here, living full of energy, surrounded by peace, silence, and new friends, with great possibilities to study and solve the immense and terrible problems that surround us. I have lived like this for centuries, absorbed in work, even forgetting that somewhere there's still another world, in which ephemeral humanity is born and dies..."

The other adept, with whom Dakhir and Supramati established a close relationship, was also a very unusual type of man, in the vigor of his years, with a copper red face, and big, dark black eyes like pitch.

His name was Tlavat, and the story of his life caused a deep impression on the listeners... They contemplated, almost with a feeling of superstition, that semi-legendary creature, a living representative of the mighty red race of the Atlanteans, whose feet stepped upon the soil of what was left of the immense continent which has remained in memory under the name of the island of Poseidon.

They agreed to always meet in the evening to talk, after their daily activities, taking turns in their rooms at each meeting.

The conversation with Tlavat was extremely interesting. The story of the vanished continent, told by a living witness of that fabulous past, acquired a new vitality.

The Atlantean's dark eyes shone passionately while he described the terrible catastrophes that had devastated his continent; facts that he hadn't personally witnessed, but the remembrances of which were vivid and clear in the memory of his contemporaries.

Tlavat described, with a touch of ethnic pride, the city of the golden gates, the capital of the great nation now vanished in time, but which left maps, visions, and detailed descriptions in the sanctuary where Tlavat was initiated, and with whose priests he migrated to Egypt before the geological upheaval, predicted by the Illuminati, which sank the island of Poseidon.

Of course, the main point of interest was the history of primitive Egypt, the pyramids they inhabited, the Sphinx, and the temple buried by the sands. According to Tavat's calculations, these monuments, erected by the initiates who emigrated from Atlantis, were at least twenty thousand years old. The same emigrants had built the underground world where they now lived, concentrating there on the realization of the consecrations and there they fabricated the powerful talismans to protect themselves from the cosmic cataclysms.

The time of rest passed quickly and one morning, after the prayer in the temple, the Grail Knights were invited to speak with the supreme Hierophant.

"I have called you here, my sons, to establish together the program of your work. You have already learned much.

On the road we have traveled, the field of knowledge that remains to us is practically unlimited. I propose that you devote yourselves to the study of the space of our solar system, which you don't know. In the same way, you'll have the opportunity to study the Planetary chain and the influence of the planets, visible or not, that surround our Earth both physically and psychologically. At the same time, you'll learn about the particularities of the cosmic laws that govern our system.

This "geography" of space, accessible to us, represents a great interest and will open unexpected horizons, a new field of the infinite and immeasurable wisdom of the Supreme Being."

Dakhir and Supramati agreed to submit to their guide's decision and, upon receiving the first instructions along with the necessary material, began their work the same day, with the passion that characterizes them.

To a simple mortal, time is a burden of regrets and failures of the past, great worries of the present, and boredom and uncertainty of the future. Peace and quiet, so precious to the wise, seem tedious to an imperfect and empty-headed being, for whom time is a cruel tyrant if not filled with torrid entertainments, intrigues, and unsatisfied passions.

And this whirlwind of mutual hostility, petty envy, and wild desires is swept through the microcosm, called the human organism, in a way that is no less destructive than the earthquakes that shake the physical world.

Through our veins run, in the purple ocean of blood, thousands of little worlds, in which are reflected the storms of the human heart, transmitting instincts, passions, and desires. If only the clairvoyant eye of man could see the devastation caused by a moral storm of his soul, by a fit of rage! There, in that rebellious blood, cosmic catastrophes take place; millions of cells and corpuscles die, drowned, and burned, and the contagious remains of these dead microscopic organisms are thrown into the aura, while man, exhausted by the internal tremors, feels heavy, weak, and desperate.

For the purified human being, who works with the spirit, sunrise and sunset only indicate the beginning and end of a day's work.

The spiritual world, silence, and the ecstasy of prayer create a beatific peace, providing the human being with physical and moral health; nothing disturbs the inner world that he controls, and the annoying presence of the human anthill that surrounds him doesn't exert any influence on him.

Enveloped in the impressive harmony of the pyramid's atmosphere, Supramati and Dakhir recovered their spiritual balance, disturbed by their earthly life, and with their usual enthusiasm began the difficult task.

His guide, for this new work, was the Hierophant Siddarta - who looked young, but whose age was lost in the misty depths of the centuries. With the art and patience proper of a superior being, He managed, little by little, to transmit his immeasurable knowledge to the two younger brothers, rejoicing in the light that illuminated them, and responding to their manifestations of gratitude always in the same way.

"You owe me nothing; I only give you what I have received and what, in turn, you will pass on to other brothers who, like us, are climbing the rungs of perfect knowledge. Brothers, my knowledge, which seems so vast to you, is nothing compared to what you have still to acquire."

However, despite their efforts, energy, and hope for the future and the support of their Heavenly Father, Supramati and Dakhir were troubled by moments that, if not of despair, were at least of weakness.

This occurred when some new truth, like a blinding lightning bolt, suddenly opened the unknown horizons of oppressive immensity, of the arcana of the Universe whose existence they didn't even suspect.

With an anguished sadness in their spirits, the magicians wondered if there was any purpose, a limit to this knowledge so limitless as infinity itself. Were they able to know, reach and accommodate all this colossal knowledge in their miserable brains?

One day Siddarta noticed one of those moments of weakness and when Dakhir and Supramati, responding to his question, expressed their fears and doubts, the wise man shook his head in disapproval.

"I'm surprised, my brothers, that you two-faceted magicians haven't yet understood that the indestructible psychic spark, created by the Higher Self, contains embryos of his knowledge and power and that our task is to develop and work on this data.

At each higher step of acquired knowledge, a new nucleus of focus is formed in the brain, a focus of knowledge and power. And this same brain, which in the lower steps of evolution was simply a mass of inert matter, with a few poorly rooted electrical conductors, becomes a special world, a dynamic laboratory of terrible power, able to control the elements and create worlds. To possess such power and remain humble, making the acquired knowledge slavishly at the service of the Divine Will: that's the highest goal of magicians and the only ambition they are allowed."

"My sons, I think it would be pleasant to animate this insipid, though very interesting, work of ours with music. Art is a branch of magic; and if you have been obliged until now to dispense with it for other more complex tasks, the time to study this great force in which divine thought is propagated has come..."

"Master, you have divined our wish," Supramati replied cheerfully. "Both Dakhir and I adore music, a gift from heaven that brings joy, upliftment, and consolation to the human being. But I must confess that we haven't studied it as a magical science."

"Spend some of your time on it. Magicians of your level must know the chemical composition of sound and vibrations, as well as the dimensions of this force. Ordinary people, with undeveloped senses, although they feel the enchantment of music, have no notion of the variety of effects it provokes. In a magician's arsenal, music is just another weapon."

"In general, I only know that harmonic vibrations calm, unite, and animate, while dissonant vibrations act in a destructive way; they provoke storms, earthquakes, etc. It's also known that musical vibrations can calm or excite human desires and even influence animals. This is all we know in this field." Dakhir explained.

"It's clear. But you must learn to control this powerful generating force consciously and to know how to regulate the rhythm, the composition, and the gradation of the vigor of the vibratory harmony, to control the astral energy, and to contain the chaotic elements, if you wish to do so; or, on the contrary, to provoke them and give them freedom. Haven't you tried using vibrations to produce dangerous poisons or to practice cures that the profane would certainly call "miraculous"? Or to fertilize the earth, not with formulas or primary essences, but with music, since everything moves and is kept in equilibrium through vibrations? The nature that surrounds the profane resounds, exudes perfumes, and shines with a thousand colors, but it isn't conscious of it because it doesn't see or feel the invisible. And now we're leaving," said Siddhartha, getting up.

"You'll hear magical music and I'll introduce you to the astral world where you would see the harmonic vibrations at work. Just as the magnet attracts iron, sounds attract sounds and harmonic waves join together in vibrations that become more and more powerful. Your task is to learn to measure, evaluate, and control this power," he continued.

And the Hierophant led his disciples to the hall of musical initiation. It was a large, round, and totally dark cave. Possessing a spiritual vision, the magicians sat on low seats. Siddarta took a crystal lyre and said laughing:

"Close your spiritual eyes and see how the music provokes the light." Then vibrating sounds of strange modulation were heard, and then a fiery torch flashed in the darkness and fragmented into millions of multicolored sparks.

As the music increased its volume, the sounds became fuller and more powerful, spreading out like sparks and crossing like shooting stars, forming incredibly different geometric designs.

These fireworks turned into sprinkles of rainbow rays which, falling to ground, fragmented into thousands of transparent drops making a watery noise. Suddenly, the cave was illuminated with a blinding light and the air was filled with a strong, but pleasant, dazzling aroma.

The hierophant stopped playing and lowered the lyre. Dakhir and Supramati, as if they had suddenly awakened, looked around and only then realized that on one side of the cave a meadow had formed. Siddarta pointed to it and play again.

The melody was different now. The blinding light lost its brightness and turned greenish, while the earth looked transparent and in it, one could clearly see various grains and embryos. Suddenly, one had the impression that the multicolored lights stuck to the earth, assimilating to the ground, and as the strength of the harmonic vibrations increased, greenish waves began to fall on the ground and the seedlings swelled and sprouted.

The hierophant paused, and silently, with his eyes fixed on space, he was absorbed, but the sounds of the lyre that were then heard were of divine beauty. The light grew dimmer and dimmer, acquiring a bluish tinge, and upon this soft and velvety background, pictures of rare beauty began to be drawn.

As in a kaleidoscope, there appeared green meadows, shady valleys, forests with gigantic vegetation, and fantastic cliffs, in whose crevices boiled and bubbled multicolored waterfalls. On the flowering branches, flitting from one flower to another were seen beings of soft beauty, - immaculate irradiation of the magician's brain, his aspiration to light...- They were also beings endowed with a known vitality that were part of the mystery of the creative force, which was ignored by the profane.

Supramati was fascinated and lost in thought, feeling nothing but delight in admiring so many wonders. Suddenly, an unexpected idea came to his mind: -Suppose I could reach and learn this with my senses to transmit and explain these mysteries to the multitudes? In what language would I speak to them to convince them, since they only want to see and understand what they can touch and perceive with their ordinary senses? They would laugh at me and take me for an adept of an insane asylum if, pointing to a criminal, I told them: Look at the myriad of demons he has created with his criminal mind and see how those worms swirl in space looking to attach themselves to someone... Or else: I will show you the pure and splendid thoughts of a hermit and abstemious, a messenger of peace and harmony... Oh, what a sacred truth Christ said: "Blessed are the poor in spirit, for theirs is the kingdom of the heaven..."

No, no, the great masters of truth were absolutely right: everything cannot be revealed to the multitudes; the initiation must be done in quiet and mystery, far from the terrible chaos of human passions; the surprising and terrible knowledge must remain hidden as treasures and the inviolable oath of silence must be kept in this sacred secret place...

When Siddhartha stopped playing, Supramati exclaimed in amazement: "How beautiful this is! Will I be able to produce sounds of such beauty and strength?" The hierophant smiled and put his hand on his shoulder.

"You don't think, by chance, that during the time I dedicate to some serious work, I use a pre-established didactic method and special rules for playing? No, the sounds you've just listened to are created from the depths of my being; they're the expression of the harmony of my spirit. Take the lyre and try..."

"But I don't know how to play the lyre. I'll destroy your ears with my cacophony," said Supramati, blushing.

"Don't be afraid. Raise your spirit to divine beauty, surrender to inspiration, pray, and the outburst of your spirit will pour out in wonderful vibrations like those you have just been impressed with."

Obedient to the mentor's words, Supramati took the lyre and, concentrating on an ardent prayer, put his fingers on the strings. His whole being was immersed in love, faith, and respectful aspiration to the supreme stays...

Without any effort, his fingers, as if moved by a superior force, played the strings, diffusing magnificent and soft sounds and provoking shapes of rare beauty, illuminated by multicolored streams of light. Harmony was forming, each time more beautiful and exciting. Surprised by the music itself, the magician listened and wondered if his aspirations for the Good were so strong to be clothed in sound and made accessible to perception.

When the last chords ceased, Siddarta embraced Supramati and said:

"Look, my son, how much your spirit has been purified and beautified. There wasn't even a dissonance that could break the enchantment of the peace achieved. Now, Dakhir, let us listen to the harmonious echo of your spirit, and then you will hear a piece of disorderly and disharmonious music, which brings harm and can even kill."

Dakhir's performance, as well as that of his friend, received the full approval of the hierophant. Afterward, he took them to the school of musical art and, calling one of the students from the class furthest behind, ordered him to follow them.

To Dakhir and Supramati's surprise, they came out of the Pyramid. It was night. The weak moonlight of the last phase enveloped the inhospitable desert with pale penumbra. All around was just emptiness and stillness.

Instructed by the hierophant, the student began to play, and, while the air was permeated with loud, high-pitched sounds, howls, and growls were heard in response in the distance. Then, out of the darkness emerged several wild animals: a couple of lions, some panthers, hyenas, and jackals. All these beasts, visibly angry and frightened, came out of dens, crevices, and abandoned dens where they had been hiding during the day.

With deafening howls, hair standing on end, and wagging their hips with their tails, the furious predators watched each other with eyes that glowed in the dark. The sharper and more powerful the sounds of the instrument, the more irritated the animals became. Suddenly they lunged at each other using teeth and claws. It wasn't a fight for life, but for death. Even the hyenas and jackals, normally fearful and thieving, went mad with rage.

No doubt the fight would have ended with victims if the music hadn't stopped. Then, submitting to the will of the magician, the beasts dispersed to their lairs.

"Do you see, my friends, " said Siddhartha when they had all returned to the Pyramid, "how sounds of this nature invoke the spirits of Evil? People of vulgar and stupid hearing cannot hear the diabolical music that the bands of demons direct at each other, while the astral mind hears and feels the dissonant vibrations of the air and is overtaken by a furious agitation."

CHAPTER III

Years and centuries passed. Dakhir and Supramati studied with fervor. Finally, the day came when they were called to the meeting with the hierophants, and the superior of the secret community greeted them with the following words:

"Friends and brothers: The studies we have planned for you have been completed. You are well prepared and equipped to begin the necessary tests for your elevation. You will go as missionaries to bring light into the darkness. What I'm about to say to you, Supramati, refers also to you, Dakhir, for except for minor differences, your mission is identical.

So, Dakhir, you will only go to the world where atheism reigns. Although they have repudiated God, and that humanity has reached a high level of culture, but their customs and laws are cruel and sanguinary. Without admitting any divine principle and attributing all creation to blind cosmic forces. Men have made selfishness their basic law of life.

Your task will be arduous because it won't be easy to preach eternal truths to these beings. However, your word and your faith should bring about a moral turnaround and a reawakening.

Your preaching, I warn you, will arouse fierce animosity, but you can never, under any pretext, use your knowledge or your power to defend yourself or make your work less hard. Your knowledge can only serve to alleviate the suffering of others.

There you'll be a poor person, deprived of everything except your acquired spiritual strength and faith in God and in your mentors. However, if you endure the trials, you'll be blessed with glory and joy in the awareness that, in an impure world, you kindled a sacred flame of love for God.

Remember that the struggle that awaits you is arduous and poignant. Human heinousness will come down upon you in all its ugliness. In return for the good you do for people; you'll receive only hatred and suffering. However, from the height of your spiritual development and the clairvoyance of the magician, you should be merciful and love the creatures who are still crawling at the foot of the ladder of perfection. You shouldn't condemn them, but put yourself at their level, as a wise man does with an ignorant one.

An ordinary human being fights with the same weapons; enmity is returned with enmity, injury with injury because the multitude is blind, the seven carnal principles prevail and compete with each other, the so-called seven deadly sins. And the one who triumphs over these sins arms with the seven capital virtues and must sow only love, return darkness with light, and offense with good.

Now, my sons, tell me if you feel strong enough to begin the trials, to overcome all human weaknesses, and to voluntarily assume all the responsibility of this difficult but glorious mission, with all its unforeseen events and difficulties.

Answer honestly and remember that you're free; we only suggest these tests, without imposing them."

Supramati and Dakhir listened pale and confused: all that remained of them as ordinary humans trembled with a painful and horrible feeling of pure men who must leave for the sewer of Evil.

Almost involuntarily, Supramati looked vaguely at the hierophant, whose pale robes seemed to be covered with diamond dust and, from beneath the Klafta, rays of light radiated - symbols of victory in the field of spiritual combat - the wise man's large and radiant eyes looked at him penetratingly and sternly.

And he felt, instinctively, that the important moment of his life had come before he took the last step that would raise him above an ordinary being, that would free him from the slavery of the flesh to become a master of light and a truly superior being.

Suddenly, a great clarity enveloped his head, a ray of faith and willpower shone in his eyes, and, extending his hands towards the hierophant, he exclaimed:

"The disciple will be worthy of his beloved masters. It is with joy and security that I accept these tests because for the spirit that has been liberated from ignorance and the weight of the body, there cannot be any obstacle. Have I not already conquered the material, extinguished the passions, and defeated the dragon of doubt? After all this, should I fear descending the ladder when, thanks to your teachings and support, I have climbed several rungs? Command Master, when shall I begin my trials?"

"And you, Dakhir?" asked the hierophant, smiling softly.

"Master, my spirit echoes Supramati's every word. Like him, I'm prepared for the trials and hope not to falter, fulfilling the sacred task entrusted to me by the leaders, and spreading the magnificence of the Creator."

At that instant, the room was filled with a mist and soft music, like the song of the spheres, spread through the air in mighty waves, and beside the hierophant's couch the tall figure of Ebramar appeared and his face radiated joy.

"Let me embrace you and bless you, dear sons of my soul. Your response is a certainty of new victory!" he exclaimed, extending his hands over them.

A torrent of golden light enveloped his beloved disciples and a radiant cross in the shape of a diamond began to radiate above their heads, as Supramati and Dakhir fell to their knees like common mortals in front of their initiator.

When they got up, they were surrounded by hierophants. In a friendly conversation, the supreme hierophant informed them that they should prepare for the tests with a special regimen because in three weeks they would be led to the cave of Hermes.

"You, Supramati, will go first. The initiates there, members of the secret brotherhood, will welcome you and direct your first moves. Dakhir will leave the next day," added Ebramar.

In the evening of the same day, Ebramar and Siddarta placed them in an isolated cave, spending long hours with them, giving them special instructions, clarifying their doubts, and preparing them for the important mission. In addition, they were taught the basics of the language of the country in which they were to work.

They were fed with a special and very aromatic substance, similar to honey, and drank a bluish and phosphorescent liquid that transported them to a state of ecstasy.

When the preparation was finished, Ebramar and the supreme hierophant arrived at the cave, accompanied by six other sages. All of them wore sacred robes and wore on their chests the insignia that denoted their ancestry. Behind the magicians followed the adepts, carrying various gargments on golden plates, followed by singers with harps in hands.

Supramati realized that the decisive moment had arrived and promptly stood up. The adepts surrounded him and dressed him in a fabric similar to silk, but as thin as a spider's web. Finally, he put on a short white robe with a red belt. His head was bare, but between the mage's two torches now shone, like a shining giant, a cross, summoned from space by Ebramar.

Ebramar and the hierophant stood on both sides of Supramati and left the cave, where a large crowd awaited them at the entrance. The procession lined up and, in front of the hierophants, four adepts carried a kind of bonfire on which burned herbs and substances that gave off a surprisingly life-giving aroma. Behind them were the priests, chanting and covering the path of the Magi with flower petals.

The procession stopped near the sacred cave of Osiris; the carriers of the fire left, placing it on the marble vat in the center of the cave. Only the hierophants and Supramati, carrying the cross of the Magi, remained. His beautiful and ecstatic face denoted concentration.

In front of the fire was an altar table and on it shone the chalice of the Grail brotherhood, crowned by a cross. The altar was surrounded by knights in their silver armor and among them was Dakhir.

Supramati knelt on the steps of the altar, followed by all present; there was a solemn silence, broken only by a low, soft chanting from outside.

The superior of the Grail brotherhood took the chalice with the smoldering essences of life and light and passed it to Supramati; and when he drank from the chalice, the superior placed his hands on the missionary's head and said a prayer.

Then Ebramar approached, and taking a strange instrument from the altar, handed it to Supramati. It was something like a harp, except that from its strings, came the colors of the rainbow.

"Take this instrument with you to comfort and support you. The divine harmony you extract from it will lift you above your daily misfortunes," said Ebramar, kissing Supramati.

Full of joy, Supramati took the instrument with gratitude and kissed the attendants with a kiss goodbye. The last and longest farewell was with Dakhir. Then, accompanied only by the hierophants and Ebramar, he disappeared behind a heavy metal curtain that hid the cave of Hermes.

There reigned a bluish darkness with swirls of silver clouds.

The magicians led Supramati to an open sarcophagus, where he lay on a stone pillow. His fingers touched the strings of the harp and a magnificent melody sounded, strange and powerful, and all the beauty of the great artist's spirit poured out in sounds created by him, which gradually faded away.

Ebramar and the hierophants prostrated themselves genuflecting and raising their hands, while the clouds gathered on high, sprinkled with sparkles. Shapes of indefinite contours, as if they were woven with white fire, enveloped the sarcophagus in which the magician lay immobile, immersed in a magical dream.

A kind of thunder rumbled in the distance; then a sudden burst of clouds, and in the midst of them a column of glowing fire rose. Instantly, the mass of clouds raised to the heights and dissipated into darkness, followed by a silence.

The sarcophagus was empty; at the bottom were scattered some white flowers, which exhaled a strong aroma.

※ ※ ※

The reddish rays of the sun illuminated a strange and wild image: a desert place, full of high and rugged blue mountains, only covered by sparse gray bushes.

Between the sharp cliffs and precipices meandered a narrow path along which two people in dark cloaks walked.

From their appearance, it could be seen that they were of different races.

A very tall, thin, but robustly built man, with an angular and beardless appearance; his eyes were of an undefined color, and his face of a surprising liveliness, as if in his veins ran white blood and not red. With agility and decision, he climbed the steep stone path, which denoted his joviality.

His companion was a young man of about thirty years of age, slim and agile, with large, clear eyes, an attractive face, as of an earthy person, and dense dark hair flowing from his lowered hood.

They spoke in a strange language: the interplanetary language, sacred to all higher-level initiates.

"Brother Supramati, you have dominated our local language well enough to start your mission."

The cave I'm taking you to is very suitable for your first appearance. There was the last sanctuary of Divinity that existed in our evil world.

The path in this part of the site was curved. The companion and Supramati rounded some rocks and entered a narrow crevice, which then widened and gave way to a wide underground gallery, descending from above through numerous winding curves.

Finally, they came to a big cavern and on one side of the cavern, there was an exit leading to a wide platform. Apparently, this place had formerly served as a chapel, judging by the fact that at the lower part, at the height of two steps, a stone altar, of a sapphire blue, topped by a cross, could be seen.

On the altar was a large metal chalice with engravings of zodiacal symbols and two triptychs with herbs.

In a small enclosed cave were a bed, a table, and a wooden bench. From inside the wall, next to the table, was a spring of pure, crystal-clear water bubbling and falling into a deep and oval basin.

Supramati's company led him to the esplanade above a large cliff, at the bottom of which a churning river was echoing and foaming.

The opposite edge of the cliff was much lower and, a little ahead, it descended steeply to an immense plain where cattle were grazing. In the distance, the tall buildings and huge constructions of a large city were vaguely drawn.

"Brother, Now, you see our capital," said the hierophant of this other planet, returning to the cave.

"Let me bless you and invoke the blessing of the Supreme Being, at whose feet you want to return your prodigal sons."

He opened his arms, and immediately above his head appeared five flares of blinding light, and his chest glowed with multicolored lights. Rays of sparks fell from his hands on Supramati's genuflection: then a swirl of bluish mist was formed, and by the time Supramati stood up, the hierophant was no longer there.

Being alone, he took out from under his cloak the crystal harp and placing it on the bench, with the leather bag he had brought, he went to pray in front of the altar.

As he prayed, two small triodes were lit on the altar; then a golden flame appeared and illuminated the purple liquid that filled it.

When Supramati finished his prayers, the night had descended upon the earth. He went out to the ramp in front of the cave and sat down on a large stone, gazing thoughtfully at the copper-colored sky, full of stars shining like pink diamonds. The longing for the distant world -his homeland- squeezed his heart and, at that instant, the task he had undertaken seemed heavy and unproductive.

But that weakness was brief, and he overcame it with an effort of will. This planet, like any other, was the "abode" of the Heavenly Father's house, whose love extends equally to all his creatures; here, like on earth, he works for the glory of the Creator and must fulfill it with joy.

In the valleys that Supramati could see from the top of his refuge, there was great agitation that day. Large herds belonging to wealthy citizens were grazing there. And several shepherds, tending the cattle, tall and strong people, began to gather in groups or to run in confusion, pointing towards the cliff. They all saw when the sky suddenly lit up with a great glow, and a sphere of fire, crowned by a strange sign, seemed to rise behind the mountain peaks at a time when in the distance could be heard the roar of thunder, and at night, under the esplanade, hovered a circle of glowing fire. What could these strange phenomena mean, and even more so near the abyss, a dark and cursed place that everyone avoided?

In the distant, remote, and mountainous valley, protected on all sides by rocks and precipices, with access only through subway passages, the initiates built their refuge.

There were the palaces of the sages, the temples, and the secret libraries, where the treasures of science and the archives of the planet were kept.

Among the inhabitants, there was a legend of a community of mysterious men who hid in the mountains, possessed great power, and remained faithful to the rejected God. But no one had ever seen them and this tradition remained mainly among the working class. The aristocracy, the scientific establishment, and the entire intellectuality of the planet, without bothering to verify the truth, laughed at all these "old wives' tales".

It was in this refuge of the hierophants that Supramati awoke from his magical sleep and found himself being surrounded by care and love.

So, he spent his first weeks in the new and unknown world, undergoing a special diet to adapt his organism to the strange conditions, including the weather. At the same time, he perfected his knowledge of the local language and studied the history, geography, and political situation of this small Earth, which was about the size of the Moon. He learned that only two races inhabited the planet: the Marautas - a hard-working population, a people of tall stature, strong and active, but intellectually undeveloped and totally enslaved by the Rudras, an aristocratic and intellectually developed people from which emerged scientists, artists, bureaucrats and all kinds of -intelligence‖. This dominant race was weak and frail and subject to certain neurocerebral diseases, paralysis without apparent cause, sudden dementia, blindness, and other maladies.

This planet was ruled by a monarch for life; however, the Marautas were governed by the viceroy, their representative. And this monarchical nation was in a totally unique situation since they claimed to come from the divine dynasties that at the dawn of civilization ruled the Earth and initiated all the sciences and arts.

Supramati spent his period of preparation all alone, getting along with only a few members of the community, among whom was a young-looking man named Sarta, who promised to visit Supramati when he had settled in the chosen place and help him study the new conditions of life.

The day after his arrival at the cave, Supramati was delighted of his friend's visit. Sarta gave him fruit and the two settled down to talk by the entrance.

"I'm not allowed to visit you brother, since you will have to do everything yourself, and the task ahead of you is very difficult, since our human race is very cruel, selfish, and absorbed by material things," commented Sarta, sighing.

"God will help me and grant me the happiness of awakening faith, mercy, and love in them," replied Supramati with unshakable certainty. "And have you never tried to guide the blind to the way of truth?"

"Of course we tried, but all our attempts were useless. Perhaps the time hasn't come yet. Besides, the laws here are so strict that people are afraid even to listen to religious preaching. Independent of this, the rumors about us are considered so absurd and laughable that, if anyone suspected they were seeing a "highlander," as we are called, they would quickly shoot themselves in the foot, because they are convinced that, going back to their primitive religious doctrine, we send them, on every solemnity all kinds of misfortunes, storms, floods, contagious diseases and all kinds of pleasures."

Both started to laugh.

"This is our destiny: not to be recognized," Supramati joked. - But tell me, brother Sarta, what were the reasons that led your human race to that fierce hatred against the Divinity, which even put up barriers of law against the Heavenly Father? I think I must know."

"It would take too long to tell everything in detail; however, I will be glad to give a brief account of what has led to this unfortunate situation," replied Sarta, reflecting a little.

I don't need to tell you that we had our "golden age" when the enlightened ones that we here and you there call "divine dynasties" reigned. It was a time of greater civilization and, of course, of the development of spiritual capacities. Then came the decadence, abuses began with the practice of witchcraft and black magic, culminating in the breakdown of the rule of the initiates.

As the practice of black magic spread, the sordid instincts of man prevailed and acted seductively. Depravity and cruelty acquired terrible dimensions and the bestial people came to practice human sacrifices. However, despite all this, there were still followers of the masters and followers of the teachings of the divine dynasties. The population was divided into two poles: that of the white God and that of the black God, assigned to a white king and a black king. Cruel wars began, which became, with the passage of time, more and more savage and bloody. Under the influence of unbridled passions, the defenders of the White God kept only the name of their party, forgetting the basic principles and laws it supposedly represented. Banditry, human sacrifices and the use for evil of all spiritual forces have created an unbelievable situation.

It was then that an extraordinary man appeared on the world scene, whose destiny was to transform the world. The cosmic disturbances resulting from the spread of evil devastated our planet; one of the continents was flooded with water and treacherous diseases claimed the lives of the population. Amocra - that was the man's name - took advantage of this distressing moment of general confusion to seize power.

His origin was obscure. In the slaughter that preceded the flood, he had lost all his relatives. To consolidate his position, he adopted a small orphan who was considered the son of the former white king.

The energetic and sensible measures he took to restore order, repair damage, and develop commerce and industry, won him the affection and confidence of the general public. Then, confident that he enjoyed unlimited authority, he initiated an unprecedented social reform that excluded even the name of our Divinity on the planet.

Any profession of faith in the supreme being, whether black or white, was eliminated. Religious ceremonies were forbidden under pain of severe punishment; similarly, relations with the invisible world, because any religion, since it was a relationship with extraterrestrial beings, only gave rise to disorder, animosity, wars, and unleashed wild passions. For if there were a world beyond the grave, let the spirits themselves, freed from the body, each one of them would arrange himself as he pleased, be rewarded or expiate his sins, provided he didn't disturb the living. Consequently, all places where visions appeared, incomprehensible sounds were heard or strange phenomena occurred were subjected to immediate burning and, ultimately, to total annihilation. As for white or black magic, the guilty were punished with the death penalty.

And we have been living like this for about a thousand years, according to this beautiful program, delighting in the astonishing civilization, is impossible to imagine. It's true: arts and industry have reached a high level, but, on the other hand, selfishness, cruelty, and injustice haven't flourished any less.

The basic principle of our "culture" is utilitarianism: anyone has the right to defend his interests, even unscrupulously; while crimes against the interests of the state are severely punished. There are terrible positive laws, but in general, the concept of justice has totally atrophied."

Sarta kept silent, sighing heavily, and in Supramati's energetic gaze continued to shine the same faith and hope.

In a later conversation. Sarta proposed to his new friend, to go incognito to the city to get familiar with the place of his future activity. Supramati gratefully accepted the invitation. A few hours later, they left the cave modestly dressed in the costumes of the people and headed for the town.

The road was well-kept, the fields excellently worked, surprising with the variety of crops. The vegetation, indeed, was lush and Supramati was interested in Sarta's explanations of the different fruit trees growing along the road. The most surprising thing he found was a tree with large fruits that looked like earthy cucumbers, but shiny as if they were covered with enamel.

"Do you see, Supramati, this tree with a thick trunk, green underneath and dark above? In autumn, when the fruits mature, the whole trunk will be dry and empty inside. When harvesting its fruit, the whole trunk is covered with a resinous mass, replaced two weeks later, and left like this for the winter. In spring, the tree begins to cover itself with leaves and flowers, as if it hadn't died."

"Everywhere nature provides us with an example of resurrection," smiled Supramati.

"I haven't told you yet that from this original tree an excellent liquor is produced and the older it gets, the stronger it becomes," added Sarta.

The capital turned out to be a huge city, divided into two totally different parts. One, the bigger one, belonged to the marauts. Apparently, they were attracted to bright colors, judging by the houses surrounded by orchards that were illuminated with the colors blue, red, yellow, etc. Of the same hue were also the fabrics that were sold in large round pavilions, hollowed out on all sides.

There were also theaters, for the Marautas liked entertainment no less than costumes and ornaments, while the Rudrassos, who used the Marautas as their servants and who had excellent purchasers in them, protected them and arranged every possible kind of entertainment. And since the working classes were accustomed to obtain everything from the Rudrassos, from whose bosom came exclusively scientists, doctors, artists, musicians, and artisans of all exquisite things, the Marautas revered and even feared them, considering it a great honor to serve them.

The city of Rudrassos was of a different kind, more elegant and artistic: small attics, decorated and finished like objects of jewelry, immersed in the shade of the exuberant vegetation; and even its inhabitants differed much from the tall and strong Marautas.

On the contrary, the Rudrassos were short, and fragile, with fine and intellectual features; but their eyes hid something cruel and diabolical, which made them seem unpleasant.

Supramati was attracted many times by the wide strips of dark lilac-colored cloth hanging from the front doors of some houses.

"Tell me, brother, what do these bands of cloth mean? They are all marked by a red symbol, and they are found in the houses of the Marautas as well as in the houses of the Rudrassos, and, what is stranger, in the houses that belong, it seems, to people of different social positions."

On Sarta's face appeared an expression of displeasure and a bitter smile.

"Those strips, dear Supramati, are a symbol of shame for our world and signify that among the inhabitants of such or such house there is a disillusioned or crippled person condemned to death, or rather, fated to be beaten on the basis of a shameful law."

"What does this mean, that sick people are murdered here? What right do they have and how can a family accept such unheard-of cruelty?"

Sarta laughed.

"By what right? For the good of society, but I have to explain it to you in more detail so that you understand the utilitarian subtlety of the law you call cruel.

You know that the spiritual ideal and everything that refers to divine laws is forbidden here. This means that free of any ethical restraint, humanity has definitively found itself in the power of the instincts of the flesh. Morality is more than weak, and from the point of view, for example, one could say that they simply don't exist; on the contrary, all kinds of shameful vices and passions flourish in profusion, and people, especially the Rudras, due to the fact that they are physically weaker, have become susceptible to different kinds of illnesses, such as: sudden dementia, paralysis, convulsions that totally deform the limbs, sores, similar to our leprosy, and finally, the permanent loss of sight. All these illnesses are extremely contagious and difficult to treat, and since doctors study and know only the subject matter, they can treat only the body, without seeking any hidden reason for the illness; illnesses motivated by obsession, the evil eye of others, spiritual sufferings, among others, remain outside their competence.

Moreover, criminality, addictions, and depravity attract evil spirits and their number grows day by day; and as blind mankind is deprived of defense against the terrible occult forces, the devastations caused by them increase more and more... For all that maintains and purifies - prayer, faith in God, the invocation of the forces of good - is forbidden and has even lost its significance.

Due to the fact that our entire governmental system is based exclusively on utilitarianism, only those have the right to life who have some utility that can serve for their own pleasure or that of a stranger. Thus, it is clear that the incurably insane, the blind, cancer patients, retarded children, in other words, beings who cannot be of any use to the government.

They only represent focal points of contagion and an uncomfortable burden to the family, as they demand at the same time unnecessary expenses, preventing them from enjoying life and attending to their affairs.

However, despite the brutalization of the population, the divine spark hidden in the depths of the human being often provokes an attachment to the unfortunate sufferers and bitterness at the realization that their elimination is necessary.

As a result of the numerous and energetic protests, the legislation was finally modified, establishing a fixed term for the treatment of the sick with a condition: if at the end of this term the hopes of cure haven't been fulfilled, this "noxious" and "useless" being must be eliminated."

"Oh, God almighty! And how are they killed?" asked Supramati, pale with horror.

"Well, there is no need to be at the ceremony! Every month, on an appointed day, a government official goes to each house with sick people and verifies the duration of the illness based on the medical determination. If the time limit is exceeded, the day of the death penalty is set. When leaving the house, he hangs a strip of cloth as a sign of certification that one of the condemned is there.

All the condemned of the current month are executed on the same day. At sunrise, they all are taken together to the abyss, under which their shelter is located, and there the same official in the company of some subordinates reads a record explaining the reasons for the capital execution, enumerating the "useless" ones, accompanied by their close relatives. Then, they are given a drink that drugs them and they are thrown into the abyss."

"What a horror! The abyss must be already almost full, if so many victims are thrown into it in the course of centuries."

"Oh, no! The current, the sound of which is heard at the bottom of the cliff, flows into an unfathomable crevice, dragging the corpses with it. By the way, Supramati, you'll have a chance to see all this for yourself, because a similar execution is scheduled for tomorrow at dawn."

Supramati was thoughtful and silent.

"Did no mother ever rebel and rise up against this monstrosity?" he asked.

"What can they do? Everyone is subject to the law and must obey it, including the king himself. Of course, there are groans and tears, but no one dares to openly resist."

"Well, if here they are severe with the sick, simply because they are useless, what punishment, then, is given to the criminals," asked Supramati on his way to the cave.

Sarta burst out laughing.

"With them, the ceremony is lighter. Those guilty of crimes of state, in the murder of useful people, the theft of money destined for social causes, etc., are hanged on summary sentence. As for vagrants, swindlers and beggars, and people in general who have abandoned the coexistence of society and don't work, wanting to live at the expense of others, these are taken to inhospitable places and then, even if there is not exactly an order of execution, if this happens, the murderer is not usually sought and consequently is not subject to punishment."

"How pitiful! - Supramati observed sadly. - I will ask God to support me so that I can dissipate the darkness and guide these lost souls to the path of perfection."

CHAPTER IV

Supramati spent the whole night praying fervently and only at dawn when in the distance could be heard footsteps, groans, and cries of the arriving crowd, did he rise from the altar steps and look out.

On the side of the city, on the path to the abyss, a large procession led by a person carrying a banner of dark lilac cloth, which Supramati had already seen at the gates of the houses. Behind them followed a group of officials, and finally, in an endless line, in carriages or on stretchers, went the condemned, surrounded by weeping relatives. The most desperate, it seemed, were the women carrying crippled, hunchbacked, and paraplegic children, who clung to their mothers' necks with their little hands.

When they reached the edge of the abyss, the macabre procession stopped and formed a large semicircle, in the middle of which were the officials in golden helmets, adorned with a bird with spread wings - a symbol of unconditional freedom - and the secretary, holding the city book, from which he would scratch out the names of the unfortunates as they disappeared into the abyss. There was even an orchestra, but its presence was supposed to silence with music the moans of those present and of the victims, in case anyone, despite being under the influence of drugs, still had the strength to scream. On a table set up ahead, the doctors began to dispense the previously prepared drink into cups.

As one of the government representatives was preparing to read the sentence, on the esplanade that overlooks the abyss appeared a man in white robes with a harp in his hand.

The first ray of the rising sun illuminated with its purple color her pale robes, her beautiful exalted face, and the crystal instrument that sparkled like a diamond.

A minute later, the slender fingers of the mysterious man touched the strings and a strange melody could be heard, sometimes soft, sometimes harsh.

The crowd gathered on the opposite side remained motionless, seemed enchanted, and all eyes were fixed on the unknown musician while he continued playing and singing. The sounds grew louder and louder, enrapturing and thrilling with their harmony in every fiber and awakening vague and unknown feelings, lifting the spirits of men and softening them like wax.

The crowd, including the audience, as if hypnotized, slowly began to prostrate themselves on their knees; hundreds of birds from everywhere flew over the esplanade and, surrounding the musician without fear, landed at his feet and on his shoulders.

However, he seemed to take no notice and continued to play. Now a silvery-blue mist emanated from him and enveloped him with a wide aura. And from this focus rays of light came out and fell like streamers on the sick, being absorbed by their bodies.

Then a magnificent spectacle took place. From the bodies of the sick arose whirlwinds of black smoke, and as the fetid miasma dissipated from their bodies, paralyzed limbs began to move, the eyes of the blind to recover their sight, the wounds to heal, and the anemic and withered faces to gain vitality.

Not believing what they saw, the mothers stared in amazement at their children, who in a few moments would be dead and now, happily, moved their injured hands and feet freely or straightened their hunched backs or hunched bodies. Not an hour passed and the wagons and stretchers were empty. All the condemned, returned now to life and work by an unknown force, knelt like everyone else, and gazed at the mysterious musician full of gratitude.

Suddenly, the sounds stopped. The stranger took down his harp, looked satisfied at the crowd kneeling down, and disappeared into the cave.

As if awakened from the spell, the people stood up and cries of joy were heard; the relatives of the condemned to death kissed their loved ones restored to life.

Perplexed by the events, the officials confirmed that there were no longer any sick persons, so there was no need for execution, and gave the order to return to the city.

An agitation and a curiosity gripped the crowd and everyone was tormented by one question: who could the person be who, with the sound of a harp only, had cured the sick with no cure? No one knew who he was or where he had come from, but after a few hours, all the capital was talking about the mysterious foreigner and his miraculous feats.

Rumors of the unusual event reached the king's palace. At first he didn't want to listen to anyone, but when one of the officials there confirmed the event, the king expressed his desire to see some of the previous patients.

Then they brought to the palace a man who had been paralytic, a leprous and blind woman, a deaf-mute child, a man suffering from convulsions whose deformed face and limbs were terrifying, and a number of previously sick people.

Convinced by his own eyes that they all were perfectly healthy, the king ordered them to describe what they felt during their healing process. They all unanimously said that, as soon as the stranger began to play, they felt an itching throughout their bodies. Then they saw rays of a bluish color that descended zigzagging down over them and absorbed into their bodies. At that instant, a current of fire began to run through them, going through them like sharp arrows, while they felt the breath of a fresh and aromatic breeze, which produced in them an indescribable delight.

In what way had the healing occurred? The beneficiaries hadn't any idea of it; but the sufferings had ceased, the eyes had recovered their sight, the hands and feet had regained flexibility, even any vestige of disease had disappeared.

When he was alone with the former chairman of the Council, a proven friend, the king expressed his concern by asking, half-heartedly, who this person was and where he came from. What objectives, ultimately, was he pursuing and what, ultimately, must they think of this whole story?

The elderly man reflected and then said a little unsure:

"I hope majesty that by force of such exceptional circumstances you'll allow me this time to express some forbidding questions."

"No doubt. We are alone and I allow you to talk openly about everything" replied the king.

"Thus, the place chosen by the stranger to practice these amazing works, leads me to draw the following conclusions. The cave, where he found refuge, was the temple of the ancient White God. In that abyss, they say, the last divine statue was thrown together with the faithful priest who had resisted leaving the sacred place. According to legend, before his death, he predicted that the first temple of the White Divinity would be founded in the same place, and that light would triumph over darkness."

"I worry that in the future he may cause disorder, but at this moment I think it's not prudent to act cruelly to the man who saved the lives of so many unfortunate people. Let's wait and see what happens," the king considered after reflection."

In the meantime, the whole city was in excitement. Flocks of visitors went to the houses of the ex-death row people, and the whole place was filled with a festive atmosphere. The previously sick - now healthy and happy - moved among friends and acquaintances without showing any fatigue and related the sensations and impressions experienced by them and their relatives, produced by the extraordinary man.

These stories caused even stronger impressions in families where there were sick people who were certain to be condemned to extermination the following month.

In the souls of these people were confronted the misfortune that awaited them and a vague hope of salvation, because the human heart is made in such manner that no illegitimate law can change it and tear out from its interior the feelings of the indestructible psychic spark placed there by the Creator.

The next day, a caravan headed to the abyss carrying sick people. On arriving at the place, they prostrated themselves silently on their knees, anxious and not knowing what to do.

In all those centuries, no one had ever taught them how to speak to God and how to pray. As a frightened herd, they knelt down looking anxiously at Supramati, who had just appeared on the esplanade over the cliff.

The magician's generous heart was filled with deep mercy for those unfortunates, cruelly deprived of any idea about God, who didn't even suspect about the powerful force lying dormant in them that could ignite the flame of faith and reunite them with their Creator.

With eyes full of tears, Supramati gazed at those disinherited and poor in spirit who, like helpless children, crowded together in fear, looking at him with sadness.

A fervent prayer arose from his soul to the omnipresent Father to give him the strength to save the unfortunate, to give them back the most valuable of gifts, the inexhaustible richness accessible to all: faith in God and the love for the Good.

At that instant, in the Supramati's heart - which was nothing more than the world itself sent there - love awakened for those inhabitants of another land and he clearly felt a fraternal affinity that united all beings from all worlds and all spheres - from an atom to the archangel - like an indivisible current that, as a shining ray, radiated from the heart of the Eternal, crossed all systems and returned to its primitive source.

Then, this was the great mystery of the divine breath that, like the flame that ignites another thousand, is never extinguished, but is transferred from one atom to another, animating the matter and extracting from the protoplasm a magician with perfect knowledge.

* * *

In that moment of great significance, Supramati understood the hidden and divine idea: At the moment of creation, in the small and fragile being, throw the powerful feeling of love that unites people and worlds, the lever of creation.

Everything that had been obscure until then became clearer; the weight of the mission was lightened; the task he had assumed was no longer an obligation, but the happiness of doing good to those he loved. Between him and the poor of spirit, who knelt before him, a powerful bond was created, thanks to commiseration, which united the beings of God. An immense joy filled the prophet's heart: his mission turned out to be wonderful and he received his reward...

Supramati's entire aura was filled with golden sparkles and her whole being breathed with a tremendous force. He picked up the harp and the sounds it produced were the music of the spheres, a very powerful vibration that subdued the elements of nature and united the worlds.

Like a stream of fire, his powerful will was transmitted to the ignorant crowd that he contemplated with love. All eyes were fixed on the white figure of the magician, the tears flowed and no one suspected that it was the awakening of the soul with the sweet dew that would rekindle in them faith in the Creator.

All the sick was healed, and the fluid of life-giving force radiating from Supramati was so strong that even the trunk of an old, withered tree by the abyss came back to life and was filled with sap.

This new "miracle" provoked great admiration and the rumors about the "unnatural" man who lived in the cave gained legendary repercussions. This excitement reached the palace once again, since still, among those who had the miraculous cure, was the young Medkha, a friend of Princess Vispala, the king's granddaughter.

The king, named Nikhazadi, was already old and his only two sons were victims of the terrible law described before. The princes suffered from an incurable disease and, despite their high position, lost their lives in the abyss. The old monarch was left with only his granddaughter, his heiress, and the daughter of the youngest son, for whom he felt an exceptional adoration.

Vispala was a lovely girl, at the peak of her youthful beauty, and Medkha had been her best friend since childhood. The thought of losing her cost the young princess many tears, and one can imagine how happy she was to see her friend completely healthy. Vispala filled her with questions about the mysterious man who performed so many miracles, while Medkha, happy about her healing, described enthusiastically how Supramati was.

"I've never seen such a beautiful man... And the surprising thing is that he doesn't look at all like our men. Although his face is pale, you can see that his blood is red, for his cheeks were rosy. Her hair is wavy and of an undefined color, of a golden hue. His eyes... It's hard to describe them just by looking at them. They seem to breathe fire, but they express such physical energy and at the same time such kindness that I could spend my whole life kneeling and admiring them," Medkha said.

"I have to see him!" Vispala exclaimed, and his eyes sparkled. "But how and in what way?"

"There's nothing simpler, princess. Every day, in front of the scarp where the healings take place, people crowd around, he stands right at the edge of the esplanade with his harp in his hands and can be seen without any trouble. While at night, an aunt told me, a bluish light surrounds the cave and the esplanade, and he stands playing and singing outside. No similar singing has ever been heard; every fiber seems to tremble, in the heart, there's desire, and the strangest ideas come to mind.

Even the animals seem to be bewitched by him; birds, for example, perch on the shoulders, knees, and in front of the feet of this strange man. One simply can't believe it."

Days later, Vispala and her friend managed to reach the abyss late at night, where there was already a crowd of people, among which they were mingled. Indeed, a strange, silvery-blue light enveloped the mage's shelter with a broad spectrum. The esplanade was empty, but clouds of birds dotted the ground and the ledges of the cliffs.

Soon after, Supramati appeared, sat down on a large stone that served as a bench, and began to sing. In the midst of the mysterious twilight, his slim white figure, his beautiful face that expressed inspiration, the unusual and unknown melodies that came from his slender fingers, and his powerful and velvety voice provoked a deep rapture. Mute, as if bewitched, Vispala looked at him; her whole being trembled with an unknown sensation and she could only return home when he came back to the cave.

Supramati's fame spread at an incredible speed: people came from everywhere to have a look at the mysterious unknown... Take care of their health and listen to his wonderful songs.

Without the strength to conquer his curiosity, the old king decided to go to the cave and question the enigmatic stranger, endowed with the incredible gift of healing. The underground paths to the esplanade weren't known to the king, but, on the outside, there was still a stairway carved into the scarp, which formerly led to the chapel, and this path, although damaged, still served as a passageway. With great difficulty, the king succeeded in ascending, and, much disturbed and agitated, stopped in front of the entrance to the cave.

The whole interior was flooded with a pale blue light, as he had been told, and saturated with a soft aroma. In the background, on the altar table, the chalice of the Grail Knights, surmounted by the cross, shone with rays. On the stone bench sat the mysterious man himself, who had wiped away so many tears and alleviated so many sufferings of others, reading scrolls.

Eager with curiosity, the king scrutinously examined Supramati, who stood up at his arrival. Perplexed by Supramati's beauty, the monarch understood as soon as he saw him that in front of him stood a different man, of an unknown race. After a few moments of mutual examination, they exchanged curtsies.

"Who are you, stranger, where did you come from, since you don't look like people from our earth, and where did you acquire this strength to snatch death from beings condemned by science?" asked Nikhazadi.

"I'm an envoy of our Creator. I've come to bring light to the darkness and to remind people of this Earth of their divine origin. The time has come to re-establish the Creator's contact with his creation; long ago your human race lost its faith. I've come to speak to the hearts of men and to interpret to them the infinite goodness of their Heavenly Father. I preserve their life and restore their health so that they may glorify the name of God and give thanks to the Lord..."

"You, miserable wretch!" shouted the king, standing up abruptly, "your intentions already condemn you to death.

Don't you know that our land has voluntarily broken off all relationships with heaven? Any envoy of Him whom you call God will be rejected here; moreover, an implacable law condemns him to death."

Supramati smiled

"I don't fear of death and the salvation of my brothers and sisters is more important to me than life. For human beings, spiritual nourishment is more necessary than material nourishment. You must only become aware that you are blind, and that where earthly science is powerless, you must prostrate yourself and invoke the invisible. Thus I have come to remind your humanity of the forgotten truths and to teach them to pray. I assure you, King, that you'll be one of the first to surrender to the powerful symbol of eternity and salvation."

Nikhazadi was livid and breathing heavily.

His soul stirred under Supramati's powerful gaze, and suddenly, he was seized by an irresistible desire to hear about the invisible, that to which a person turns in the difficult moments of life.

A minute later he sat down on the bench and gasped:

"Tell me what you intend to preach to my subjects. I have the right to hear it first."

When, an hour later, Nikhazadi left the cave, a wrinkle formed on his forehead, and his gaze showed dark thoughts.

In the following weeks, there was nothing special. The healings continued and the crowd that gathered at the border of the terrible abyss, which had already gobbled up so many victims, grew even larger. Now, however, the mood of the people had changed somewhat; the music, the strange singing, and the excitement caused by the return of health and life moved the souls.

In these people, who had lost even the notion of the Good and of spiritual perfection and who only lived according to their desires and pleasures, the aspirations were awakened to join something lucid and pure that radiated from the one who cured them and to know a little, if possible, his wonderful science.

As a result, seven of those who had wanted to become Supramati's disciples one evening climbed the old stone staircase and timidly stopped at the entrance to the cave. They were deeply impressed by the sight of the altar and the radiant cross. The incredible enchantment that reigned in the magician's refuge overwhelmed them all and the pure radiations that saturated the air made them dizzy.

When Supramati appeared on the step of the white cave, the brave men knelt down and supplicantly stretched out their hands in his direction.

Approaching quickly, Supramati helped to stand them up and said in an affable tone:

"Welcome to you, the first ones thirsting for the light of Truth. Do you wish to be my disciples? I accept you gladly, because your poor world is in great need of preachers who will teach them to rediscover the way of perfection, although, my friends, it's my duty to warn you that the task you propose to yourselves is very difficult. The teachings that I'm going to transmit to you must be transmitted to your brethren even at the risk of your lives, since faith without actions has no sustenance. Reflect, then, if you feel strong enough to assimilate my teachings in practice."

Deliberating among them for a minute, one of them stepped forward and said without hesitation

"Master, we are so weak, so ignorant and blind, that we think it too brave to promise something we may not be able to assimilate. Be magnanimous, put us to the test and we promise to do our best to be worthy of your teachings."

"Your answer gives me great hope. He who acknowledges that he is blind has before him the possibility of knowing the eternal light, while the vain will remain blind because he only sees his pretended greatness. I say it again, my friends, you are welcome! You will stay here with me, but first I must purify you and remove the wrappings of miasmas."

He took them to an adjoining cave, ordered them to undress, enter the tank and kneel down, which they did without objection. Then Supramati stretched out his hand, drew in the air a cabalistic symbol, and at the same moment a broad beam of light appeared from space and under their bowed heads multicolored lights flared up like an igneous dome, which then seemed to be absorbed by their bodies.

Noticing that their faces expressed dread and perplexity, Supramati explained: "Don't be afraid. This purifying fire of ether will permeate you and eliminate the bad fluids that surround you."

Afterwards, he gave them ordinary white robes and shoes of woven straw and brought them to the altar, where they knelt, and then let them kiss the chalice and place small aromatic wooden crucifixes on their chests.

From that day on, the morning and evening hours were spent in teaching. First of all, Supramati explained the dual nature of man - material and astral - and the immutable law that united people with the invisible world, from which they came out to incarnate and returned when they died.

He showed them the invisible population of space and explained its dangers to the soul and bodies of the mortals.

Later, like an obvious deduction, he pointed out the only effective weapon against these risks and began to teach them the great art of prayer.

"This force, as powerful as the elements of nature and in the image of lightning, ignites the divine flame in the altars, fertilizes the earth, penetrates the depths of the ocean, and crosses like a hurricane space, ignoring the obstacles. The prayer, the first of the sciences, is an extraordinary power, a magic talisman that unleashes unknown forces. And not only a magician, but anyone who possesses an ardent and pure faith can use this enormous force, control the elements of nature, calm storms, stop epidemics, gather and collect fine and delicate elements for the cure of diseases...".

Astonished and enthusiastic, the students listened reverently to the magician. And these men, who until that moment had lived only for the pleasures of the flesh, humbly and with full faith bowed down before the cross and tried to pray.

Countless times they suffered failures, became tired and fell into discouragement, because the ability to pray is not as easy as one might imagine. It has three aspects: first - it demands concentration; second - it renounces all material things that burden the soul and chain it to the earth; and, third - it requires a strong willpower that ascends and releases a pure flame, dispersing the aura of sinful man to the perception of divine radiations.

Nevertheless, thanks to their efforts and the magician's support, the disciples improved quickly. Now they knew that they had a discarnate spirit whose main destiny was perfection.

They discovered the mystery of existence and the great law of love that dictates the obligations of the human being regarding his neighbour. Step by step, Supramati prepared his disciples for their mission: to spread the light of faith on the darkened souls of their carnal brothers.

"Your duties are to return what you yourselves have received. It's hard, of course, to inculcate in people the great laws of Good, and to stop them in the trodden path of abuse and vice. They will hate you, and they will pay good with evil, but this cannot frighten you; and if your mission is marked with blood, it will be a victory of the most glorious kind. Know that our blood is a life-giving dew that will be shed upon the barren earth of unbelief and selfishness, and that remembering you as an immortal flame will kindle faith in the souls of many. So, dear brothers, don't fear death, for the death of a martyr is a heavenly aroma that dispels the pestilential miasmas which surround the atmosphere of an evildoer."

"Master, while I have understood your teachings," observed one of the disciples, "we must never repay evil with the same coin in our defence; but since our laws encourage vengeance and the destruction of everything that can be an advantage, then we'll be killed in vain."

Supramati smiled.

"It's precisely your preaching that must put an end to your savage and unjust laws, but don't think that you'll be disarmed. Those who preach the truth, inspired by the love of their duty and armed with the cross, are invincible."

"Master, explain to us why you believe that the cross is possessed of a special power. I know very well that this symbol was once highly venerated here, but I cannot understand the origins of this devotion." asked Khaspati, one of Supramati's most zealous disciples, to whom he'd become very attached.

"As you mature and advance in the sciences, you will learn to understand, at least partially, the benevolent peculiarities of this symbol of eternity and salvation. The cross, my son, terrible in its power, is a symbol, a weapon of attack and defence. Being both artificer and destroyer, it's the compass of the illumined one. Wherever it's, in all the visible worlds of the firmament, the cross reveals its power, because its lines, being oriented towards the four sides, permeate the universe."

One evening, Supramati was sitting on the esplanade with his disciples and he was teaching them the art of developing the mastery of will, demonstrating by practical examples the power of this energy. Under the action of his thought-force, he made a withered bush to blossom and unleashed a storm, which calmed down at his order.

"You see, my sons, this developed and conscious will brings the cosmic elements into submission, making them malleable as melted wax. Of course, to reach the level of my power requires much time and work; but this is possible through persistence and an understanding of the objectives to be achieved."

The disciples contemplated him with a mixture of fascination and almost superstitious fear. Khaspati asked hesitantly:

"Master, tell us who you are, where you come from and from whom you have acquired this colossal knowledge. Explain to us why, in the course of so many centuries, nobody has come before you to reveal to us the great truths which you have propagated."

Supramati reflected for a while looking into space, and replied:

"I come from a far distance; I'm a humble son of science, sent by the guardians of good and truth to dispel the darkness of human misunderstanding and to return to the Father his prodigal children because you're all his children, indestructible and divine particles from him. Seeing you lost in the uncrossable jungle of ignorance, enslaved by the flesh, cruel and full of vices, the great guardians of humanity sent one of their faithful servants, armed with the cross and with love to guide you on the path of truth. And my coming won't be in vain: I'm not alone, I already have loyal disciples who will transmit my teachings to their brothers and continue my cause if I perish."

"What do you say, master, will you, who is the benefactor of the suffering saints, perish? That would be horrible. What will happen to us without your teachings? We won't be able to continue your cause. - exclaimed Khaspati with tears in his eyes, embracing his consecrator."

Supramati caressed his disciple's bowed head.

"The cause of saving the soul from the death of ignorance and disbelief isn't often paid for with life. But this doesn't matter; the seed of truth planted by me, the liberation from the centuries-old shackles of brutal atheism advocated by me to my brothers, will survive my carnal existence. Whereas you, my sons, shouldn't be afraid when you are without leaders. Invoke the mentors who reside in the mountains in spiritual retreat and they'll bring you in profusion, the spiritual bread and wine which will nourish your souls."

"Why then have they not appeared so far to enlighten and heal us?" said one of the young disciples, visibly annoyed.

"Avoid making unfounded judgements about what you don't understand," Supramati admonished. "How would you know, what if his appearance had been before his time and had caused a painless death? I've come to prepare the way for you, to prepare the foundation for an initiative that will later be developed by my brothers. It'll be they who will revive their ancient faith, restoring what has been distorted or forgotten for centuries. And then, if necessary, others will appear and defend the truth. Their path will be illumined by beams of light. Like me, they will fulfill their designs: they'll share with their brothers the truth and the light, obtained in turn from others."

Supramati's observation embarrassed Khaspati.

"Thank you, master. The next time I'll be more cautious and hold back from jumping to conclusions."

CHAPTER V

Supramati watched with great satisfaction the rapid progress of his disciples, whose personal capacities were becoming clearly noticeable. While one was interested exclusively in music, another in the study of the occult power of the planets, and a third in the wonders of the starry sky. All those aspirations, without exception, to study the mysterious and mighty force of will, that great lever of cosmic forces, the motive force which governs the elements of nature, converged into one. The will, developed and disciplined, represents the force similar to the very elements of nature.

Now Supramati, in the company of his disciples, sometimes went out of the cave performing healings in the surrounding towns and villages, eventually preaching and impressing his listeners with the need to love God so that in the trials and sufferings of existence they'd look to Him for help and support.

The fame surrounding the supernatural man ended up protecting him, and no one dared to arrest him for insolently violating the law that prohibited even uttering the name of God.

So, conveniently, everyone was silent, while on the sly, the mage's enemies became united and their numbers grew rapidly.

In the front ranks were the doctors, who felt they were hurting financially. As well as being wounded in their self-respect as -scientists. No less discontented were all those who found it more comfortable not to be constrained by a norm of morality, conscience, or duty since the concept of God and his laws were hated for becoming a restraint on their disorganised and animal passions. And so the number of these adversaries became legion.

Supramati, who could read the human soul and the thoughts of others, obviously saw the hostility growing, but he did not pay attention to it and continued with his healing and preaching.

One day, returning from a visit to the forest, the master and his disciples sat down exhausted to rest and eat a little. In the dense forest, overgrown with bushes and undergrowth, Supramati saw behind a pile of broken branches a pile of ruins.

"Do you see those ruins of the destroyed temple? I hope it will be rebuilt and under its dome the sacred hymns will sound and that united prayer will draw to the believers the mighty and renewing waves of the divine bliss."

"Master, you really know everything and can see into the past. How else would you have guessed that those formless ruins were once one of the most majestic temples of our country?" exclaimed Khaspati in surprise. "Everyone avoids this place because, during the destruction of the sanctuary, a large number of priests who looked for a hiding place were annihilated here," continued the young disciple. "They even say that the place is haunted, but no one recognises it for fear of being punished."

"What horrible times those were! I hope they will never occur again," said one of the young men present. "But tell me, master, will you return to the priesthood again, when finally, the worship of God is restored?"

"No doubt. This office requires priests, and I suppose that you, my friends, will take on this great and arduous mystery in accordance with your responsibility," replied Supramati seriously.

"Don't think that everything will be solved without a fight," he continued. "Good always has adversaries, because darkness hates the light.

Out of the drain will come a thousand-headed monster of unbelief and doubt, covering everything with its poisonous saliva in the name of -science.

Obviously, the monster will attack the temple and try by all means to shake its foundations; but one of the responsibilities of the warriors of faith is to defend the sanctuary, which represents the idea of Divinity and is for humankind an inexhaustible source of salvation for soul and body.

Woe to those initiated priests who allow the treasure that has been entrusted to them to be desecrated, humiliated or plundered.

A priest is the first cultivator of God, a direct intermediary of the divine forces of the invisible world. A singular mystery envelops the servants of the altar, the focus of light into which the divine power descends and concentrates. Their life must be pure and their thoughts turned towards heaven, their life should be chaste and their thoughts aimed to heaven, since they're the vessels into which the bliss of salvation is poured and from which it's distributed to mortals.

Woe to the priest who, being impure in soul and body, dares to approach the altar to grasp the Heavenly light; he would only darken and obscure it, denying it to those who seek help and salvation.

The priest's mission, as a true cultivator of God, is great and sublime. His task is to preserve in the heart and to practice all the truths he has spread, so that the believer looks up to this agent of light from below.

Don't forget, my children, that the decay of religion begins from the moment when in man's soul there insinuates contempt for the priest of God. Just as a shepherd is responsible for all the sheep of the flock, so the shepherd of the flock of Yahweh must know the soul of his sheep."

Khaspati leaned over and kissed his guide's hand.

"We'll never, honorable master, forget your words and we will ask God that He transforms us into true priests, like you have just described us."

As the number of his followers grew, Supramati became more and more open. Preaching his sermons even in the capital, he managed to unite the believers into communities that gathered for joint prayers and wore small wooden crucifixes, made of aromatic trees, and distributed by their adored master.

It's clear that all Supramati's enemies - which were numerous - foamed with hatred when they saw his impunity. Some members of the Monarchic Council openly demanded in meetings the arrest of the mage and his trial by the court, since his insolence was growing day by day, while his "lectures" threatened to provoke disturbances and undermine the laws in force.

"If the majority of the Council opts for detention, I won't speak out against it," Nikhazadi replied. "However, think very carefully before you make your decision to ensure that the arrest of the man who saved hundreds of people from death doesn't provoke the disturbances you fear so much. The stranger has undeniably powerful means of healing, and which of you can guarantee that tomorrow he won't have to resort to the healer's help?"

A silence filled the room. The last argument was indisputable and the final decision was postponed.

However, this postponement infuriated the most intransigent, so they decided to go underground and eliminate the "mage" at all costs. In the meanwhile, the appearance of a new fact confirmed their ignoble intention.

After seeing Supramati, Vispala was seized with a burning and wild passion for him, typical of the people of that perverted world. Every night she went with Medkha to the edge of the cliff to spy on the mage as he talked to his disciples, played his music or sang. Spellbound, she couldn't take her eyes off Supramati's beautiful countenance, illuminated by an unusual light blue that seemed to irradiate from him. Her passion was growing every day. Taking advantage of the mage's visit to the city, Vispala managed to send him a message. In her letter, she declared her unmeasured love for him, saying that she elected him to be her husband, which would give him the right to the throne.

"My grandfather has no male successor and I'm his only heir and my husband would be given as king, because I have the right to give the people a monarch, without power, however, I'll govern myself."

This message, as well as the second one of the same kind, was left unanswered and, consequently, Supramati stopped appearing on the esplanade at night.

Vispala thought she was going insane. Day and night she thought only of the unknown prophet; her blood boiled in her veins and plans - one more daring than the other - bubbled in her agitated head.

Once, she managed to get close to the magician when he was in the city. It appeared that Supramati hadn't noticed her, but the moment she wanted to touch him with her hand, she felt a strong shock that threw her to the side, as if she were being blown away by a gust of wind.

Vispala lost sleep and appetite and fell into such desperation that she ended up getting sick. The long and continuous emotions caused one of those terrible nervous illnesses for which the doctors had no cure. The young woman lost her sight and terrible convulsions contorted her arms and legs.

Nikhazadi became desperate and even the people shared his misfortune, because everyone was too fond of the charming woman. Because of this, a retinue of representatives from the various classes of the population went to the cave. If there was anyone who could save the princess, it was, without a doubt, only Supramati.

The magician promised to visit Vispala and ordered his disciples to pray in his absence. He then went to the palace, where he was immediately taken to the sick woman's room.

Terribly deformed by evil, Vispala was lying on the bed, and Supramati gazed with pity at this creature, a victim of the contamination of her own impure radiations, who was perishing in the prime of her youth.

Her sensual and disturbed love was repugnant to him, but he had not come into this world to dispise his inferior brethren. He must love them, polish the diamonds in the rough, and, with examples of pure affection, ennoble the congested sentiment, where, in despite of the various shadows that obscure it, there remains, nevertheless, a sublime feeling called love.

Supramati noticed at first glance the sticky, fetid mist that enveloped, like a gelatinous cover, the sick woman's body. Disgusting beings drawn from beyond by her carnal passion crawled over her body and sucked her vitality like leeches. Supramati ordered them to leave her alone, and when everyone had gone, he filled a small bowl with water and placed in it the ring he'd removed from his finger.

The water turned bluish with a silvery tinge. Immersing a towel in the bowl, Supramati rubbed the young woman's face, legs and arms with it. Enclosing the patient in a magic circle, he crossed her, and almost immediately the circle he had drawn caught fire and surrounded the bed with a multicoloured flame.

Flickering and sparkling, the fire from space began to absorb the black and sticky atmosphere surrounding Vispala. Whistling and writhing in whirlwinds, the abject beings were torn apart or swallowed up by the flames.

Slowly, the dark cloud vanished and gave way to a wonderful red light that filled the whole room, illuminating Vispala's body who lay lifeless. While the renovating forces were at work, he had lost consciousness.

Then, from inside the sick woman's body, clouds of black smoke began to rise, quickly absorbed by the red light.

Once the phenomenon had stopped, Supramati wet another towel that looked like it had been sprinkled with diamond dust, wiped it all over the patient's body and covered her.

Then, he took the harp, sat down by the headboard and began to play.

Sounds of extraordinary harmony arose and the room was filled with a soft aroma. The marvellous light seemed to fade, to be replaced by a violet glow. And upon this dark amethyst background appeared transparent beings, as if they were deformed by the same mist, surrounding the bed of the princess who lay motionless. Their aerial forms oscillated around the motionless body of Vispala. Slowly, the visions began to fade and dissipate into the mist.

Meanwhile, Supramati continued to play, and an expression of captivated joy was frozen on his face. At that moment, when one more time he had succeeded in bringing back to life a being who had suffered and been condemned to death, he delighted in the fruits of his labour. The delight produced by the melody, the gift of commanding the powerful agents of scent and colour, filled his heart with happiness and gratitude.

Surrendered to his thoughts, Supramati didn't notice that Vispala had opened her eyes and, standing up slowly, was watching him with a shy and loving gaze.

She felt recovered, but her entire being experienced a startling transformation. The impetuous and voracious passion that had lacerated her heart had disappeared, giving way to a comprehension of the abyss that separated her from the superior being she loved, and this awareness was presented to her with complete clarity.

Meanwhile, her whole being was filled with infinite gratitude and deep happiness at being able to see him there, next to her.

Getting down from the bed, she knelt before him and, raising her hands in prayer, murmured in an embarrassed voice.

"Master, how can I thank you for saving my life?" Supramati stopped playing, blessed her and, standing up again, said to her:

"It's not me you should thank, but God, your Creator and Heavenly Father. Be worthy of the spiritual and carnal health that you have been granted. Don't forget that in the carnal dungeon burns an immortal flame that will show you the way to the light that illuminates, supports and protects all that exists."

He raised his hand and pointed to a clear cross that in the air sparkled like a diamond.

"You, benefactor of all the misfortunate, teach me the great science: to believe and to love, not with the body but with the heart!" murmured Vispala.

"Believe in your Creator; have faith in His mercy; love Him with all your being and you will find the way of salvation. While your soul is purified, you'll learn to love with your heart and you'll dominate the impure passions of the flesh. And now, go into the arms of your grandfather, who went through fright and suffering during his illness."

Vispala grabbed Supramati's hand impetuously and placed it to her lips. Then she got up and ran to the king's chambers, where the king, surrounded by a few acolytes, waited in fearful anticipation for the results of the cure. When he saw his granddaughter completely healed, the king was overjoyed, and when he and his entourage wanted to thank the magician, he'd already disappeared.

The next day at dawn, the king went to the cave to express his deep gratitude for Vispala's healing. The old king was deeply touched. He spent a long time in serious conversation with the magician, after that, as Supramati had predicted, he knelt humbly before the altar, professing Divinity and pronouncing the name which the law forbade him to pronounce.

The healing of the heir to the crown caused an enormous repercussion and the magician's popularity increased even more; for the same reason, practically, the hatred of his adversaries grew. The straw that broke the camel's back was the rumours of uncertain origin that began to spread in the population.

By word of mouth, it's true, but rumours about the future king were everywhere, because Nikhazadi was an old man and his end was near, by virtue of which, the general opinion was that Supramati should be his successor.

Could the princess choose a better husband than this benefactor of all suffering? - It was spoken in society. - He's young and handsome; of course, his origin is obscure, but at least the princess is of noble lineage. Besides, he's poor... But that only shows his lack of self-interest, otherwise... If he were more practical... he could be the richest person on the world. How much would people pay him to save a loved one from certain death?

The conclusion of these conversations was that it would be preferable for the future monarch to be a kind, handsome and wise man.

But if the people's yearnings to have their king in Supramati were huge, the mere possibility of such a combination provoked a real storm of opposition and attracted quite a number of people to their ranks. Among them were some young men who, because of their origin and high position, nurtured hopes of being chosen by Vispala. But the young woman's passion for the handsome magician was no longer a secret, and in this the national aspirations could be succeed.

The surest way to avoid annoyance would be to eliminate the danger, and so, in a secret meeting, the enemies decided to finish him off, whatever the cost.

The conspiracy continued. Supramati was surprised by an attempt against his life as he was leaving a farm where he'd just been treating animals suffering from a malevolent disease. However, a hasty blow didn't hit him in the chest, but only in the shoulder. The evildoer tried to flee, but the indignant shepherds stopped him and brought him back. Later, it turned out that he was one of the people Supramati had saved from death.

No doubt the crowd would have lynched him, but for the interference of the magician, who declared that no one had the right to punish him, since he himself forgave the guilty. However, the criminal would have gone after one of Supramati's most fervent followers, if he hadn't prevented the scoundrel, even helping him to escape.

The second attempt was much more ingenious and they chose an animal to do it.

It was a beast that lived in the swamps, half lion, half bull, but of extraordinary strength and intelligence. Smaller than the bull that inhabited the planet, it had a mane similar to that of a lion. The uru - as it was known - had three horns, straight and sharp as daggers, a huge mouth full of strong teeth, and its paws more like monkey's feet.

The domestication of this animal was impracticable, but the public always enjoyed watching the uru fights, which were in vogue in the old days. What made the spectacle even more interesting was that this animal was difficult to dominate, in addition to being an endangered breed. That day they'd just brought out of the swamp two of those exceptionally huge and ferocious beasts, chosen to treacherously end Supramati.

The beasts were locked in iron cages, watched in an open shed. At the exact moment when the mage was crossing the street, accompanied by two disciples and a large crowd, one of the animals escaped from the cage and, blind with fury and incited by the screams of pursuit, ran towards the mage, ready to seize him with its horns. The danger was inevitable and mortal. The enraged beast flew towards Supramati, while the crowd, in panic, scattered to every corner.

Suddenly, however, two steps away from Supramati, the animal stopped suddenly, sniffed the air and turned towards one of the disciples; Supramati, meanwhile, raised his hand and the uru collapsed with its legs folded, as if it had received a heavy hit on the head. The spectators listened in amazement as the magician pronounced some unknown words, strangely repeated by all, and then played the harp.

Hearing the music, the uru, as if enchanted, slowly came up to Supramati and lay down at his feet. The magician stroked its head, gave it a piece of bread, taken from his pocket, and the animal began to eat it. Without stopping his playing and half-singing, Supramati entered the shed, followed by the uru who, obeying his order, entered the cage submissively.

"Next time be more careful and don't leave the cage open. Im not the only one on the street and how many innocent people could fall victim in my place," Supramati calmly warned the guards, who were visibly embarrassed.

This event caused a tremendous commotion and at the same time discontent among the population, who began to suspect an attempt on their benefactor's life.

The conspirators calmed down, suspending their bloodthirsty intentions for a moment. Hating their "enemy" even more, they decided to wait for an opportune moment while collecting more supporters.

Some time later, Nikhazadi died suddenly. The old king was much loved and his death caused a general shock.

Only those who accused him of weakness and of allowing Supramati's preaching rejoiced at the monarch's death.

For Vispala it was a very hard blow. The recognition of being alone in the world tormented her.

The entire period of mourning was spent in total isolation, surrounded only by a few friends who had recently converted.

Finally, there came a day when, according to the law, Vispala had to announce the one she chose as husband and king, for, as mentioned above, she herself couldn't rule, but she had the right to choose a monarch from among the young men of the high nobility.

The whole Council of State was gathered when Vispala arrived and, with humble dignity, took the monarchical seat, announcing that the only person that she considered worthy in the world to succeed her beloved and unforgettable grandfather was Supramati, the benefactor of the nation who had restored health and life to thousands of people.

The embarrassment of those present was evident.

"Queen, your choice is contrary to all laws," replied the president of the Council, recovering from his shock. - You want to elect as our king a person who is certainly worthy of it. However, his origin is unknown. He belongs to a totally different and unknown race, who could contaminate your descendants with impure blood, inferiorising your ancient and glorious dynasty, of which you're the last representative. Think it carefully, our beloved queen, and don't decide anything without mature reflection."

"I've analysed all this before coming here and my decision is irrevocable," Vispala declared firmly. - I also know that the Council can accept my choice or not. Your conclusions may even be fair, however, in my opinion Supramati's many good actions are the best example to confirm his nobility. Im prepared to submit to the Council's decision; but in case of refusal, I renounce all my hereditary rights to the throne and will retire to private life. That the Council and the people choose their king, according to their laws and for the welfare of the nation. In three days you'll give me your answer."

Leaving the councillors in total perplexity, Vispala left the room and returned to his chambers.

A heated discussion took over the room. Opinions diverged; some didn't even want to hear Supramati's choice; others were afraid of riots in case of a refusal, considering the people's love for the young queen and the adoration of the prophet and promoter of healings.

Tempers were heated. The mage's enemies claimed that with the accession to the throne of this unknown "sorcerer" new religious disturbances would begin, since it was clear that he would want to re-establish the old cult, reinstate the symbol once rejected - the cross - and demand the reverence of the forgotten God, who, thanks to the "wise laws", was the best way to live without.

Opponents countered by saying that their ancestors had lived with faith in God for many years and that times were better, the laws less cruel, more just, and that in any case, according to the prediction, the white faith should be reborn.

In order to calm down the agitated atmosphere, a respected dignitary proposed the election of a qualified candidate to the throne, putting an end to useless altercations.

At first, the proposal was unanimously accepted, but when the time to choose came, the party spirit, personal ambition and passions became so heated among those people who had grown up in the middle of total selfishness, that no one was chosen.

In a tedious, irritating and nervous meeting, convened by majority vote, it was finally decided to send a retinue to Supramati with the Queen's proposal, many abstaining from the vote who preferred the option for the unknown to the detriment of their peers, whose promotion might affect their own vanity.

In view of this decision, shortly after twelve o'clock that same day, the entourage, composed of the highest dignitaries, departed for the cave.

Supramati listened quietly and thoughtfully, and only smiled when they began to describe all the honours that awaited him. He replied with dignity that the proposal was too important to take a decision without analysing it, and asked the commission to wait until the next day to get a definitive answer.

When he was left alone, he ordered the disciples to retire to the little cave, then, he knelt down before the altar, and became immersed in exalted prayer.

His whole spirit aspired impetuously to join its disciples and obtain their advice: should he assume such a responsibility?

A long time ago his purified spirit had been free from any shadow of ambition, but at this moment he didn't know if his ascension to the throne would be desirable and useful to the mission. His whole spirit yearned for advice or any visible instruction from his leaders.

Suddenly, Ebramar's familiar and beloved voice resounded in his ears, as if it were a remote and soft music:

"Move forward without hesitation, worthy son of the light. To achieve your goals, you'll have to accept the crown of power, which may then lead to martyrdom."

Supramati prayed a lot and when he got up he was calm and determined, knowing what he had to do.

At dawn, Supramati gathered his disciples and, announcing that when he became king he'd have to leave them, he imparted his final instructions.

Shaking the hands of each of his disciples and saying long prayers, Supramati blessed them and gave each one a small wooden crucifix.

Wherever you settle, my friends, raise up the symbol of salvation and eternity in three dimensions: high, wide and deep. This sublime sign, the seal of God Himself, the cross, must remain on the doors of your houses and in your hands. With it, you'll cure illnesses, expel demons, tame storms and avoid catastrophes. But don't forget that the miraculous power of this mysterious instrument will only act according to your faith and your love for God; the stronger the faith, the more tremendous will be the power of the cross.

Preach and, above all, demonstrate by your actions your love for every creature, since love eliminates hatred and crime, dignifies man and increases his strength. Love God more than anything else and, in every living being, love the divine spark that vivifies it.

CHAPTER VI

When the retinue returned the next day. Supramati announced that he'd accepted the governmental power conferred to him, immediately he was showered with flattering and servile compliments and expressions of joy from the dignitaries present. They couldn't suspect that the magician's discerning eye read their hypocritical hearts, their hostile and envious thoughts, and their treacherous intentions.

But Supramati's beautiful clear eyes didn't reveal anything. He returned their greetings in a friendly manner, let them dress him in a short white robe with gold embroidery and a blue cloak, and placed on his head a large golden crown incrusted with precious stones. Once this was done, he made his way to the royal palace.

At the bottom of the stairs. Supramati was awaited by his bride. Shaken by the feelings she was experiencing. Vispala timidly raised her teary eyes, looking at him with affection. And when he, with an affable smile, took her hand, kissed it and pronounced a few affectionate words, her eyes shone with happiness and, radiant with joy, she went with him to the banquet hall.

The wedding was set for six weeks later; however, the controls of government soon passed into the hands of the new king; after presiding over the Council meeting for the first time, Supramati retired to his chambers.

To assist him in his personal services, Supramati called two of his disciples, a fact that created new enemies for him. The courtiers, thinking that such functions were their inalienable rights, were ignored on the "whim of this "outsider" who dared to prefer people as ignorant and miserable as himself.

Supramati knew that his illusory reign wouldn't last very long. So he tried to leverage the most of the time he had to introduce changes and lay the foundations of a religion that would return the people to the Creator, who had been a renegade for so long.

Thanks to his energetic action, he finally succeeded in repealing the repugnant law that condemned the sick to death and, later, in suppressing other legislation that was less important but equally cruel and unjust.

With difficulty, barely concealing their discontent, the dignitaries listened to this man, a total stranger, who spoke to them of mercy, forgiveness, kindness, and then, with his bold hand - as they called it - overthrew the socio-political system of the long existing state. Good or bad... Everyone had become accustomed to these laws and most had an interest in their maintenance.

The discontent of the privileged classes grew as new followers were recruited. Supramati seemed unaware of this fact, and continued his search for transformation. Devoting daily a few hours of the night to Vispala, he transmitted his teachings and developed his mind.

Already aware of her inferiority compared to her chosen husband, the young queen aspired to reach his level of intellectual development. She begged Supramati to enlighten her and inculcate the doctrine professed by him, and naturally there was no more devoted, convinced and fervent disciple than her.

Meanwhile, the most vile and alarming rumours about the new king started to spread among the people. First, he was slanderously accused of witchcraft, with whose help he'd murdered the old king and bewitched his heiress to usurp power. The harp, with whose help Supramati promoted cures, was also a weapon of sorcery. He'd undoubtedly appeared as a dangerous agent of the highlanders, who intended to re-establish old prejudices and witchcraft, which were punished by death, with his help. The rumours became so intense that the Supramatifriends considered it appropriate to warn Vispala that a revolt was being prepared.

Supramati was working when his fiancée, pale and trembling, rushed into his office. In a cracked voice, she told him what she'd just heard.

"I know everything," Supramati said calmly, making her sit down.

"And you do nothing to avoid the mortal danger that awaits you?" Falling to her knees, she extended her hands to him and pleaded:

"Hide, Supramati, until your enemies are eliminated. I'll unmask and punish the miserable ones, and after they're thrown to the bottom of the abyss, you'll be able to return without any obstacles."

Supramati hurried to lift her up and spoke to her, shaking his head:

"What a good example I'd set instead of putting my teachings into practice. Do you really think I'm a witch?"

"No, not at all! But you have so many enemies who hate you…"

"You must understand that the great truths which I profess and which must take root in you provoke the fury of the inhabitants of hell, and here they unfortunately find instruments to serve their purposes in people who are perverted, if unconsciously. It wouldn't be worthy of me to run away from destiny. Be calm, Vispala, I fear nothing: only can happen what must happen."

Sad and with bad omens in her soul, the young queen retired.

Emboldened by Supramati's apparent stupidity and inoperability, the conspirators became more audacious and energetic and, feeling quite strong, decided to fix the day of the royal wedding to carry out their plan. But despite all their efforts, Supramati had many supporters among the poor and especially among the working class. The conspirators decided to add a very strong narcotic to the delicacies to be served at the solemnity. In this way, Supramati's supporters would fall asleep and not obstruct the execution of the plan, and by the time they awoke, recognising what was happening, their beloved prophet would no longer be among the living.

At last the wedding day arrived. The civil ceremony was celebrated with great splendour, and afterwards the bride and groom walked through the streets of the city in procession, enthusiastically acclaimed by the people, who then dispersed to various parts of the city, where food, feasts and gifts were prepared. In the king's palace, a table with two chairs was already prepared for the newlyweds, and an expensive, aged wine was placed in a finely finished golden jar.

Supramati was calm, while the queen looked sad and worried...

As soon as they sat down, Supramati leaned towards his young wife's ear and whispered:

"Don't drink this wine, or you'll fall into a dangerous sleep."

"Is it poison?" she asked, frightened.

"No, it's a very strong sleeping drug," Supramati replied, pretending to drink and returning the guests' cheers.

The party was in peak. Enjoying the sound of music and conversation, Supramati leaned back into his wife's ear and said in an affectionate but firm tone:

"Gather your courage, Vispala, and arm yourself with a sense of dignity as a woman and a queen. A difficult time is coming," he squeezed her hand tightly. "They'll separate us, and probably my time has come..."

"Then I'll die with you!" Vispala muttered under his breath, trembling with dread.

Supramati nodded in disapproval.

"No, live to continue and maintain my mission. Remember me with love. Even though I'm invisible, I'll always answer your call..."

He was interrupted by noises and shouts from outside and into the hall came a large crowd of armed men, led by the old pretender to the princess's hand.

"Capture this witch who by his vile sorcery has taken the throne, killed Nikhazadi and blinded the queen's heart!" he brandished, pointing to Supramati who stood there, held tightly by Vispala.

A hellish commotion broke out in the hall. Supramati's supporters leapt to his defence, fighting around the royal pedestal. But as the rebels were more numerous and still finding their co-religionists in the hall, they were victorious and the leader of the conspirators climbed the pedestal.

Meanwhile, Supramati took off his king's crown and said in a low voice:

"What's all this fighting about? I'm not defending myself."

"This is of no importance. The question now is not that, but your defence before the court," the rebel leader argued with a laugh.

Vispala cried out in a muffled voice, knelt down and began to beg, in tears, for her husband's release.

Supramati quickly held her up and whispered in her ear:

"Shame on you to ask for mercy…"

For a few moments, under the influence of the mage's powerful force, Vispala appeared to calm down and Supramati used the moment to kiss and bless her.

When the time of the removal of the deposed king came, she clung to him again, but was abruptly separated from her husband; then, she lost consciousness and was removed from the scene.

A provisional Supreme Court, formed by the most fervent enemies of the prophet, assembled hastily in the noble hall of the Council.

Standing in front of this Areopagus, and effervescent with hostility and passions, Supramati gazed sadly and thoughtfully at the brutalised faces of his jealous judges, who hadn't given the necessary value to a superior being, thrown by destiny at his mercy.

Perplexed and suspicious, the president looked at that bluish haze enveloping Supramati, but, recovering quickly, he shouted angrily:

"Defend yourself, daring usurper, from the terrible accusations against you. Using your sorcery, you dared to restore in our planet the symbol of the cross, that was rejected many centuries ago. You had the courage to invoke the God we have denied, whose worship is forbidden on pain of death. You seduced the crowds to enter into delictuous contact with the unseen world, you uncovered the veil that covers discords and other funereal mysteries. With your strange music and your poisonous scents, extracted from the ether, you bewitched and seduced the people to such an extreme that you ended up seducing the heart of our queen and she chose you as her husband and king, a foreigner of obscure origin. And now, confess before all, who are you? person of unknown and strange race? Where were you born? Who are your parents? Where did you learn this evil science which you use to destroy us, because your doctrine will undoubtedly provoke an internal war."

Supramati listened quietly to his judge's malicious accusation and, when he kept silent, replied calmly:

"Im a child of light. My Father is also your Father. I was generated by the same divine spark that gave life to you and my supernatural powers are a result of the supremacy of a wise man over an ignorant one. A blind and ignorant person is a slave to contingencies and to all calamities that happen to him. A wise man foresees future events and is able to prevent their consequences."

"How wise are you, then, that you cannot predict our intentions and their harsh consequences?" laughed one of the pseudo-judges, gritting his teeth.

"You're wrong, Ragaddi. The very day I healed your only son, I already knew that you were attending a meeting where my death was being discussed. Which of us was fomenting discord? That, however, doesn't matter: I'm here by the will of my masters to sow love and faith among you. The light with I illuminated the darkness won't be extinguished any more. My mission is fulfilled. Do now what you must do; break the chains that tie me to this world. This is the destiny of the prophet: to mark with his own blood the teachings he preached."

"You have become so much more docile, great witch, why don't you defend yourself with your sorcery? If you can turn wild animals into lambs, why don't you use the powers at your disposal, or is it that you dont have the harp and all your power lies in that talisman?"

"You don't care where my energy is, since I don't want to use it anyway. I repeat, do what you have to do, kill the prophet so that his blood will purify this impious environment."

"So let's not waste any more time to avoid disturbing the purification of the atmosphere," the president quipped, and pronounced the sentence: Supramati must be shot with arrows and then burned."

"At dawn, your sentence will be executed, and when the wind spreads your ashes and there's nothing left of you, we'll root all your wrongs sown," he added with an expression of deadly hatred."

With the same calmness, Supramati let them chain him and they take to an underground dungeon where he was locked up.

When he was left alone, he lay down on a pile of straws in the corner, how contrasted his luxurious and festive clothes with the musty, dingy, underground setting!

As he pondered, he was struck by a strange mood.

He'd heard that the supreme initiation requires the sacrifice of the adept as proof of victory over the body and the self... But, being immortal, could he die?

It's true that he was in another world, of a different chemical composition, where the original matter of the planet may not have produced the normal effect. In the first attempt against his life he had been wounded and he had even suffered from the injury, though his scars had closed exceptionally quickly.

In case of death, he would be carnally separated from his masters, for example from Ebramar, and consequently, he would be deprived of the possibility of going to a new planet, where his brothers would go as legislators. Where and in what way would he then apply the knowledge he'd learned?

Without a doubt, by means of science, the masters could collect a new matter in his astral body, but that would already be something unusual, in other words... the future was uncertain and the path wasn't even planned or clear...

Supramati was ashamed of feeling some anguish; a weight seemed to oppress his spirit and his head felt slightly dizzy. It seemed to him that the air was scarce and, possessed by a sudden weakness, he rested against the wall. In his semi-conscious state, he heard remote voices:

Why did you abandon the refuge of the Himalayas? Where did your insatiable thirst for perfection lead you? Seeking an imaginary and vain glory of becoming a prophet, you must now die and remain on the path. The masters you revered have simply deceived you, pushing you to trials that will liquidate your body, while the fruits of the reward will be reaped by others. And what a terrible end awaits your perfect and spiritualized body! The wind will disperse it into atoms that will end up in chaos...

Shivers ran through Supramati's entire body. Suddenly, he felt as if sharp needles were piercing him, causing him terrible pain. Near him a bonfire was lit, giving off an unbearable heat, and the flames moved towards him and licked his feet, which trembled under the fire...

A mocking voice murmured in his ear:

"Are you feeling how the arrows pierce you and the flames devour your body? You have the power to calm the elements of nature. However, this is denied to you...You don't dare use your knowledge to defend yourself! What a shame! Ha, ha, ha, ha, ha!"

Horrified by the inhuman suffering that was tearing him apart, an icy sweat covered Supramati's body and something shuddered, rebelled, and became indignant inside him.

With a vague look he watched the bonfire that seemed to disappear under an opening abyss. And above the voracity, like a black cloud, floated the fateful accomplice Sarmiel, the Dragon of Doubt, accompanied by a retinue of monsters, begotten of darkness and usually surrounding those men enslaved by the flesh. There dragged the disgusting and infamous dread, the degrading weaknesses that paralyse men, and the oppressive anguish in the face of the unknown...

The Dragon on the threshold - the sign of doubt - is a dark enemy. Scrutinising carnal weaknesses it approaches determinedly to the child of light as a common mortal. From the bottom step of the ladder of the shadow of all that exists, a fateful shadow as much for a prodigious being as for a common man.

In every hard moment of disappointment and suffering, the diabolical voice whispers:

Stay under my protection. I'll give you everything and free you from the knowledge and conscience that torment you. I'll remove before your eyes the mistakes that make you perish...

Supramati's weakness increased more and more. Insufferable pains tore at his body and his thoughts became confused. Despite everything, he understood the danger and, by a strange effort of the will, he shook off the weakness of the disillusionment that overwhelmed him and the sickening doubt that overtook him, and the mighty and pure spirit rose up again. Yes, that doubt proved to be a terrible and cowardly enemy. No surprise that his mentors warned him of this treacherous and voracious swamp, into which he might succumb, making useless his work in all those centuries.

"My masters and leaders, don't abandon me," he cried, and at the same moment, in the darkness of the underworld, a glowing cross shone out."

Supramati stood up as if he was electrified. A heavy rock seemed to slide down his back and, raising his arm, he ordered:

"Get back and get lost, you creature from hell! You might tempt me, but don't confine me. With faith and love, I entrust my fate into the hands of my leaders and my soul to my Creator. May His will be done now!"

He fell to his knees and began to pray with such fervour that he didn't notice the chains falling from his arms and legs, and then any pain disappeared; and the voracity disappeared into the black clouds along with the thunder of the storm.

Suddenly, the subterranean floor was illuminated with a soft silver light, and before Supramati appeared the overseer of the Grail brotherhood. His vestments seemed to be woven of diamonds, and the cloak, falling from his shoulders, was lost in the darkness as a silver mist. In his hands, he held the chalice, decorated with the cross.

"Our Lord sends you His divine blood to empower you and help you to carry out the mission you have begun. Drink from the fountain of eternal life."

Happy and full of faith and enthusiasm. Supramati drank the purple liquid which extended in a fiery stream through his veins, giving him strength and a sensation of unspeakable tranquillity.

The vision vanished and he began to pray with such enthusiasm, that his spirit was taken from the earth and rose to the spheres of harmony and peace...

The armed guard who entered the dungeon brought Supramati out of his state of ecstasy, but the blinding light that enveloped the prisoner caused everyone to panic.

The head guard hesitantly ordered Supramati to follow him, while his commanders stared in fear at the chains that lay on the floor.

The dawn enveloped the planet with its whitish latent light. The prisoner was led into an adjacent courtyard, surrounded by high walls. The back door was locked. As soon as he had taken a few steps, a woman, wrapped in a blanket, emerged from the shadows and threw herself, crying, on her knees in front of him, and embracing him.

She was Vispala. Supramati got up and kissed her, trying to comfort her, happy to see her again.

"They gave me permission to say goodbye to you, but I don't want to survive your absence. I don't have the strength! It's too terrible to lose you at the moment when we were united forever. I understand all my insignificance in front of you, but for love there's no distance. Miserable as I'm, I love you more than life..."

Tears suffocated her.

Supramati lifted her lowered head and looked at her lovingly with eyes full of tears.

"You're right. The pure love which I taught you knows no boundaries, and spiritually you cannot be separated from me, for your love for me has united us indissolubly forever and ever. This divine union will always carry your thought to me and bring you my answer; so please, don't sadden me in this great hour with your thoughts of suicide."

That would distance me even further from you. Instead, live and honor my memory with acts of mercy, productive work, and spreading teachings, and every lost soul that is guided by you to the Creator will be a precious gift to me.

A joyful faith shone in Vispala's beautiful eyes.

I'll live Supramati, to make myself worthy and come closer to you, the wonderful being that God has graciously given me the opportunity to know and love. All the rest of my life, I'll dedicate to spread your teachings.

She hugged Supramati and kissed him, shuddering at the same instant.

"Your lips are dry, my dear, thirst torments you! Those monsters didn't even give you water... I suspected... Take this!"

She took out of her pocket a juicy red fruit and gave it to Supramati, who was very thirsty. He tasted the fresh, aromatic fruit; he held the leftover, as big as an apple, in the palm of his hand for a few moments and then, bending down, buried it in the ground.

"To commemorate this moment of my gratitude for the kind sentiment of your intention to strengthen me, I'll leave here a tree, whose fruits will serve as a source of health for the poor and disadvantaged. And now pray with me."

He stretched out his hands over the place where he had sown the seed and rays of multicoloured light came from his fingers; also, clouds of vapour began to rise from his palms and, falling to the earth, were absorbed by the soil. He seemed to be transformed. From his eyes flashed blinding lights and from somewhere a surprisingly melodious music was heard.

Vispala knelt down and, with her heart pounding, gazed in ecstasy at the phenomenon before her. She felt the earth tremble and break and saw the first stem grow into an impressive tree she'd never seen before.

Its white trunk was phosphorescent and translucent, so that red sap was visible flowing through its bark.

Supramati lowered his arms and addressing Vispala told him:

"The tree will blossom and bear fruit all year round. I've provided it with beneficial medicinal properties and whoever approaches it with faith and love will find in it the health of body and soul. And now, my dear, goodbye, or rather, see you soon. Now they'll come for me," said Supramati, raising Vispala, dissatisfied and excited.

He gave him a blessed kiss and, taking a cross of himself, he placed it around Vispala's neck.

"This cross will be your support and protection. I leave you also my harp which was hidden by my disciples. You'll place it in the first temple that rises to God. My ideas and my will are engraved on this instrument, and its strings will sound, when it's necessary, producing only the songs of peace that strengthen all, morally and physically."

He's interrupted by the sound of the door opening with the arrival of an armed guard. Two soldiers carried the unconscious queen, while the others escorted Supramati, who looked calm and content, as if he were going to a party and not to be executed.

Not far from his captivity, a small group of disciples and loyal friends waited on the road to say goodbye to their benefactor. The leader of the guards, acceding to their supplications, allowed them to approach the condemned man. Supramati kissed and blessed them one by one, and saying goodbye in a firm tone:

"Instead of weeping, contemplate my death. Probably more than one of you'll have to mark with your own blood the truth I've spread. Prepare, then, to bear that hour with dignity."

As if in cruel mockery, the bonfire was lit on exactly that spot, in front of the cave where Supramati lived. The means by which the execution was carried out suggested that he himself was stronger than the fatal abyss from which he'd managed to save thousands of people. The current at the bottom of the precipice had never roared so loudly or foamed with such intensity and fury. It seemed as if it had been possessed by rage against the monstrous injustice that men would perpetrate.

Supramati made no resistance when he was tied to the post. His countenance glowed with a deep, calm and exultant faith. Nothing now could shake the tranquillity of his soul; that terrible and repulsive monster - the doubt - which approaches every one who's about to die, constricting and obscuring the sublime moment when the enigma of life is solved, had been defeated. The mage, without any remorse, went to meet carnal death in order to be reborn in eternal light.

As the fire crackled, his soul was filled with jubilant prayer, and as he ascended to the light's abode, the visible world disappeared and left him. He felt neither the arrows piercing his body nor the blood flowing from his wounds. His blood seemed clear and bright, not dense and heavy as it does in the veins of ordinary men. The invisible opened before him and translucent beings surrounded Supramati, while in the air saturated with soft scents the music of the spheres played.

Suddenly, the sky was covered with black clouds, a gigantic blinding lightning dissipated the darkness, the earth shook and people fell to the ground. A purple start came out of the fire and like an arrow it ascended to the heights and was lost in the clouds.

Later it was discovered that where once there had been a mineral spring and a reservoir, the earth had formed a wide crack, from which the sapphire-coloured water gushed forth, as if sprinkled with phosphorescent sparks.

Vispala, removed from the dungeon, soon regained consciousness. Without returning to the palace, she covered her face with a veil and followed the macabre procession. Meeting a group of disciples and friends on the way, Vispala stopped them and begged them to incite the people to save the king and benefactor.

No matter how chimerical the hope, all his friends - two of them in particular - clung to the possibility of saving their master and rushed to different corners of the city. Meanwhile, under the effect of the sleeping elixir, the population slept without suspecting that at that hour their friend and protector was being carried off for the terrible execution. The daze, however, had begun to wear off, and the news of the event shocked and provoked a furious rage in the city.

At the queen's call, some hurried to the cliff, while others attacked the houses of members of the Monarchist Council - Supramati's enemies - and ended up killing them.

It was impossible to describe the despair of the crowd who, on reaching the abyss, realised that everything was already over.

The first ones to arrive with Vishpala and Khaspati could see, for about a minute, the prophet on fire, the unleashing of the storm, an igneous star bursting into space and finally, a strong current coming from the cave, dragging from the platform the last vestiges of the torpid murder perpetrated there.

At first, the crowd was astonished, followed by a wave of furious despair; people were tearing their hair out, and rolling on the ground, but their shouts of rage and groans were silenced by the roar of the hurricane.

But if the disposition of Supramati's supporters was so latent, the prophet's enemies, who had gathered in considerable numbers, were not prepared to allow the people to vindicate them summarily. A bloody struggle followed and Vispala found it very difficult to avoid the worst. Kneeling at the edge of the abyss, she prayed as if she could neither see nor hear anything.

"Queen, try to put an end to this carnage, a consequence of the words of the accused witch," shouted one of the councillors.

You're the ones who started the discord, so you're the ones who will have to put an end to it," the queen replied with disdain.

But turning to Khaspati, she asked him if the master hadn't instructed him, in case of absence, about how to calm the human passions. Khaspati thought for a while and said:

Let's quickly go to the cave. The harp of the master is hidden there. He once told me that if I prayed fervently and uttered some words in a strange language that he taught me, the harp would produce sounds, as if played by him, which would be heard by all, because on this harp his voice and his music were engraved.

Quickly, using subterfuge, they reached the opposite shore and, climbing the difficult stairs because of the water pouring out of the cave, they stopped inside; taking the crystal harp from its hiding place, Khaspati and Vispala headed for the esplanade.

On the opposite side, the fighting continued, but the storm had already passed.

After a fervent prayer, Khaspati raised the harp, pronouncing mysterious words, and a bluish cloud enveloped the instrument. Vispala had the impression of seeing beings with vague, transparent outlines.

Suddenly, oh, miracle! The strings sounded softly, accompanying the velvety and strong voice of the mage in his marvellous song. As the amazing chanting progressed, the excited passions of the troublemakers subsided, the clashes ceased, and the crowd fell perplexed to their knees. When the singing ceased, the people, calm and thoughtful, made their way to the city, where the telling of what had happened provoked a great reaction.

The next day, the members of the Council of State who had managed to save their lives met and asked Vispala to appoint a regent until she could calm down and choose a new husband and king.

"I don't want to govern. My misfortune will only end with my death," she replied resolutely.

There was nothing to convince her to the contrary. Vispala retired to the cave, where Supramati lived, and there she built the first temple to the Divinity, as the old priest, the last cultivator of the shrine, had prophesied.

A period of revolt followed. Supporters of atheism tried to establish the old, more "comfortable" order, but the latest events had a positive effect on the population.

Supramati's death produced a very strong reaction in souls. The number of devotees of the prophet's doctrine was growing day by day and the marvellous healings performed at the cave contributed to this. The water gushing from the spring was found to be miraculous and devotees came flocking from far and wide to seek help or to listen to the preaching of Vispala and the disciples of the revered magician.

A few months after Supramati's death, the forest temple was rebuilt, and soon after many others. The struggle against atheism wasn't over for good, for the evil had taken deep root; nevertheless, the foundations had been laid: a torch of faith was lit and the way to God was found again...

Tied to the stake of the fire that was to finish him, Supramati thought neither of his body, about to be abandoned without mercy, nor of the devastating fire. His soul, full of faith, love and aspiration for God, only was immersed in ecstasy.

With the vague impression that his body, melted in an ocean of flames, was being freed from an enormous weight, it looked to him as if he was being taken up by a strong wind and grey, unrecognisable beings were swirling around him, carrying him.

Even less clearly, he felt himself flying at vertiginous speed through layers of clouds, falling into an unfathomable abyss and then losing consciousness... Then, sweet and unusually soft sounds woke him up.

He hadn't yet realised what had happened to him; only waves of harmony lulled and held him, while his exhausted gaze wandered over the familiar scene of Hermes' tomb, as always illuminated by a silvery-blue light.

Suddenly, his memory came back and he stood up. He was inside the mysterious sarcophagus, where he had been placed to fulfil his mission. Surrounded by flashes of blinding light, above Supramati was the great primeval founder of the world: Hermes Trismegistus.

Now Supramati could bear that light and look at the wonderful countenance of the protector of Ancient Egypt.

The radiant vision held out its arms to him, which seemed warped with light, and Supramati stood up:

"Come into my arms, my dear disciple, and accept the reward for your work," said the melodious voice, but as if damped by distance. "The first mage's torch you received for defeating the beast within, the second for acquiring knowledge, and the third for loving humanity and God to death."

The transparent hand touched Supramati's head and forehead, and, between a torch of bluish light and a green one, a third one shone: a purple light of golden hue. He felt a kiss of vision on his forehead, and then the image of Hermes dissipated into the bluish mist.

A current of vital and energetic forces seized Supramati, and he, with a look of radiant delight, examined the tomb.

And there were gathered the Hierophants, Ebramar, Grail Knights, and among them Dakhir, also with his luminous gaze, also with three beams of light from the mystical crown of the mages.

Supramati quickly jumped down from the sarcophagus and threw himself into Ebramar's arms, who, with tears in his eyes, pressed him to his chest.

"Dear son of my soul! What a moment of happiness you have given me!"

Soon after, everyone present embraced and congratulated Supramati. The most emotional encounter was with Dakhir, his faithful companion on the difficult road to perfection.

When the initial emotion calmed down, all those present fell to their knees and in a prayer of fervour thanked the Lord for so many graces received.

At the end of the short prayer, both heroes of the event were led into a chamber where a modest celebration was prepared.

The mysterious abode of the mages had a festive appearance that day. There were wreaths of flowers everywhere, the disciples decorated the floor with flower petals and, during the banquet, beautiful voices of young adepts cheered the visitors with songs.

At the tables, they talked animatedly. It seemed that the spirits of these extraordinary people were full of satisfaction. Ebramar was happy and proud of his two heroic sons, the fruits of his knowledge. They, in turn, experienced an indescribable delight in feeling that they were dignified in the tasks assigned to them and full of love and gratitude to the wise and patient mentors who made them what they now were.

After lunch, Dakhir and Supramati heard that Ebramar would take them to stay in the Himalayas to rest in one of the initiatory palaces until they were called to fulfil their last mission on earth, already condemned to death.

Dakhir and Supramati knelt down and thanked the Hierophant for all they'd acquired and learned under his guidance.

Then they said goodbye to the Hierophants, to Siddhartha and to all the members of the brotherhood.

An hour later, a spaceship was taking Ebramar and them to the Himalayas to rest, until, according to the mages' motto: Onward to the light... they started a new journey.

CHAPTER VII

In its rocky depths, the Himalayas hide countless astonishing secrets. There, for hundreds of kilometres, like a spider's web, a network of galleries stretches out. Some of them lead to unknown valleys, with their beautiful initiation palaces; others give access to temples and underground cities; and some finally lead to gigantic caves, where in chests, desk drawers and shelves are archived collections of the most diverse historical writings. Any one of these would have caught the eye of a modern scientist lucky enough to be able to peer into the unknown maelstrom of the past. It contains the material archives of the planet, the maps and history of the vanished continents and the people who inhabited them. All this is written on animal skins, papyrus, palm leaves and on clay or metal plates. But... no profane foot has ever walked on the floor of these enigmatic hiding places, no curious eye can glimpse the marvellous works of art and the history of earthly mankind gathered there...

In the underground world there was an uncommon movement. The main and largest temple of this amazing underground city received numerous retinues in silence. Through the galleries came, in pairs, young women dressed in long transparent robes and under cloaks of light green, sky blue, red, violet and white. Their heads were adorned with wreaths of luminous flowers. Majestic and silent, they arrived, climbed the stairs and entered into a large, colonnaded cave, decorated with statues of gods and goddesses. At the back of the hall, in the shape of a semicircle, was enclosed by a heavy but flexible metal curtain, and beside it were two wide stone steps where the women who arrived just now could be accommodated.

From various ways came new processions. Young men in oriental costumes and muslin turbans entered; then came a long line of knights in silver armour, winged helmets and wide white cloaks. They were followed by the women of the Grail confraternity, and on the chest of each was a chalice decorated with a cross, decorated with gold embroidery. After, the procession of the sons of the mages - of both sexes - appeared with little golden harps and other musical instruments. Then entered the women mages of truly angelic beauty, in white robes and long veils, sprinkled with diamond dust.

All who entered, who numbered a few thousand, moved in masse into the temple, and as soon as they took their seats, from the open gallery in front of the curtain, the procession of mages appeared. They were enveloped in a broad golden aura, and the number of lanterns on their heads indicated the degree of initiation they'd reached. On the chest of each shone a magic star.

When the representatives of the great science stood in a semicircle before the lowered curtain, this opened in two parts, revealing a platform of a few steps, and the whole room was illuminated with a soft blue light.

On the platform, the senior mages presided over the Areopagus; a blinding light shone from them, especially from their heads and even from their robes, but a white haze covered their features. The person in the centre radiated six torches from his forehead and commanded the Areopagus.

As the curtain opened, music of indescribable harmony and beauty was heard. The head mage stood up and blessed those present. After the blessing, all in chorus sang a hymn and then concentrated on a short prayer. It was impossible to see their features, but their sonorous, metallic voice carried melodiously and clearly to the back rows.

"My brethren and my children! Today, the coming of the great moment unites us. The end of the planet we live on is near. Our Earth, the mother of all, which nourished us and which was the school of our youth and on which we have passed difficult trials in the great ascent towards the light, is dying."

In this case, our Earth obeys only to a general law, for everything that is born must die, and after having served as a refuge for billions of human generations, the planet is exhausted and its nutrients have been consumed, and it can no longer offer its ungrateful children anything more than the grave."

I call humanity ungrateful and even blind because it has exploited without mercy the mother that sustains it, sucked the marrow from its bones and broken the balance of forces that provided it with life; and finally, it has affronted it with crimes and dishonesty, whose consequences are chaotic catastrophes that will finish it long before the limit to which it could and should reach.

This coming moment should be of concern, above all, to us, the immortals who live thanks to the life of the planet. We'll have to leave the Earth, which was our cradle, but it won't be our tomb. We'll break thousands of ties that bind us to it and we'll seek another world for our home. There, my brethren, we'll be immortal and we'll remove the wrapping that our amazing destiny ordered us to wear.

However, I've called you not only to announce to you the coming catastrophe, but also to tell you of the last mission we'll have to take up on this dying Earth, for which, for the last time, we'll have to make contact with mortals. You know that a large number of souls of a very specific type have now incarnated. They're all those who by their actions, examples and inventions have contributed to the devastation of the planet; they're all those who have rejected, committed sacrileges and fought against the Heavenly Father, destroyed the temples and desecrated the altars; they're all those who, by their sophistry and distortions of the truth, have seduced their fellow men, teaching them to despise law and belief. Finally, the leaders of states, instead of dignifying, purifying and disciplining the bestified peoples, instead of preserving and supporting the laws of morality, which ensure balance, have given to the stupid or to criminals the power to do harm, to rob the poor and to negotiate justice and the interests of the people. The implacable law of karma has brought and gathered all these criminals, who sold themselves to Satan, in the place of their crimes, to participate in the catastrophe they've prepared. In this final judgment, predicted by the inspired prophets, they'll be forced to account for their murdered and degraded victims, for the spilled blood of the innocent, which feeds hell. What a terrible punishment it'll be to witness this scene and feel the agony of the world, to witness terrifying phenomena announcing a catastrophe in which the invisible will be the visible and fear will dominate even the most courageous! May their destiny be fulfilled and their karma catch up with them!

But among the criminal multitudes, who will be punished for their actions, there are chosen souls who have resisted against the temptations around them, speaking bravely in favour of the truth, enduring the taunts and persecution of evil-doers, and, in spite of hostility, disdain and insults, they bravely carry the light into the region of darkness.

Faith in God has never been extinguished in their hearts, they have never rejected the Creator for the pursuit of ephemeral earthly advantages, even though they have been despised, abandoned and persecuted. You, the mages, will identify these humble workers of pure heart and ardent spirit, and prepare for them a place of honour in the new world, towards which we're moving. It's a great task that's incumbent upon you at this important time. Go, my brethren, sisters and children. Spread the truth, support the weak, and comfort the suffering, because mercy is our duty, and knowledge will give you the powerful means of rendering this help. But be careful in choosing those who will go to a new world, where we'll sow the religion and the knowledge which we ourselves have acquired, as well as teach the divine laws and establish the human laws. Beware of bringing, whoever is contaminated by crime or bloodthirsty abuse, with a brain poisoned by hereditary hostility to the Divine and its laws.

These general instructions are enough to draw your path. Then they'll fulfil their difficult but sublime mission; may the Creator guide, teach and strengthen them!

The great hierophant became silent, and for a few minutes a profound silence reigned. The beautiful and spiritual countenances of those beings who lived, one could say, outside of reality, were sadly concentrated. All that remained of their humanity suffered at that moment the near separation from that Earth where they'd been born and to which they were linked by a thousand hard and happy memories on the way of ascension.

For the last time, the hierophant's voice was heard:

Goodbye, brothers and sisters, may each one go to the place indicated for their activity! At the great hour, we'll join you with the guests that each will bring with him.

He blessed those present. All chanted a prayer, the metal curtain closed behind the magician' areopagus, and immediately the crowd dispersed into the galleries of the underground labyrinth.

✳ ✳ ✳

Nothing had changed in the beautiful valley where Ebramar's palace was situated. As before, there were lush green orchards, fountains silently murmuring, and numerous flower beds brightened the view and filled the air with sweet scents.

On the terrace, next to the table with papers, was seated the sage. He wasn't working, but deep in his thoughts, resting his head in his hands.

Ebramar was more handsome than before. The soft silver light that radiated from him enveloped his figure as if by a light mist, while in his large black eyes shone such strength and ardor that it was difficult to bear his gaze.

Suddenly, Ebramar's face lighted up with a cheerful and friendly smile. He got up and went to meet three people approaching the terrace. All were dressed in the long white robes of mages and on the heads of two of them shone three beams of light, while on the head of the other there was only one.

"Welcome Dakhir and Supramati, dear brothers." greeted Ebramar, kissing them warmly.

Then he embraced the third one warmly, blessing him.

"Narayana, prodigal son, finally you have brought me happiness by making yourself a wise man, making good use of time and even deserving the first torch of our immortal crown."

"I'm no less glad to hear a compliment from you. And you, my dear master, have tried even harder; you have become so luminous that to look at you, like at the sun, one needs blue spectacles or dark glasses," replied Narayana, visibly happy and joyful."

Ebramar couldn't contain his laughter.

"Incorrigible even in the role of a magician. I can imagine the original company he'll bring us."

"Exceptionally beautiful women I'll try to save from death. They'll be needed on the new planet and you know that I'm a master in the art of winning women's hearts."

"I see you haven't forgotten this branch of science and you're going to offer us a surprising and unusual spectacle: a mage in the role of Solomon with his harem," Dakhir remarked mischievously."

"Doing what? Even on the new planet, even King Solomon will be useful," Narayana replied, full of sympathy. - But, at this moment, I'm just a magician and I'm happy to be with you," he added."

Everyone sat down at the table and began a lively and friendly conversation. They talked about Narayana's initiation and he recounted his work:

"Well, no more talk about me. I haven't yet congratulated you, dear friends, on the third torches that adorn your foreheads. Are those difficult medals you won during your excursion to the neighbouring planets? Was the trip a good one?"

"In any case, very enlightening!" replied Supramati.

"And very sensitive," added Dakhir.

Narayana laughed.

I think it was even spectacular! Face it Supramati, sometimes you thought that crossing the limits of the worst of the trials was "easy stuff". Nivara told me that those miserable wretches were about to burn you alive and that you were already at the stake.

"That's true. But faith hadn't deserted me either in the dungeon or at the stake. I believed that the supreme test, imposed by the leaders on the magician, is death by condemnation," replied Supramati seriously and thoughtfully.

"I experienced a surprisingly good time at the stake," he added. I didn't want to invoke any incantation that could prevent what was about to happen and just concentrated on a fervent prayer. Suddenly, I felt a nice, refreshing breeze that enveloped me and didn't let the smoke touch my face. Then I was illuminated by a red cloud, as if sprinkled with lightning, while the earth and air trembled with the rumble of thunder. The fire moved away from my feet and then seemed to melt and disappear: and I was lifted up by a hurricane and in a warm whirlwind carried off into space. I lost consciousness, regaining it here at home."

"Ha ha! I can imagine the shock of the poor crowd who dared to burn a magician. And you, Dakhir, it seems they wanted to finish you off too," said Narayana."

"Good. I also had to fight a fierce battle with the high priestess of a satanic temple - very beautiful, by the way - and by her order I was thrown off the cliff."

"I bet she fell in love with you and chased you away in jealousy," observed Narayana, winking mischievously. "And what happened to her?"

"She lost her mind and threw herself off the same cliff, thinking I had perished."

"Brr! What a "hellish" passion! But frankly, I'm surprised about the apathy of the initiates there. What did they think when they saw their visitors, the earth mages, tortured and even about to be killed? And they slept peacefully instead of taking care of them and protecting them from the savagery of those animals," Narayana said.

Ebramar, who was listening in silence, smiled.

"Moderate your anger, my son. The initiates, our neighbours, are not guilty of having slept while Supramati and Dakhir were tortured and prepared to be executed. No, they acted in agreement with us, and our two mages during this ordeal - which I recognise is difficult even for them - must necessarily be left alone and deserve the third torch from their crown. However, you must also know that immortals don't have access to ordinary death."

"And now they'll go like me, rest peacefully and study contemporary society," laughed Narayana.

"I think this break won't be long and less pleasure will be given to us from those degenerate people. But, master, where can we gather information about the present state of the earth before we set foot on it?" Supramati asked.

"Nivara asked him for the honour of initiating them into modern life. By the way, he adores you, Supramati, and looks forward to meeting you," Ebramar replied.

"I've seen him and even had a brief conversation with him; what he told me about today's society is pretty disgusting. I can even give you some interesting background information," Narayana declared enthusiastically.

"That shouldn't surprise you, my son. Don't forget that we're on the eve of the end of the world. It's like the end of a great kingdom that the enemy is passing through with iron and fire, and such catastrophes are always preceded and accompanied by various horrors," Ebramar observed.

"Yes, yes, our dear contemporaries have already disunited too much. Nivara told me how they've denied God. There's no more place for the altar of the Creator and the symbol of expiation no longer preserves humanity. It means that there are no more Christians and the consequence of this state of affairs is that all laws have been eliminated except one: the law of the strongest. For the same reason, there are no more judges or prisons; any crime or cruel act is tolerable and not penalised, because they're considered to be the fruit of personal freedom.

Internal wars, cruel revenge, savage persecutions are normal phenomena. Blood flows, but nobody cares. You don't mess with the strong and powerful for fear of reprisals."

"What a wonderful little world we'll have to go to! Are there any states, republics, empires, or anything like that left? Are there any arts or temples?" Dakhir asked.

"Only the temples of Satan, in which the bestialised people worship their passions and vices. As for the arts, these are cultivated, it seems, in their forms and obscenities that exceed the limits of cynicism."

"Judging by what you say, all the sacred places have been eliminated," shuddered Supramati.

"Of course! They have destroyed all the holy places that the profaners managed to penetrate," Narayana observed. - But Nivara told me that the Christians still exist, even if in rather small numbers. They're persecuted like criminals and go into hiding, but they're inspired by an exceptional and jubilant strength of spirit. They're people of unshakable faith and heroic courage. They've managed to preserve from desecration a number of marvellous icons and exceptionally venerated sanctuaries, which were hidden in inaccessible caves. The secret of these isolated places is inviolable and only true believers have access to pray there and renew their strength at the source of the divine light and warmth.

By the way, Nivara told me about a remarkable case in Lourdes. It's a place venerated for the many miracles that take place there and has provoked exceptional hatred on the part of the minions of the antichrist. Finally, it was decided to suppress the sacred cave and the fountain, blowing up the first and crushing the second.

To perpetrate this profanation, a veritable army of evildoers set out for the site, but on the way the sky was covered with dark clouds, the heat became scorching, and the air thickened to the point where it was difficult to breathe. An earthquake and a fearful hurricane followed and torrents of lava gushed out of the earth and covered all the attackers; and when the storm subsided, everyone saw that on the site of the ancient cave there was a large lake and in the middle of it stood a solitary rock in the form of an island.

The water of the lake became salty and bitter in taste, full of bitumen like the Dead Sea, and the air became saturated with sulphuric evaporation. To sum up, the area became a desert that everyone avoided.

And then one day a young shepherdess discovered in the cliffs a natural gallery leading down to the bottom of the lake, and led her to the cave of the Blessed Virgin, who had emerged unharmed in a truly inconceivable way, as if she'd been brought there by a benevolent hand. The miraculous fountain was still, as before, pure as crystal, flowing through the sand.

When the news of this miracle spread, the supporters of Satan wanted to try again to destroy the holy place, but they failed, because several of them were suffocated to death in the gallery by poisonous gases."

Silence fell and Dakhir and Supramati were deep in gloomy thoughts. But, Ebramar who was watching them, to change the subject, said jokingly:

"Well my sons, don't dream for the moment of the delights of your excursion. Soon you'll see the people, the things, and the drained earth, whose fertility is only artificially maintained by electricity, which will also lead to the final and fatal blow."

"Talking of the final blow, I wonder if you could show us the air fleet that will take us to our new home. I know the ships are being built by hierophants and senior mages and I look forward to seeing them," exclaimed Narayana.

"The fleet is not ready yet, but I'd like to invite you to see what I've built, which is almost finished. We just need to go up a bit," Ebramar replied, smiling.

"Oh, thank you! We'll go with you to the spheres if we have to!" exclaimed the three of them with such enthusiasm that Ebramar burst out laughing.

"Come on, friends, I'll serve you dinner on our campaign ship."

He led them to a laboratory and opened a small door, artificially camouflaged in such a way that it was impossible to suspect its existence. The laboratory went into the mountain and, through a small corridor, they entered a small room, dug into the rock, from whose ceiling rose a dark tube and below it was a lift. When the four had entered it, Ebramar activated the mechanisms and the machine, with vertiginous speed, started to move upwards. The lift stopped on the rocky, craggy platform where a spaceship was moored, and the mages entered it.

"Now," said Ebramar, "lets go where no living being or mortal has ever been: the lost and inaccessible glacier."

A minute later, the spacecraft landed on an immense glacier, surrounded by dark and sharp cliffs.

In the middle of this valley, covered with snow, as if sunk in a white mist, a long object shone in the pale moonlight like a cut crystal.

On closer inspection, it was a huge, elongated spacecraft made of a strange, transparent, phosphorescent, material similar to crystal. At the tip of the ship was a single entrance. When Ebramar turned on the lights, he saw that the interior consisted of three rooms and numerous cabins, small but comfortable, luxuriously finished.

In each cabin there was a window, made of the same material as the ship, not too thin. The window can be closed with a curtain of a material as flexible as the wind itself, but waterproof as leather, which Ebramar demonstrated to his guests. Everywhere, in the rooms and cabins, there were stands with large vases of the same crystalline substance.

"In the holds there're compartments for the necessary provisions and the things the travellers will take with them."

"And what will they take with them?" Supramati was interested.

"The most valuable things, what is preserved in laboratories, hermetic libraries and works of art as samples. All this must be removed because it will be needed to build new palaces of science and of initiation."

"Is there a device that can lift that colossal weight into the air?" Supramati remarked.

"I'll show you later, because I haven't yet finished the construction of these devices that will transport us, and you can convince yourself that they're capable of carrying and lifting a very large amount of weight.

For the moment, the list of everything to take on each boat is ready, so that you don't forget anything indispensable or take the same thing two or three times. At the right moment, when all the travellers are gathered, this door will close hermetically and we'll only breathe the original essence, which will be lit in all the candelabras."

So talking, they boarded the ship, but Dakhir asked for more explanations, while Supramati paused to wait for them and, bowing his head, was immersed in sad thoughts. All that was left of him that was "human and earthly" was shaken in that minute and he felt his heart squeezed by indescribable anguish... For the moment he crossed that threshold for the last time and the door of the spaceship closed behind him, the world into which he was born would crumble under his feet, that extraordinary work of the Creator, with its immense and wonderful past, would disappear...

At that moment he felt a hand on his shoulder and raising his head he found the deep gaze of Ebramar, which with its luminous glow penetrated his saddened eyes.

"Don't fear Supramati, and invoke wisdom to assist you. The future oppresses you, because you will witness the end of the world for the first time."

But the time will come when, like a swallow, you'll fly easily from one world to another, from sphere to sphere, and you'll become accustomed to contemplating the death of a planet, like the death of a cell in any organism.

What seems so significant and moving to you now is nothing in the grandiose All of the universe.

Look at the Milky Way, - he raised his hand - where millions of suns and their planetary systems revolve. Worlds crowd there like dust in the sun's beam, yet in each of those atoms of space, human generations are born, live and die. Only our profound ignorance, in all respects, and our mean selfishness obscure them.

We panic and tremble, thinking that something will happen that will bring down the universe. The truth is that nothing of the sort will happen: only one of the countless atoms of the great infinite will be extinguished

Supramati raised his head and admired the celestial sphere as if sprinkled with gold and glitter. At that altitude, the air was exceptionally transparent and the stars, in the dark blue of the sky, shone with surprising radiance.

Suddenly, from one part of the sky, a beam of sparks blinked and spread out like an exploding rocket. For a moment, the sparks glowed like a swirl of reddish light and then faded.

An enigmatic smile appeared on Ebramar's face.

"By any chance, Supramati, would you have heard any noise or bang? Did you feel something, at least a movement of the air? No? Yet this sparkling whirlwind indicated to us the end of a world whose existence we witnessed from a long time.

Yes, my son, greatness and insignificance are relative concepts; we're great in our own eyes. An ant, perhaps, may also consider itself very secure in its mound at the foot of a high mountain, and will only realise its insignificance the moment it climbs to the top of the mountain. So we are - fragile beings - insignificant little dusts of space, despite the flames of the mages who crown us. The only thing we could boast of, without blushing, is that we're only useful bees in the great hive of the Eternal."

Supramati lowered his head and covered his eyes with his hand. He realised that he too had believed himself great and mighty when the third torch flared on his forehead, but Ebramar's words destroyed the mage's pride and reduced him to nothing. In that instant, he felt insignificant, a pitiful ignorant; would he ever reach the remote and vague heights of perfect knowledge? Doubt, bitterness and despair - three enemies he'd always considered vanquished - suddenly came upon him.

"Beware, Supramati, and drive away such weaknesses! Be on guard, because the enemy is near!" pronounced Ebramar rigorously in his sonorous voice, and, raising his hand above Supramati's head, he applied a torch of silver light to her.

Supramati shuddered, looked around and saw a black figure that appeared behind him, then stepped back and leaned against the cliff that surrounded him. There the black shadow seemed to grow denser, illuminated by a purple aura, and against that bloody background the tall figure of Sarmiel came clearly into view, coming closer with his black jagged wings: in his characteristic countenance, disfigured at that moment by clear disillusion, there was hatred, envy, and infernal hostility.

"Look that this servant of chaos has even dared to close to you," said Ebramar. "Go away and disappear, creature of hell, who dared to declare war on the Almighty. The Eternal only tolerates you as a testing stone for human souls, while you dared to test even the Son of God and now you stalk the pure cultivator of Good."

Sarmiel's figure began to melt and finally, with a horrible hiss, disappeared in a swirl of smoke, dotted with fiery flames.

"Do you see how danger is always near? The diabolical tempter waits for our slightest carelessness, and only those who resist him can continue their ascent to light. The weak, however, are led by him to the abyss of darkness. Don't ever doubt yourself, Supramati, nor underestimate the virtues of your spirit. However miserable the elevation of man may be, he's already halfway to the ascent. Every good action, every prayer and spiritual work for the good of others, every good intention, the desire to improve and overcome the carnal in man, will be the links in the saving chain which will unite you to the Divine and, at the same time, gather together all the weak and humble in our association; and this effort for good will sustain and guide these beings to the extent of their spiritual strength."

One can lift only a few kilos; an athlete will lift hundreds, but this is not important: because nothing can be underestimated. Everyone is given what is necessary, and if at a moment he is short of strength, his own effort and the merit of that effort are of equal value."

"You personally, Supramati, have no reason to despair," Ebramar added earnestly. "Ambition is inherent in any person, while noble ambition is a worthy sentiment.

Before your ambition opens up a wide field of work and science. Supported by the light of the knowledge you've already acquired; you'll ascend the magic ladder that leads to the sanctuary of perfect knowledge. In time, you'll become the genius of the planet, the protector of the whole system, and you'll rule over the chaotic primal elements to bring them into harmony and create worlds upon them.

You'll investigate and direct the cosmic forces: you'll rule over the phalanxes of higher spirits; your mind will be able to apprehend and judge: your will of discipline will maintain the balance of the spheres and you'll become a wise servant of the Supreme Wisdom.

As a form of the ultimate test, it's up to you to courageously cross the last barrier that divides you from your

Creator to finally comprehend Him in all His greatness and infinite wisdom. Is it not enough to satisfy and evaluate the knowledge acquired? Lift up your head, Supramati, and spread your spiritual wings. Never look down; there's the abyss and there lies the doubt and misunderstanding. Look up to the luminous heights and your wings will carry you to infinity, where harmony reigns.

Supramati blushed slightly, his eyes sparkled and he extended his hands towards Ebramar.

"I thank you dear master, I'll never forget this moment. Your words have strengthened me and made me realise how close is always the terrible danger that lurks even in the soul of a prepared mage. We must always be on our guard against the skilled and insistent enemy that pursues us!"

Ebramar shook his hand and said in a cheerful tone:

"Enough of serious thoughts. Let's go inside the spaceship. I promised you a dinner, remember?"

He led them to one of the rooms, where they sat at the table. Ebramar took a basket of toast from the wardrobe, which was exceptionally light, tasty and very nutritious. After the toast, he served vegetables, pastries in flour dough and fruit jam, which they ate while drinking wine.

Narayana returned to his usual mood and everyone, more cheerful, talked animatedly and quietly about the great journey.

Your dishes are pretty light, and not bad at all," he said laughing, " but they cannot compare with a dinner of roast boar that I once ate at King Richard's palace: and no doubt none of the beauties of that time would approve them. But for so long a journey, one doesn't save wild boar.

"Besides, wild boars don't exist any more," Dakhir laughed.

"Well, we'll find them in our new home. I predict we will do well there. As soon as we land, I'll immediately put all our rescued people to work, I'll confiscate the local herds and build a palace," Narayana decided.

"What a good shepherd you'll be! As for doing well, I know you won't fail! Ebramar commented in a slightly humorous tone.

"My God, they must be occupied! Because if everyone is only going to go just to eat and drink and to roam around the new planet, they'll fall into sin. You yourself have told me a hundred times that idleness is the mother of all sins. Yes, since there will be no theatres, no restaurants, no newspapers, and no big shows, everybody will begin to die of boredom and enjoy working."

"Of course. I see that you're going to be an exemplary administrator, dear Narayana; and once we divide the planet into nations, we'll certainly make you king."

"I thank Ebramar and I hope to be worthy of his trust. And so a legend will be formed about me, as about Rama or Hermes, that I was an example of wisdom and knowledge, and that under my sceptre the golden age reigned," Narayana concluded, jokingly.

"These are all distant dreams," he added sighing. Now I'm worried about the present. The time for our presentation in society is approaching, and I have no idea where to order our clothes. Maybe there aren't even any tailors and I'll have to sew something, because in this robe, precious for mages, I won't take the risk of appearing in a hall.

Settle down, there're still tailors and Nivara has been instructed to see to your personal grooming and to dress you in such a way that no one will suspect your origin," calmed Ebramar.

I hope the 20th century lady who left us such a complete description of our people didn't predict that we would appear with the coming of the end of the world. She has a bad habit of being too precise in her predictions," Supramati said.

In any case, it's our duty as knights to verify that he doesn't reincarnate at this critical moment. In that case, she will be able to describe us as lawmakers and geniuses of the new planet," Dakhir added.

Everyone laughed.

"Saints don't make miracles. So does this poor lady. If people had believed her prophecies, they'd have corrected themselves and humanity wouldn't now be on the eve of its end," Ebramar observed, getting up.

They left and fifteen minutes later they were in Ebramar's chambers.

Nivara was waiting for them there and he eagerly rushed to embrace Supramati.

Supramati hugged him and thanked him for his affection.

"I'm happy to see," he added, "that you have worked spontaneously and have already taken a big step forward."

Narayana immediately caught the young adept's attention and began to ask him about dress and modern customs; and as Dakhir sat and listened very attentively to the conversation, Ebramar took Supramati to his laboratory.

It was a large round room with columns, filled with strange instruments of strange shapes.

Ebramar showed his disciple a part of the equipment that was supposed to transport into space the ship with the terrestrial emigrants.

After a lively conversation, the sages went to a dark room in the annex, illuminated only by a faint bluish light.

This room, with a roof as high as a cathedral, also had an unusual appearance. In the centre was a huge table of solid gold, and on it was a vertigo-inducing artefact.

In front of it appeared to be a huge clockwork mechanism; small crystal or metal and shiny little wheels of various sizes spun rapidly and spread multicoloured sparks.

Long and thin as hair, the hands ran along the discs, and from the long tubes, widened at the ends, came phosphorescent ribbons, that spiralled, rose and disappeared in the darkness of the dome. The whole thing rattled, creaked and trembled, while little hammers tinkled in rhythm like little bells. On the edges of the table were a series of coloured buttons connected by electrical wires to the mechanism.

"You already know part of the mechanism of this telegraph, even though you haven't seen it in operation," said

Ebramar, showing his disciple the details of the apparatus and explaining how it works.

"With the aid of this machine we keep in touch with the initiation sanctuaries of the planets of our system and we communicate with the Hierophants of distant worlds."

"The principle of operation is identical to telegraph without wires; its only necessary to know how to control the vibratory waves and to capture the desired direction. All the sanctuaries in our system are in permanent contact, because the same cosmic construction maintains the mutual balance between us."

"It's totally unnecessary and even dangerous to divulge this secret to the multitudes. If the profane knew about our means of communication with neighbouring humanities, they would undoubtedly become brave, dream of conquering the new planets and even try of conquering our space fleet; then they would take our place in the journey," Ebramar concluded, smiling.

"You're right, master. The hierophant friends had sound reasons for keeping their science of secrecy. The terrible forces of the elements of nature in unprepared hands do more harm than good. The enormity of the discoveries, badly used or employed for evil. This is exactly what contributed to the devastation of our planet long before the time established for it," said Supramati sighing.

"Tell me, master," he added a minute later, "would they allow us to use our knowledge there to organise our life in a similar way to the way it's now?"

No doubt. For our work and study we must have a quiet and comfortable refuge; but, of course, we won't abuse our science or keep it, as usual, in impenetrable secrecy."

CHAPTER VIII

An hour later, Supramati was talking in his room with Nivara, who opened a large basket of clothes on the table and placed it on the sofa.

"It's clear that you want to groom me personally, my dear Nivara. Frankly, the need to replace my light and comfortable white robe with this ridiculous modern garment is pretty much a punishment," Supramati remarked.

"Yes, I consider this an honour to serve you and I will gladly be your secretary, my dear master, while the youngest adept assigned to you can be my assistant," said Nivara, looking at him, friendly, with his eyes bright and cheerful. Supramati stood up and shook hands with him.

"Well, let's put on the costume, I see you've already opened your business," he added, laughing.

"First, the black silk knit, the main garment, since shirts are no longer worn. Don't worry, it doesn't fade, it's top quality; however, I thought you might not feel comfortable wearing black, so I also brought a very fine white knit, which won't embarrass you."

"Thank you for anticipating my wish. I confess I don't like these black clothes," replied Supramati, putting on his garment.

"And here are the boots. They're not leather nowadays; the herds of cattle are too few to clothe all mankind. But look what a great imitation, very sturdy and elegant."

Supramati pulled on his boots and tightened his wide leather belt; and Nivara made a big bow with the silk scarf around his neck and handed him a wide-brimmed hat, a wallet and a watch, tied to a gold chain and kept in his waist pocket. Then Nivara dressed him in a sleeveless coat of a black cloth, very soft, fine and shiny like satin; the lining, quite thick, looked like velvet. It had no collar or cuffs.

"What about my hair - has the giraffe haircut gone out of fashion?" Supramati asked curiously.

"A long time ago. Now they wear their hair loose, without worrying about length: only men grow their hair down to their shoulders. Your haircut will be fashionable."

Supramati approached a large mirror and looked at himself curiously, finding himself strange. He didnt like the clothes: there was something eccentric and insolent about them, with their very loose silhouettes. Still, Supramati looked very good; the knit emphasised his tall and slender figure, though the thick tufts of dark hair gave him a youthful air. Of course, no mere mortal could suspect that this handsome young man with flaming eyes was a mage of three beams of light, on whose shoulders rested so many centuries. However, a more attentive and, above all, a more sensitive observer would recognise that in the depths of those clear eyes was hidden something that made this man a being totally different from other mortal beings.

Supramati was trying on his hat when Narayana and Dakhir came in dressed like him, accompanied by Niebo and three young adepts of lower rank destined to be secretaries, assistants or messengers of the mages. Narayana was very happy. He was bragging and clowning in his tight-fitting costume and his big eyes sparkled with mischief and boastfulness. He introduced the three adepts to Supramati, explaining that each of these magnificent young men was at most two hundred years old.

"They're still children. And now, let's say a quick goodbye to Ebramar and leave. We have to hurry to get to the station before the train leaves," he said.

"So, did the railway come back? - No, Your Highness," one of the young secretaries hastened to reply.

"Now we use the air trains, very fast and comfortable."

After a quick and effusive farewell to Ebramar, the mages and their court took the aerial train and soon fell asleep with the sleep of mortals.

When they woke up, it was dawn. As soon as they had finished washing up, the train stopped near a huge and strange building made entirely of metal and glass. It was a series of huge square towers, as tall as the Eiffel Tower, separated by large chambers. Inside were lifts for passengers and luggage, restaurants, ticket offices and other modernities, all operating automatically.

The tops of the towers were joined by a huge metal bridge, which was a mooring next to which, tied together by airlifts, something like an enormous snake hung in the air.

In fact, the aerial train looked like a snake. One had the impression that the head opened into a gigantic throat, inside of which a huge electrical apparatus roared and sparked and under the belly of the aerial monster were hundreds of spheres and on its back a kind of mobile and transparent wings.

The passengers, guided by Nivara, boarded the train via one of the access bridges and examined it quickly before taking their cabins.

The corridor through the wagons - if you could call them that - was wide enough to accommodate shelves in some parts and bars in others.

The small cabins, with two or four seats, were cheap. The more expensive ones had two rooms: a lounge and a bedroom, more or less large. It was one of these larger cabins that Dakhir, Supramati and Narayana occupied.

The place had all the comforts and refined luxury.

Overall it's not bad, but I suggest, my friends, that you go out into the corridor and have a look at the ladies' toilets," proposed Narayana, after examining everything with the air of a knowledgeable expert.

Dakhir and Supramati couldn't hold back their laughter and suggested him that he call Nivara to guide them on this excursion, but Narayana didn't even listen to them and dragged them away almost by force.

As they passed the bar, they saw two women approaching and, with the help of a vending machine, filling their glasses with a fizzy liquid, similar to sparkling water.

They were young and beautiful, but Supramati thought their costumes were indecent and inelegant.

One of them, a tall, dark-eyed brunette, wore a pink knit that gave the impression that she was naked, and over the knit she wore something like a kimono with wide sleeves, made of a pink fabric with silver embroidery and white lining. Over her beautifully combed black hair she wore a pink velvet beret with a shiny clasp.

The other was blonde, of medium height, wearing a black knitted jumper and a kimono, also black with blue lining. A blue beret with white flowers covered her head.

"It wasn't bad either, really, just a bit exaggerated," Narayana remarked with slight irony when the travellers had left.

"That's right. Old dresses are no longer worn," said Nivara, when they returned to the cabin.

"Don't tell me that old women also wear those ridiculous and disgusting clothes?" Supramati asked, sitting next to the window.

"What old women? There are no more old women or old men because science has completely eliminated old age. One of the latest inventions has made artificial teeth unnecessary. As soon as a tooth falls out, another one is born in its place..."

"In the same way the electric baths work, with different types of massages that remove wrinkles. As for the hair, it also grows like grass and in the preferred colour," explains Nivara.

"Damn it! These people are in better condition than us. They enjoy their eternal youth without the burden of immortality." exclaimed Dakhir with a laugh.

"But there's also the other side of the coin. All this artificial, ultra-intellectual and fake youth is weak, feeble and nervous, susceptible to serious illnesses. On the whole, this is a generation doomed to failure," Nivara sighed.

"What a pity, hard times for poor humanity! - commented Supramati. - And would it be different in a world without God, without church, without law, without truth; in a world where only animal culture reigns? By the way, Nivara, Narayana described the miracle of Lourdes and said that there were still some Christians, I mean believers. Will there be many of them?"

"No, there're very few. Christians are a very poor and persecuted sect. They live in isolated places, devastated by earthquakes, on abandoned islands or in underground places, in other words, practically in deserts, where the " benefactors " of our time would not stay even for a day. They settle in places close to ancient sacred sites or near hiding places where miraculous and highly venerated relics or icons are kept."

"Nivara, could you tell us about other sacred places that are left apart from Lourdes?" Dakhir asked.

"Thanks to a miracle even greater than that of Lourdes, the Church of the Holy Sepulchre has been preserved. I have to describe this very interesting event to you. You know that a sacred place that has accumulated hundreds of years of prayer broadcasts provokes deep hatred in Satanists. This source of light and warmth, which has renewed and strengthened so many souls, didn't give them rest and the conversions to faith in God which took place there drove them completely mad. And one of these conversions, a particularly brilliant one, happened to a repentant man, precisely from their own ranks. That was, I would say, the straw that broke the camel's back."

At the meeting of the Luciferian chiefs with the unbelievers in both God and Satan, the last were convinced that this nest of fantastic people was polluting their minds with "obscurantism". It was then unanimously decided to blow up the temple and the Holy Sepulchre, proffering at the meeting all kinds of sacrileges and blasphemies, impossible to repeat.

In sum, the criminal plan had many supporters. An army armed with bombs and other means of destruction, chanting sacrilegious songs, in the style of holy songs, advanced on Jerusalem.

As they drew nearer to the spot, the excitement of the bestified crowd increased. At the head of the procession was the statue of Baphomet, while the "Sabbath Queen" performed a shameless dance. This was because, before destroying the sacred place, they intended to desecrate it by celebrating their satanic Sabbath there.

News of the approach of this satanic troop arrived in Jerusalem, leaving the believers horrified and astonished. They were gathered in relatively large numbers, preparing to celebrate the Passover, a secular custom. Everyone knew perfectly well why the sacrilegious ones had purposely chosen the holy night to seize and destroy the temple. At that time, the bishop of Jerusalem was an elder of great asceticism, religious fervour and heroic courage.

The announcement of imminent danger didn't disturb the courage or the firmness of his spirit. After spending the night in prayer at the tomb of Christ, he called the faithful together and, with an eloquent speech, persuaded them not to be cowards and not to escape, but to defend the sacred place as best they could and to leave the rest to the will of God.

His words had the desired effect, and a feeling of enthusiasm seized the devotees. They knew that they would pay with their lives for their faithfulness to the Saviour, but their enthusiasm didn't decrease. Kneeling and with lighted candles in their hands, they all sang the resurrection hymn in chorus. Their faith was so ardent and their cry to God for help and support was so loud that the combined prayer rose like a pillar of fire and became a radiant cloud over the temple.

The whole temple sparkled with astral light, but the faithful, immersed in prayer, weren't aware of it; even less so the Satanists, who didn't notice the immense invisible force that was concentrated in the sacred place they intended to destroy. Finally, the diabolical horde arrived near the temple and their indecent chants and shouts could already be heard from afar. At that moment, the faithful chanted "Christ is risen" and the chaste bishop, holding the crucifix and raising his eyes to heaven, prayed with euphoric faith.

And just when the Queen of the Sabbath and the statue of Baphomet were entering the courtyard of the temple, the sky seemed to catch fire, the earth trembled and split open, forming huge cracks that spewed out flames and smoke. It's said to be something horrible; the subterranean tremors, alternating with the rumbling of thunder, were unheard of. The satanic armada was literally swallowed up by the abyss that opened beneath it: the mountain on which Jerusalem stood seemed to crumble.

The next day illuminated the horrific picture of divine wrath.

At the place where the mountain with Jerusalem rose, a deep valley surrounded by black rocks and ravines. The great and exuberant city was completely destroyed by the earthquake, and the surrounding area, once full of vegetation, was reduced to ashes, turned into an inhospitable and barren desert.

However, the most interesting thing is that during the catastrophe the rocks formed a kind of wall that safeguarded and protected the part of the temple where the Holy Sepulchre was situated; it seemed that the whole temple had collapsed along with the earth and, except for minor damage, it didn't seem to have suffered any damage.

The faithful without an inner self became unconscious during the catastrophe when they fainted, as if suffocated, coming to their senses only a few hours later.

Among them was also the old bishop who, without having fully recovered his strength, said a mass of thanksgiving. From that time on, the remaining Christians gathered in that inhospitable valley. There are two small secret communities, one male and one female, who spend their lives fasting and praying, but don't dare to leave the valley or the confines of the church walls, for the place is avoided and feared by Lucifer's cultists.

"This means that the evil is deeply rooted, as even the obvious demonstration of divine power and protection failed to convert the infidels or lead them to repentance," Supramati observed, thanking Nivara for the interesting narration.

From the conversation that followed, they learned that they were going to Czargrado. Then Dakhir, claiming fatigue, retired to his lodging. Supramati, who intended to visit all the places where the faithful remnants of God dwelled, stayed a while longer and talked with Nivara and Narayana about the past and the future.

All the mages had little hope, knowing that the struggle would be arduous and exhausting, because the Satanists, convinced of their impunity, didn't even suspect the approaching end of the planet. The great recent discoveries had awakened an inordinate pride in humanity, and the spirits of darkness, taking possession of the masses, greeted them with the hope of greater conquests. In their opinion, life should be a total and infinite feast, not to be spoiled either by old age, sickness or death.

Darkened by their own pride and their mad thirst for pleasure, the human flock enjoyed the benefits on the edge of the abyss, without suspecting that those who incited them to commit crimes, blasphemies and sacrileges, will sooner or later suffer the colossal hecatombs that the end of the world was preparing for them. How much pulsating human flesh, how much steaming blood, how much vital fluid would serve as a feast for the vile scavenging hyenas of space.

Narayana made a remark in this regard and Nivara exclaimed:

Ah, how fortunate we are! What a priceless reward we'll receive for our work: the possibility of moving to a new world and achieving a happy ending for the light of the higher sphere, instead of enduring a terrible punishment and becoming the prey of the vampires of hell!

Yes," replied Supramati, "the Creator's mercy is made his wisdom, and to show him how grateful we are, we must do good and save the children of Christ, ratifying the parable of the seven wise virgins and the seven foolish virgins.

This parable fits perfectly today. The wise virgins endured the trials stoically, their love for God didn't weaken and they waited resignedly for the Last Judgement, while faith and prayer, like constantly burning lamps, illuminated their souls. But the foolish virgins forgot their divine origin, denied their Creator and were enveloped in darkness; they extinguished the heavenly flame that leads to God and illuminates the thorny path of ascension. Poor blind women! What a terrible punishment awaits them, with no light to illuminate their souls during the imminent chaos," the magician added sadly.

The conversation continued for some time on the same subject, Narayana, perceiving that the compartment was loaded, regretted that it wasn't possible to open the window.

"At the end of the train, near the machines, there's a small, covered counter and I can take you there" proposed Nivara.

Immediately the three of them were in the narrow corridor in front of a large and wide window, against whose sill they leaned.

It was necessary to have a strong head in order not to feel dizzy when looking out, because as far as the eye could see there was nothing beyond the sky and an ocean of clouds that covered the earth. But the immortals knew neither fear nor vertigo; calm and curious, they enjoyed the truly thrilling sight that opened before them.

In all directions, airships and aerial trains crossed each other, resembling immense serpentine monsters, shaking the air with noises and whistles, and the multitude that crowded inside those black, yellow or green serpents, blindly surrendered their fate to the ingenious mechanisms and most of the mechanics, as they used to surrender to the divine will.

"What a huge step forward our discoveries have made since our last world tour!" Supramati wondered.

Oh, you have seen little of the "miraculous" inventions. It's safe to say that man has subjugated and placed at his service all the elements of nature. The mind is refined, while the divine soul submits and the flesh celebrates victory; it's master of all; it has reduced labour to a minimum, levelled lordship to the servant and enslaved the forces of nature," Nivara explained.

"That's correct. The moment they go to celebrate and consider themselves masters of the elements of nature, the cauldron will crack and against them will rise up the same servants with whom they sought to control god," Narayana observed ironically.

After a breath of fresh air, they returned to the cabin, continuing the subject of their stay in Czargrado.

"And you, Nivara, where do you want to be sent to work? Wouldn't you have a preference for a country or a village that you would like to save and protect?" Supramati asked, smiling.

No master, to me the whole earth is repugnant and my beloved ones will be safer under your tutelage. Therefore, my only desire is to continue to be your disciple and executive," replied the young adept, staring at him with his bright and grateful eyes.

Czargrado still existed. Thanks to its incomparable location, the city has survived all the catastrophes that have afflicted it over the past centuries.

Obviously it was changed. It had been extended and had acquired modern characteristics. But the old Supramati palace was still standing, miraculously preserved despite its age, serving for centuries as a shelter, first for the victims of the earthquake, followed by the flood that devastated half the city, and then as a refuge for widows and orphans. Later, as charity became increasingly unfashionable, a pornographic museum was set up in it, only to be destroyed by fire a few days after its opening.

After a while, the property was acquired by a foreigner who made the necessary renovations, but rarely resided in the palace. Gradually, the city's most chic entertainment venue changed location and the former Supramati palace remained isolated, no longer attracting attention. Apparently, the owners didn't want to rent it out or rebuild it.

Suddenly rumour spread that the palace had been bought by a Hindu prince named Supramati, who apparently intended to take up residence there, for the property began to be renovated. Some outsiders arrived, men of dark complexion, under whose supervision the palace premises were luxuriously furnished and the gardens renovated. The fountains began to function again, the gardens were covered with flowers and statues appeared among the vegetation. In short, the old palace was revived, adorned and its luxury aroused the curiosity of the idle, well-fed masses who were only interested in other people's affairs.

One day the news spread that the owner had arrived, unseen and to the great disappointment of onlookers, in a simple air train, accompanied by a brother and a cousin and rumour told that the three Hindu princes were young, handsome and rich, real multi-millionaires. With them came their friends and an entourage of administrators of the vast estates and three secretaries.

The Basbaque people were even more disappointed when they learned that the foreigners were nowhere to be seen or leave the palace walls, and could only be seen when they went for a walk.

In fact, the mages avoided appearing in society for the moment, struggling to study the cosmopolitan language, history, customs and the general picture of humanity at the time when they were about to begin the fulfilment of their difficult mission.

The panorama before them, old and new, left much to be desired. In a few centuries, which passed imperceptibly in parallel to their strange and mysterious life, the world suffered terrible upheavals and geological revolutions considerably altered its geography in some places. The political changes were even more horrific and funereal, shaking even the foundations of society.

The evil sown generously and richly among the masses of humanity by Jews and antichrists bore fruit. Terrible revolutions broke out everywhere, undermining customs and destroying all that remained of the ancient precepts that dictated the way of life of humanity. This devastating crisis generated a new society that would have seemed incomprehensible and repulsive to past generations.

The pretensions of false humanitarianism destroyed all punishment and turned the whole institution of law, with all its mountain of flexible laws, obscure to the masses. All this wasn't only a consequence of the unrestricted and unbridled freedom of conscience, which slowly dethroned any notion of religion; there were no more prisons, no more God, no more churches, where the "uncomfortable laws" were preached to the masses. No one recognised any mutual obligations and everyone lived as they pleased, making their own self-criticism according to their animal instincts.

There were no longer borders, armies or nationalities; there was a single human herd, run by communal municipal administrations which, moreover, had little authority.

Population was reduced to a dangerous level, as women refused to take on maternal responsibilities and two-child families were a rarity; changes in the way of life were no less. Scientific and industrial inventions eventually transformed not only the appearance of the earth's surface, but also the habits, character, needs, manias and way of life of the human race, virtually eliminating individual labour. There were no longer any workers, only specialists, who were paid enormous salaries to work on machines or drive spaceships.

But with less work came more leisure, which gradually became a mass institution. The Roman maxim of the age of decadence, "Bread and circuses! reappeared in gigantic proportions; everybody craved for the enjoyment of life, without obstacle or rest; and as this kind of orgiastic life was expensive, the most shameless deception was openly employed, and for a little gold, any means, indiscriminately, were good and lawful.

It's understandable that in such a society, consumed with vices, laziness and decaying "civilisation", any mental effort would be difficult. The human masses were suffering from a crass ignorance hidden behind a veneer of supposed education.

And - what a strange situation - perhaps because of the law of atavism, the secular intellectual work of this vanishing humanity sometimes crystallised, and from among the ignorant and insolent multitude, brilliant people appeared, who made magnificent discoveries and provoked real revolutions. But, unfortunately, these prodigious minds were led precisely by the left-handed spirit, and whatever they invented was, above all, conducive to the increase of evil power, the spread of vices, laziness and sordid passions.

Parasitism, which served as the basis of the entire social organisation, also altered the educational system. There were no schools except elementary schools and "specialised courses" in which young people were trained in selected subjects and taught superficially, because, through lethargy, most of them refused to work intellectually and seriously.

There were only a few institutions where select minds gathered and from them emerged great inventions, diabolical but brilliant scientists or specialists worthy of the name, who supervised the construction and operation of complex machines. But these were in the minority and all enjoyed great prestige in their locality. The crowd, on the other hand, were entertained by science for sport and were content with the superficial study of basic knowledge. They were content with the international language, with which they could travel around the world and make themselves understood from end to end, while those who continued to study linguistics laughed and considered them retarded or maniacs.

Along with the fall in moral and intellectual level began the decadence of art and literature. The former only produced terrible imitations of old works of art, adapting them to the cynical taste of the time, and the second, even more miserable, limited itself to reading newspapers with the latest gossip about everyday events and racy scandals. Nobody had the time or the inclination to read the great works anymore. People were joking, enjoying life and having fun on the edge of the abyss. It was a true pastoral idyll, which was only lacking in innocence.

To satisfy the need for entertainment and to find a substitute for the old literature and reading, people opted for theatres. These multiplied so much that every street had its own. Cinemas also proliferated as never before. And, as always, they reflected the customs of the time. But true dramatic art disappeared, only crude farces and vaudeville were in vogue, in which cynicism was taken to the point of absurdity and performing them required no effort from the artists, which was essential. The audience burst into laughter, "killing" a few hours, which was also the essential.

Life passed in theatres, restaurants or satanic temples, where depravity triumphed in unbelievable orgies. Contaminated by the gangrene of morality, the ingenious minds of the age invented and sought ever more intense, perverted and enervating passions. Scientific criminals maneged humanity. The evil forces of occultism, which could only be done in hell, were studied and applied. People who had lost God, deprived of the heavenly help of their Creator, sank deeper and deeper into evil, leading to death. And then blind, distracted and deluded multitudes of Satan's spawn flocked to the diabolical temples.

And readers shouldn't think that the author wrote this under the influence of some infernal nightmare. If you look critically and coolly around you, you'll clearly perceive the embryos of all the horrors that will spring up profusely in the future. Arm yourself with microscope and scalpel, my conscientious and impartial thinker, and upon the deceptive varnish of our "brilliant civilisation" you will find the baleful embryos of fratricide, fanatical atheism and laziness, that monster which popular wisdom has aptly called "the mother of all vices and sins".

Haven't the reduction, at any price, of the working day together with the increase of wages become the watchword of the masses and the aim of men as they seek to attain them by any means, lawful or otherwise? The laziness which has taken hold of the youth and spread like a typhus epidemic has become the fertile soil in which the great aspirant will grow and flourish. It will lead souls to suffering, to long atonement and to the destruction of the planet.

Our world, in summary, is tiny. It's only an imperceptible grain of a whole, an atom in the infinite plane of the Universe. Big is only the idea of evil, which manifests itself in all its fullness in this polluted cell of the celestial body.

This story, by the way, isn't new. Before and after us, in the extinct worlds and in the worlds of the future, the same infernal tragedy of wayward souls, deceived, swallowed up by the voracity of continual suffering, with atonement as hard and bitter as the sin is more repugnant.

The understanding of ancient traditions has been obscured or lost over the centuries; thus, for example, the legend of original sin, which has a deep and mystical meaning: temptation through libertinism, hell which instills insubordination in man, which promises him easy knowledge and the cursed science which annihilates souls by banishing them from paradise, depriving them of divine order, peace and protection. And men, banned to a world of misfortunes and sufferings, become servants of hell, which incites and torments without ceasing with impure desires and rages with the impulse to practise evil unceasingly.

To conclude the description of the society in which the mages will have to appear to fulfil their difficult mission, it remains to underline one facet, though insignificant in the face of the general picture, but which possesses its curiosity.

When the first of the "levelling revolutions" broke out, the plebs, conquering power, satisfied their age-old greed and repressed hatred by sweeping away everything that seemed to them to be innate privilege, social position and even wealth.

However, since absolute equality is nothing but an unattainable utopia that no arch-revolution can ever achieve, evil has dampened the political storm and society has been rapidly transformed, from which an old principle has re-emerged, but with a new face: vanity.

Although the servile hierarchy with its patents and honorary titles, decorations, nobility or any privilege no longer existed, still - oh, what a cruel irony - there were titles of nobility.

This happened this way. When all was quiet, rich and poor re-emerged, and vanity quickly made up for the old distinctions, the luxurious crosses and magnificent ribbons of ornament that once so gracefully adorned the chests and cuffs of illustrious persons. It was difficult and risky to recover all that, but there was still one ancient distinction, forgotten and unowned. This distinction could be used without the slightest danger, because the freedom to choose a name was unlimited, allowing it to be changed and altered at will. The descendants of old noble families were the first to take the risk, becoming again counts and marquises, and later so many imitators came along that even in the apogee of feudalism there weren't so many "counts", "princes" and "barons" as in this democratic society of different calibres, where anyone who wished could name himself with a noble title which gave him no rights, but which sounded very nice...

On several occasions, Dakhir and Supramati smiled sadly as, while studying the documents, pictures similar to those briefly described above appeared before them; while Narayana laughed out loud as he read to his friends the hilarious episodes of the past, especially the story of the revival of noble titles.

"From the looks of it, we won't get many honours, since being a prince is as common these days as being a porter used to be," he added, wiping away tears of laughter.

Without the magicians showing themselves to anyone, the curious imagined that they'd many acquaintances, even compatriots, and so preferred to entertain themselves in their company, as a large number of aerial vehicles often landed at the back or in the palace gardens and left at dawn.

In fact, from time to time, the mage-missionaries came to discuss with their friends the various details of the general plan of action, in different parts of the world sentenced to death.

In Supramati's palace, a select society gathered: men of sober beauty, with radiant and deep eyes, whose inspired heads were enveloped by a vast aura.

One night, in Supramati's workroom, fifteen mages and a score of young adepts gathered to definitively establish each one's place of work.

"Friends, it has been decided that initially we'll study the battlefield where we'll fight, and visit the sacred places where the defenders of the faith hide and vegetate," said Supramati.

"True," replied one of the mages. - First of all, we must go to the places where sacred communion still connects men with the Divine; in these places the mages will reveal themselves to their brothers and together they'll organise meetings to preach the approaching end of the world and organise processions, accompanied by sacred songs, the sounds of which will purify the atmosphere."

"Our task is hard, but it will also be hard for those who respond to our call and want to be saved," Dakhir said. "Where atheism and Satan worship have broken all contact with God, only blood can establish this union. Like the early Christians, we will have to demonstrate our faith in God through martyrdom and, by faith, make them worthy to follow us."

"Yes, this path to salvation, despite its difficulty, is inevitable. Only those who have never denied God and havent wavered in their faith, despite all the tests, can avoid suffering martyrdom, if they themselves don't want to accept it voluntarily, in order to purify themselves and reach a higher level," Supramati explained.

"Yes, the satanists will have a lot of trouble and sorrows, as soon as we disturb their sweet tranquillity," exclaimed Narayana with a glint in his eyes. "I can already sense the time when the vibrations of joint prayer and holy chanting will strike them like a deadly poison, causing convulsions, nervous breakdowns on the verge of insanity and other psychic ailments."

"But they won't die for it," argued one of the mages, "they will have to endure the terrible punishment of the last days, which will anticipate the end of the world, to whose destruction they have contributed by their misdeeds. The weaker will remain here, for their presence in the new world would be a germ of death. They have experimented with the cursed science created by the outcasts of heaven to pollute souls. They have forgotten that the children of Earth must love and respect their common mother, which was their cradle and will be their grave, without desecrating their sacred nurse, as this infernal generation that populates it's doing at present."

"God forbid that one should fall so deep and stumble, for the path of ascent is difficult and narrow, and the shining beacon of total wisdom, which indicates rest to the weary traveller, shines far away in the mist," said Supramati. "And this tortuous path passes between chasms where many temptations are found. "Homo sum" we are human beings and subject to various weaknesses of the flesh and spirit; inside us lurk a thousand unfulfilled desires, all the indignities of unbridled pride, and the only support of the balance of sense is that in itself."

"I say this," Supramati added, "for the young adepts present. They must pray and concentrate so no weakness will disturb them in that gale of evil we are heading for."

After the farewell dinner, the mages, knights and adepts took their leave to begin their preliminary round before meeting for the last time in the Grail Palace.

CHAPTER IX

Two days later, Dakhir travelled with Narayana, who preferred to work with him first, while Nirvana stayed with Supramati. On the advice of his faithful secretary, Supramati initially decided to visit the city to examine, in person, the new institutions and to see in situ what he had only learned in theory so far. They decided to make this first tour of the city during the day because they felt freer, they didn't want to be disturbed by the crowds, for in that time of decadence things were topsy-turvy.

Satan worships darkness and hates light, so his admirers also began to live at night, with most of the population sleeping during the day and having fun at night. As saturnalia, sabbats, orgies and satanic sacrifices were preferably held at night, everyone who was able retired to sleep at dawn and got up at sunset. The tallest buildings in the huge capital had a clock with a gigantic black cockerel, which with its high-pitched crowing announced to all those around it the arrival of the closing hour of the black festivities and the time for rest. The walk through the empty city and the streets with only a few passers-by left Supramati with a sad impression.

The shape of the buildings hadn't changed; however, the building material was different and was mostly made of thick glass and iron. Glass of the most diverse colours was used, and whatever the house, it was intended to look like a palace.

As already mentioned, there were a large number of theatres, which were notable for their large dimensions: on the frontispiece, allegorical groups or pictures, disgustingly indecent, gave an idea of the spectacles that were presented on those stages.

There were also a large number of satanic temples and idols in honour of Lucifer, Baphomet and other princes of darkness. The huge temples imitated ostensibly the heavy, massive architecture of Babylonian buildings. Their bronze doors were wide open, and inside was an immense statue of Satan, surrounded by candelabra with black candles. In the innumerable triptychs smoked herbs and essences, whose strong caustic aroma was unnerving and could be felt even in the street. There were also the so-called chapels, probably built as a mockery, in the style of Christian chapels or Muslim mosques, with their beautiful minarets or Gothic towers.

Obviously, Supramati and Nivara didn't enter any of these pagan temples, but as they passed close to one of them, a strong windstorm began to blow inside the diabolical lair, whose roar and dull roar spread under the vaults of the enclosure.

"To get to know the real life we have to wait for the night," Nivara observed. "Then we can also see the new breed of servants: humanised animals," he added in disgust.

As night fell, a great bell began to ring from the high tower, and in the deafening sound, which was to wake people to life and activity, there was something dismal and sad.

This time, instead of the aerial vehicle, something like an automobile was made available to Supramati, which Nivara deftly drove through the countless vehicles and pedestrians that now congested the well-lit streets. Every house seemed to be illuminated, in every tower there were huge electric suns that filled the city with light. Everywhere, in the air and on the ground, the bustle of the crowd could be heard; vehicles with men and women passed each other in every direction. To his astonishment and disgust, Supramati observed that most of the ladies and gentlemen were accompanied by animals of unusual size, generally belonging to species of wild beasts, uncommon at the time of his last time in the world. However, the appearance of these tigers, monkeys, leopards or lions looked altered: their heads had something human about them and their complexion denoted strange anomalies; all were particularly agile and seemed to play the role of servants.

"You see, master, these mutants, half-man, half-animal, are today's servants," Nivara observed. "Since their similars no longer wanted to be servants, practical humanity created them to be a special kind of servant."

"Many animal species served very well for this adaptation. These creatures - as I have already said - half-man, half-animal. They are highly intelligent, but dangerous because of their savagery, ferocity and fiendish fury, though they were kept under severe subjection, which didn't prevent them from eagerly seeking human love. Human beings possess the need and instinct to command and to be served; but when they invented complete equality and freedom for their fellow-men, they thought of creating species of submissive creatures so inferior to them as to fear them and to endure their ill-treatment, and yet intelligent enough to understand and serve them."

"You're right, Nivara. For this satanic age only the species of inferior beings was lacking," Supramati remarked bitterly.

The next day, Nivara proposed to Supramati to visit a renowned scientist, an expert on avatars.

"Professor Chamanov transplants the souls of old rich people into the bodies of boys, which he manufactures by a chemical process. It's very interesting."

"Of course, but why does he transplant old satyrs into children's bodies instead of into adult bodies? And does he also transplant old coquetes into girls' bodies or does he only know how to make boys?" - asked Supramati curiously.

"No, he does both sexes. He's a great chemist. I'll let him know we're coming. He uses children's bodies in his avatars, because it's assumed that these artificial bodies don't live to maturity if there's no astral. We'll be able to visit him even during the day, as Chamanov's clients can wait until night to make the "change". He pays his assistants so well that they accept to sacrifice some hours of the day for the sake of science."

In the afternoon of the same day, Supramati's aerial vehicle landed in the garden of a grand palace. The visitors were taken to a luxuriously furnished reception room, where shortly afterwards the professor appeared to greet the Hindu prince who was keen to visit his establishment.

Chamanov was a man of mature age, broad-shouldered, strong, with a big head and a high forehead of a thinker; his eyes were deep set in their sockets, but the look in his eyes was cold, cruel and devilish. He exuded great pride and self-esteem.

He received Supramati with bows and affirmations of immense satisfaction at having him as a visitor.

"I m pleased, prince, to be able to show you at this moment one of the avatars of your interest. The client is now fully prepared and I'm about to begin the operation."

Nivara stayed in the reception area, while Supramati followed the professor. The operating theatre was large and equipped with various devices; in the centre were two long tables and on one of them was an object covered with a white sheet.

The professor asked Supramati to observe everything from behind the curtain so as not to embarrass the patient and went to the armchair which was next to an empty table. There sat a man, dressed in an apron, and Supramati thought he had never seen such a repulsive being in his life.

This, no doubt, was a dying man, and, besides, an old man whom science has preserved with a youthful appearance: but the approach of death has marred his fictitious aspect, and created something horrible. The thick black hair fell in various parts of the head, forming bald patches, and the cheeks of the face were sunken and earthy in colour.

When Chamanov approached the disgusting old man, the latter straightened up with great effort and asked in alarm, grabbing the scientist's arm:

"Dear professor, will you start the operation? Are you sure it will work?"

"No doubt, duke, we do many operations and all with success"

"And you chose for me a healthy and strong body? You know that for me money is not the problem and I want you to give me the best."

"Judge for yourself the qualities of your "new home" - said the teacher, removing the sheet from the other table.

There lay the body of a boy of 12-13 years of age; he looked healthy and strong, but his extreme pallor, the closed eyes and the total absence of expression on his face, immobile like a mask, made a strange and suffocating impression.

"As you see," continued Chamanov, "this body is very well made, flawless, strong and powerful as a young oak. After about four years, which are necessary for the assimilation and development of the organism, it will again enjoy a long and happy life. - Don't be afraid, dear Duke. Take courage and drink this, it's time to begin. When you wake up, all your present pains will be gone, everything will be new and the machine will start to work absolutely rationally.

He took a cup served by one of the assistants and held it out to the dying man, who eagerly dried it.

After a few minutes, he fell deeply asleep.

"Let's get to work" said the professor, making a sign for Supramati to come closer.

With the help of his assistants, he undressed the client and placed him on the operating table, which was made of crystal.

The naked body, looking like a corpse, was covered by a glass bell with some tubes connecting it to one of the apparatus, and put to work. The glass bell filled with steam, completely hiding the body.

"It's a special steam and serves to open the pores and facilitate the exit of the ethereal body" explained the professor.

After twenty minutes of steam bathing, the glass bell was removed and a thick glass tube was placed in it in the shape of a U. One extremity was placed in the mouth of the dying man and the other in the mouth of the child... On the old man's body were installed small electrical devices that fluttered and fluttered like bird's wings; the devices were connected to a larger one, which worked noisily like a steam engine. Next, the two bodies were covered with glass covers.

All this had gone on for about three-quarters of an hour when suddenly there was a snapping sound, the old man's body contorted, and out of his mouth came a misty, bluish phosphorescent mass, like a jelly, the flame of a candle that seemed to reflect from the inside out. The whitish and vaporous mass filled the tube completely, and when it passed into the boy's mouth, the tube was quickly withdrawn. The old man's body turned a greenish colour and his mouth remained open. He was definitely a dead body; they covered him with a sheet and carried him away.

The professor in control of the operation leaned over the boy, whose body was trembling and shaking as if he'd received an electric shock.

"I believe the operation was a success!" he said, pleased with himself.

"Look, prince," he added, turning to Supramati, "how simple it all is, and how ignorant were our ancestors who, to relieve pain and save a life, swallowed terrible compounds or even underwent horrible surgical operations, lying under a scalpel. Wouldn't it be more comfortable to adopt a new body? It's the same story of Columbus' egg."

"Our ancestors weren't lucky enough to have a great expert like you, Professor, who made this amazing discovery."

"I thank you prince, but I cannot take the glory of the discovery exclusively for myself; I have only succeeded in definitively putting into practice the work of many generations of scientists."

"And how many avatars of this type are made?"

"Relatively many. I have students who practice the operations in most large cities; however, it costs a lot and only very wealthy people allow themselves to do so."

"And when will your client come to his senses?" Supramati asked.

"Normally they are unconscious for three or four hours, depending on the circumstances, but I'll see if it's possible, to satisfy your curiosity, to get him to say a few words right now."

He carefully removed the thermometer from under the child's arm and listened to his heart.

"The temperature is normal and the heart is beating regularly. That means we can risk it," said the professor, uncapping a small bottle and holding it up to the boy's nose."

He shuddered and, after a moment, opened his eyes.

"So, Duke, how do you feel?" asked the professor smiling.

"Well... But a little uncomfortable - replied a weak voice and the eyes closed again."

He'll remain for six weeks in my clinic so that I can personally monitor his full assimilation and unconditional rest before he returns home.

Without suspecting that he was dealing with a scientist, the professor gave Supramati a series of explanations.

"If you wish, Prince," he added, "I can show you the latest achievement of science, our laboratory for recreating human beings. You'll see that not only have we triumphed over death, but we can also create life. In short, we have at our disposal all that our ancestors, in crass ignorance, attributed to the power of their God - Creator, the Lord of the universe. Ah-ah-ah! We no longer need this God either to die or to live, nor do we impose on women these terrible sufferings."

Supramati thanked him, saying that he was very interested in those wonderful discoveries, and the happy professor took him to another part of the huge establishment.

They entered a large circular, windowless room, immersed in a dim, bluish gloom. There were long rows of tables, with narrow passages between them. On each table was a sort of long box, covered with a sheet, and connected by wires and tubes to large electrical apparatus, installed at two ends of the room.

The ones on the left will be less interesting to you. These receptacles contain only embryos in the first stage of fermentation and formation.

"You see we have achieved the possibility of recreating the human body thanks to a chemical amalgam of the male and female principles. This is still the beginning and the last word will be said when we succeed in extracting from the vital atmosphere the -rational substance. But I'm convinced that we'll succeed."

"You're referring to that substance which has passed from one body to another, am I right? Has not your highly developed science yet found the key to determining the composition of that which you call rational substance?" asked Supramati.

Unfortunately, not yet. We only know that this substance is infinitely diluted, we'd say rarefied fire, but until today the strange substance remains imperceptible and cannot be researched. And now, prince, look at this.

He went to a table on the right, removed the blue sheet covering a dark glass box, turned an enamelled knob and then

Supramati noticed a hole or a small circular window at the end of the box, through which the professor wanted Supramati to look.

He saw that the interior was illuminated by a kind of bluish light, and on a mound of gelatinous substance lay the body of a small child, apparently well formed and appearing to be asleep.

Through little glass tubes, a faint white mist passed into the little body, which the body seemed to absorb; it was probably the child's artificial nutrition. The child breathed well, the organism functioned and the chemical work of art was a real success.

"Your knowledge is superb, professor, but something is missing in your masterpiece..."

"What, for example?" Interrupted the professor animatedly.

"He has no soul."

"It can be said that it lacks "rational substance". But I have already told you that we don't yet know the secret of its composition. Temporarily we use the method I have just shown. The situation is made all the more regrettable for me by the fact that similar substances, stripped of the material body, whose origin we don't know, are fluttering in the air..."

"And don't you know how to attract them to these human forms, which you do with such art?" asked Supramati and an enigmatic smile appeared on his face.

Meanwhile, he noticed that in the dark corners of the room, the eyes of the worms glowed, amazed by his presence;

their dark bodies snaked around, eager to possess such a body.

"No," lamented the professor, "there's no way to attract them, they come by themselves... they are mysterious beings. I can't understand the reason for their damage either, because as soon as they enter the newly formed body, it starts to decompose as if it had gangrene, and then it dies. But these are small details. The important thing is that science is on the way to discovering the secret of man's creation, and therein lies, no doubt, the great glory of our century," concluded the professor proudly

Supramati looked thoughtfully at the "priest of science", endowed with a privileged brain, who was able with his knowledge to solve the difficult question of the creation of the human or animal body, but who couldn't give them a real life. This was the true representative of the dark and fatal science of the end of the world.

"Professor, you're a great sage and artist and, I recognise that you deserve this name. However, this... this "something" that you search for and cannot find is the human soul and this you'll never be able to recreate, because it's a work of God, that God who was torn away from the heart of men. The soul is the divine flame, marvellous and indestructible, which has made you a great wise man, a courageous and untiring researcher. It's the spirit that animates your brain and makes it more receptive to learning everything."

Lose hope of ever submitting to analysis this divine spark, whose chemical composition always eludes you. And don't even seek it, for its secrets are summed up in the plenipotence of God. And however much mankind may deny His creative being, He exists, and no infernal sentence, no ignoble sacrilege will take from Him even an infinitesimal particle of His absolute power.

The professor frowned and, in turn, he looked scrutinisingly at the haughty figure of his interlocutor and at his big, bright blue eyes, whose gaze seemed to be oppressing him. But the enormous self-esteem overcame this impression. He straightened up haughtily and replied, with contempt mingled with anger:

"Prince, you surprise me; you look like an enlightened man, and yet you believe in God, to whom you attribute unlimited power. These absurd convictions served the ignorant peoples of past centuries. Today, when each of us can compete with this legendary God, such ideas, you will excuse me... are, to say the least, amusing."

Supramati's eyes sparkled and his voice sounded serious and strict.

"Unfortunate! Diabolical pride is leading you to the abyss. You dare to compare yourself to the Almighty, who creates and controls the infinite universe! You consider your poor knowledge to be equivalent to the omniscience and wisdom of God. Just wait! And when the divine wrath is unleashed on this criminal humanity, when the uncontrolled elements thunder around you, then you'll understand that, before the Almighty, you're a miserable atom or a particle of dust that the storm will pick up and carry away. Think and be ashamed of your ridiculous pride, unworthy of an authentic sage."

The professor paled. Anger and affronted self-esteem were fighting within him against a strange sensation of a sudden and indefinite awareness that the person before him represented a force, the dimensions of which were beyond his understanding.

"You consider my knowledge despicable" he said, after a few moments. "Perhaps you, using your knowledge, could put a soul into this body?"

"I cannot. I, like you, don't have the power to create a soul. I can still draw a spirit from the ether and force it to animate this body, but this spirit would be a larva or a wandering spirit and I know that to do so would be dangerous and purposeless."

So could you. But could you say how long this vital force would last, if it possessed all that was necessary for the actions of the spirit, and if it possessed, in its chemical composition, all that was necessary for the assimilation of the astral and the material? You know nothing of this.

The professor lowered his head. He - a researcher - knew that he still had a long way to go to perfect his work, and in those many years of concentrated work he had failed to capture and investigate that mysterious psychic spark which the Hindu called "celestial fire".

"Who are you, stranger, who has an absolute faith in God, so long forgotten by all?" he asked, after a moment's thought.

"I'm a missionary of the end-times, since the hour of destruction is coming and deaf and blind mankind dances above a volcano that will swallow it up."

The profesor lowered his dead and smiled.

"Wow! Are you a prophet of the end of the world? It's a strange fancy, prince, for a man who is young, handsome, rich, and moreover, seems educated."

"Strange it may seem to you, but the end of the planet is near. Humanity itself anticipated this time, breaking the harmony and balance of the elements. People have reached the crucial moment and in their arrogance have raised their unholy and sacrilegious hand even against the sanctuary of God.

I won't deny that I possess knowledge. The Eternal One arms submissive and faithful servants with the power of science, who step by step climb the ladder of improvement towards the light, and all the knowledge acquired is only used by the divine will." replied Supramati, bidding the scientist farewell.

This visit left a very bad impression on Supramati, who was sorry to see the misconceptions into which so remarkable a mind had fallen. He remembered that head and the prominent forehead, characteristic of a thinker, which didn't harmonise with the ruthless look and the cynical and animalistic expression that usually exists in people who have swept the ideal from their soul, giving freedom to the animal that hides in the human being to direct his actions...

However, this meeting also awakened in Supramati a desire to know what the health of this strange humanity was like, to know what kind of illnesses afflicted them and how they were treated. This question was of particular interest to the physician Ralf Morgan.

When informed of his wish, Nivara suggested that he visit a doctor who enjoyed great notoriety. In society he was considered a freak and almost a maniac, as he studied ancient languages; Nivara, instead, saw him as a true scientist. The doctor, having been forewarned of Supramati's visit, received him courteously and took him directly to a large terrace, attached to his office, which was decorated with climbing plants.

Dr. Rezanov was still a young, thin, pale-skinned man, serious and calm, with large, thoughtful eyes that betokened intelligence.

"I'm at your disposal, prince, and I'll be happy to provide you with any information I can," he said as they both settled into their comfortable bamboo armchairs. "What specifically do you wish to know?"

Ah, many things, doctor, and for this I fear to abuse your kindness. For example, how does the human organism cope with this unnatural life? How does it assimilate this excess of electricity and other substances which are good for strong and healthy organisms and not for the beastly people with frayed nerves, such as those you treat? What kind of diseases and epidemics are caused by this state of affairs? How do you treat them? And is the mortality rate high?

"You're right, it is a very broad subject, Your Highness," replied the doctor with a smile, "but I'll try to give you an overview first and then detail the points that are of most interest to you."

"I must say that, in general, hygiene took a giant step forward. Order became a compulsory law and electricity, with its powerful discharges, destroyed infectious sources. Epidemics such as bubonic plague, cholera, tuberculosis and others so lethal in ancient times disappeared completely. And yet, unfortunately, mankind has become neither stronger nor more immune, and the present race that populates the earth is abnormally nervous and weak."

There has developed such an ethnic miscegenation that today it's practically impossible to find a person of pure race to determine what kind of person he or she is: German, Italian, Arab or Russian. Only nationality designations remain, but there are no more characteristic racial differences.

I'm convinced that such an amalgamation of such different elements is fatal for humanity; this is because not only each race, but each people has its psychic peculiarities among the others, which, due to frequent miscegenations, are lost and sometimes cause the appearance of very strange beings, and finally lead humanity to total extinction.

This is the present state of society, composed entirely of abnormal people, and the evil whose flourishing we now witness has very ancient origins. You see, I had the patience to study the ancient languages, now replaced by international jargon, and read the works contemporary to that remote past. The study demonstrated the depth of the roots of the main disease that afflicts us and which is called -demential. Imagine that even in the 20th century there was a tendency to explain many symptoms as diseases of the brain. An Italian scientist of that time, called Lombroso, considered that all genius people are psychically abnormal and that all crimes are products of madness. But what was or seemed to be only a paradox in that century has now become a sad reality. And the population in every corner of the world is composed of insane people, of greater or lesser dangerousness.

Do you seem surprised, Prince? But I still maintain my point of view. I too am mad like the others; in many ways my brain is not normal.

It's extremely curious to study the beginning of social dementia, not even considered a terrible and dangerous psychic epidemic and which revealed itself in different ways. Initially there was uncontrolled speculation, the gold rush and speculation on the capital market, which made people rich or poor in a few days, and sometimes in hours, shaking even the foundations of people's nervous systems. Gambling had the same result. Later, this craving for new sensations gave rise to a craze for all kinds of sports: bicycles, cars, aeroplanes, speed contests, etc.

As the force of evil increased, there arose an epidemic of murders, suicides, unnatural vices, orgies and erotic follies. The revolutions with their cruel and bloody explosions, senseless killings, human hecatombes, excited the passions, and the spirit of destruction took possession of the masses. War was declared on the Creator, his temples were desecrated, his worshippers killed, and all this was done under the aegis of supporting -freedom. This was carried out by hordes of demented people, who didn't take over. Many of them were considered intelligent people.

Unfortunately, among the people who remained, healthy, there wasn't a hand firm enough to stop the gangrene. They let it develop and it took over the world. With an indifference and apathy, absolutely incomprehensible to me, contemporary society allowed these facts, watching all the unnatural acts, and, besides not repressing them, didn't lock up those madmen in hospices, in short, it didn't treat the sick with every possible means to provoke in them a saving reaction. In this way, this fatal "great neurosis" appeared, grew and spread over the face of the Earth, just like the worst of poisons, and nobody reacted vigorously against the frenzy of freedom, orgy and denial.

The great invasion of the yellows provoked a certain reaction, but only for a short time; the evil was deeply rooted and then it was reborn even stronger. And again all those who could and should have had an influence remained indifferent. This psychosis set the whole world on fire and burned everything on the social ladder from end to end. No one fought it, and everyone simply looked on and admired the grandiose sight of this uncontrolled rage, unwilling to reflect on the danger and giving it superb and pompous names. The present society has emerged as a consequence of all this...

The professor fell silent, shook his head thoughtfully and sighed deeply.

"I'm sorry prince, for getting carried away with my thoughts," he apologised, after a minute of silence and wiping his forehead with his hand.

"It is natural to reflect. Everything I have said is too sad not to think about it for a long time," Supramati argued, sighing.

"Because in order to understand the present, I have studied in depth the past of peoples and have come to the following question: are we at the limit of the earth's existence, or at least on the eve of some terrible catastrophe that will alter the appearance of our world? Without a doubt, humanity today is doomed to die. They are unnatural people, like plants without roots, or even artificial vegetation grown to flourish and, when it finishes flowering, dries up for lack of vital sap."

"Everything around us indicates decline. The land, once so fertile, is becoming more and more barren and depleted and the desert is advancing all around; the climate has become so altered that sometimes it seems as if the seasons have blended; mortality is growing at frightening levels, the birth rate continues to fall and it is clear that it won't be the people manufactured by Doctor Chamanov who will give us a race with powerful physiques and morals."

With the exception of an extremely limited number of scientists who still work and enjoy science, all the rest shun intellectual work, wanting nothing from life except pleasures and the satisfaction of their animal lusts and instincts.

Sometimes I bitterly regret the past, with its belief in God the creator, with its castes, its love of country, its ambitions and even, if you like, its wars, bloody, of course, but full of glories and heroism. Life was better then than it is now, without wars. And why? Because terrible weapons were invented with such destructive power that during the last decades they destroyed entire cities with all their contents and even entire armies with cold mercilessness."

"I see, doctor, that you have a strong principle of atavism," smiled Supramati. "Besides, I agree with you completely: in the old days, life was better in the old days. But now, please tell us what kind of diseases have caused the current state of society. You say there is no more cholera, bubonic plague or diphtheria. What do we have instead?"

Diseases are always a consequence of the causes that caused them. In the old days, cholera and bubonic plague were caused by a lack of hygiene on the one hand, and the absence of a cure on the other. Nowadays, constant excitation of the nervous system and excess electricity cause disease of the nerve centres, lethargy and general weakness of the organism.

We combat these illnesses by making the patient fall asleep artificially for a few weeks or even months, waking him up only to feed him. In this way, by prescribing unconditional rest, we give rest to all the functions of the body and recover the patient's strength. The sick is also sent to the mountains, to the snowy region, where the harsh, fresh air renews them. Those suffering from excessive electricity, on the other hand, are buried up to their necks in fresh earth or given special baths. The medicine that existed in past centuries no longer exists. But homeopathy is still used; then appeals were made to medicinal plants; vegetable oils are also much used in all epidermal diseases. Here is the summary, prince, of the physical and moral situation of humanity.

Why do we still need this festive - intellectual - mob, which has spent its nervous energy, tired of living, with its brains in tatters and seemingly destined for extinction? Only the future will tell. But, I repeat, I am convinced that we are approaching a catastrophe.

Supramati looked curiously at the intelligent countenance of the young scientist, one of the last representatives of science on this dying Earth, covered by the debris of fallen empires and toppled temples, taken over by sterility and the grim cult of darkness and evil, as an indicator of human trend.

After discussing some matters of interest to him, Supramati took his leave. The city air was oppressive and infected; only at home did he feel well.

During dinner he communicated to Nivara his conversation with the young doctor, and opined that they should endeavour to save that worker, who would be useful in the new world, since in his soul some sparks of good seemed to be kindled.

Oh, many will still convert and repent when the days of horror come, when the divine light will no longer illuminate the Earth and men will have nothing to warm themselves with. Of course, by then it will be too late. However, master, you're right, Doctor Rezanov deserves to be converted in time.

CHAPTER X

After a few days, which were spent touring the city and its surroundings or dedicated to various visits. Supramati decided to visit some remaining sacred sites, among which, first of all, Jerusalem. Nivara's account of the strange and wonderful catastrophe that had occurred there aroused his interest.

As the ship took off over the capital, Supramati gazed pensively and sadly at the city, flooded with electric light. - When I return here again and the glowing cross shines above my palace, marking out the refuge of the mage-missionaries, then the hard and decisive battle of light against darkness will begin. How many will triumph and how many will succumb, only God knows," he thought, sighing.

Jerusalem has changed a lot. The hill on which David once built his fortified city broke in two as a result of the earthquake, and that part where the Holy Sepulchre stood collapsed, forming a gigantic depression, in whose interior now stood the old sanctuary. Various debris had accumulated around the rock, forming a sort of wall to protect the deep valley, and there, around the temple, blackened by time, was a little Christian town. It was not large and consisted of poor little houses of faithful servants of Christ, in the midst of dense vegetation of cypress and fig trees.

Beyond the boundaries of the rocky wall, the land seemed abandoned and only in some places in the distance were fields or orchards with sparse vegetation visible.

These places provoked an inexpressible sadness. Satanists avoided them because of the terrible episodes, and if they eventually saw themselves there, they would end up feeling a prolonged uneasiness; moreover, an incomprehensible inner fear kept them away from the place.

The rocks surrounding the valley were as crowded as the city. In every great crevice, in every tiny cave, lived a hermit, spending his life in fasting and prayer.

In all those shelters there was a crucifix or an image of the Saviour and a lighted lamp; the looks of its inhabitants denoted that ardent and infinite faith that moved mountains.

Next to the gate, formed naturally by collapsing rocks that prevented any other access to the valley, there was an old man standing guard. He also served as a guide to the foreign pilgrims who came to pray or to escape persecution.

Supramati and Nivara declined in thanks for their services as guides, and proceeded to the temple. Unfortunately, nothing was left of the old grandeur and wealth; a dim gloom reigned beneath the ancient vaults, and the costume of the priests was as simple and poor as the ornaments of the church. The office was conducted by an aged bishop in a vestment of white cloth. For a long time, masses were celebrated continuously. Day and night, the faithful waited in line for their turn to attend the holy office. The lack of space was due to the damage suffered by some parts of the church due to the collapse of the rock, which collapsed for good, saving only the part of the church where the Holy Sepulchre was located, which was unharmed.

In the interval, after the celebration of mass, Supramati approached the bishop and asked for permission to talk alone. Both went to the priest's cell and talked at length. In the evening of the same day, a strange crowd filled the church. The people of the town and the crags had gathered there at the bishop's request.

When the doors of the sanctuary opened, Supramati appeared, accompanied by the bishop. For the first time before mortals, he wore the garb of a Grail knight and his head was enveloped in a broad aura.

The people, who filled every corner of the temple like a compact mass, fell to their knees, imagining that they were in front of a saint from heaven.

When, by order of the bishop, all stood up, Supramati approached the steps of the pulpit and began to speak. In eloquent words he described the state of the world, painted a picture of the misfortunes and bestialities of humanity, who, forgetting their divine origin, had allowed themselves to be dominated by the spirit of evil.

And now, brethren," he continued, "the prophesied times are coming: the end of the world is near. During the terrible minutes, according to prophecy, the invisible will become visible, a judgment will be made, and the pure sheep will be separated from the impure, just as it is in the scriptures. Those who have never declined from faith and honoured God, those who have always remained united by the luminous and invisible him with their Creator, will receive in that minute a reward for their loyalty. They will see Jesus and the spirits of the planet, who will illuminate them with the heavenly light, and they will hear the rigorous condemnation of the diabolical hordes of sacrilegious and seductive people who have blinded and misled so many souls, breaking ties between the God-Father and his children.

It's evident that it would be easy for the Eternal Almighty to break and annihilate the rebellious spirit which considers itself so powerful along with its hordes of supporters, but the Lord has given them the freedom to choose, for evil is an obstacle which tests the good, and the temptation to evil is the supreme test of the soul. You, brethren, are considered "faithful" to the Lord because you have kept your faith in Him and have been the untiring guardians of the altar and of His divine sacraments. In your souls you keep burning the sacred flame that illuminates the tortuous path of men towards their Creator, and you sing the sacramental hymn of the Resurrection. Until today you have stood firm, enduring the poverty and persecutions of these trying times, when Satan has raised his standard upon profaned altars and insolently offended the Creator and His laws. Now, brethren, it remains for you to fulfil your last duty on this doomed earth.

You have to leave this refuge where you perform your prayers and sacraments to appear again among the people and fight against evil. You must preach the word of God and call people to repentance and prayer, tell them of the approaching hour when there will be no more time for salvation. You must be courageous and fear nothing, not even death, for you will fight for the salvation of human souls, and every soul saved will be a priceless treasure which you will lay at the feet of the Eternal. The responsibility resting upon you is sublime and difficult. The sinful kingdom is at an end; the satanic hordes have already tried and destroyed too many souls; their temples will be razed to the ground and purified with the blood which the martyrs will willingly shed. Answer me, my brethren, do you consider yourselves strong enough to fight this great battle, without shrinking from any sacrifice, and to contribute to the victory of the divine light over the darkness of evil?

While Supramati was speaking, the crowd gradually came to their knees, without losing sight of the wonderful, inspired face of the speaker, who, in his target suit and with his silver aura over his head, seemed to them a spirit of the spheres. When he fell silent, a unison exclamation was heard in response, all extending their hands towards him.

Yes, we want to fight and put our strength and our lives to save our brothers and sisters! Help us, Lord, to fight for the glory of your Name - hundreds of voices were heard. Everyone's faces exuded courage and energy; a burning faith was reflected in their eyes and an unexpected inner beauty seemed to transfigure everyone's appearance.

At the end of the mass, all present took communion, vowing to fight against Satan, not backing down from any danger. Then Supramati spoke again.

Brothers and sisters! It only remains for me to tell you that the moment a cross appears resplendent in the sky, the grotto of the Holy Sepulchre lights up like a fire and the bells begin to toll on their own, it means that the time has come to enter the holy combat, armed with the cross and with your unshakeable faith. And until that time comes, pray, prepare yourselves and gather all the moral strength you can.

At the end of the last prayer, the faithful dispersed, while Supramati, Nivara and the priests gathered in the bishop's cell to discuss the situation in Jerusalem and other Christian communities in Palestine. At this meeting, Supramati learned that a real underground city had formed in the mountains outside Sinai.

A wanderer in the desert stumbled across large caves that formed labyrinths, soon occupied by Christians fleeing persecution. There they built churches, houses, cemeteries and opened new passages, carefully hidden and known only to the faithful. In these inaccessible shelters were kept the most venerated relics, miraculous icons and all the shrines that managed to escape the sacrilegious wrath of the Satanists. There lived a unique and ascetic population, imbued with an energetic faith, who spent their time in uninterrupted fasting and prayer. The region seemed to be divided into two layers: on the surface, a raging Satanism reigned, while underground, sacred chanting, masses and religious festivals were held. By a strange twist of fate, it was precisely in the catacombs that the Christian faith had grown and acquired its unshakable strength; and now it was preparing again to emerge from the depths of the caverns, as clear and strong as at birth, to receive a new but final baptism, through the blood of the martyrs.

All this was told to Supramati by the priests, one of whom recalled that some years ago a small female community had been formed in the caves, whose prioress was a young woman so benevolent and devout that she was unanimously elected to the position.

This is an unusual creature," continued the old man. - His intelligence and strength of character are not commensurate with its age. Her parents were believers and belonged to an old Christian family, but unfortunately they succumbed to temptation and fell into Satanism. However, Taíssa, who was only 10 years old at the time, stood firm in her faith and escaped from home. Her escape was particularly miraculous. It is said that an angel brought her here in a small and fragile canoe. At her request, she was brought to the community she now leads. Her great faith and exemplary life have always delighted and amazed her colleagues. Taíssa has an astute spirit and has visions. She is convinced, for example, that her life is a supreme test or a mission and always seems to be searching for something or waiting for someone.

Hearing the story, Supramati smiled. He knew who was this girl who, through trials, sustained by unwavering love and conscious faith, was making her way to him.

Then the conversation turned to the personality of a man who troubled the faithful too much. They saw in him the embodiment of evil itself and the most dangerous creature that ever existed on the face of the earth.

Supramati had already heard of him in Czargrado, and was convinced that his extreme influence over minds was growing every day. Supramati, however, wasn't able to see him, because Shelom Iezodot - that was his name - was then living in another city and was returning from a tour of inspection of the world, for he considered himself the lord of the planet. His unlimited power over people, in all respects, entitled him to be so called. Interested to hear opinions about this man from mere mortals, Supramati asked to hear all about him.

Shelom Iezodot's origin was mysterious and already surrounded by legends, the most likely of which was that he was the bastard son of a Jewish billionaire who gave him a dowry and made him his heir.

He claimed to be "Satan's only son", mockingly adding that he looked like Christ, called the Son of God. Otherwise, he let people talk whatever they wanted. Coming from Asia while still young, full of energy and devilishly handsome, he began his triumphal rise. He practised "miracles", turned stones into gold, performed miraculous healings, unleashed and calmed storms, summoned demons. In other words, he seemed to dominate nature and apparently possessed inexhaustible treasures, judging by the amount of gold he threw in handfuls into the air and distributed to all who approached him. One of the priests, who had seen Shelom, said that there was something truly bewitching about his countenance and his gaze was undeniably subdued and domineering.

"Then, brother Supramati, since you say that the final hour is coming, is not this man the prophesied "Antichrist"?" asked the concerned old man. Supramati didn't answer and took his leave. His intention was to travel to Sinai at dawn and visit the underworld, which served as a refuge for the army of Christ.

With great concern, Supramati entered the galleries where the persecuted Christians gathered their valuable treasures and hid them from the sacrilegious. The refuge of the women, who lived alone, was completely separate from the refuge of the single men and had separate entrances. The families occupied special buildings in this huge underground city. Supramati and Nivara stayed in the residence of a family who asked them to accept their hospitality. The owner of the house - a young and enthusiastic devotee - showed them the caves.

Full of surprises, they had admired the settings sculpted by nature itself and the great churches, tall as cathedrals, where spiritual treasures saved from destruction were kept.

A woman who had a relative in the community being led by Taísssa offered to take Supramati there, since he was a prophet who predicted the end of the world. Nivara wasn't allowed to enter. Because of the slanderous rumours spread by Satanists about Christian women, no men were allowed in, and only on the great festivals, commemorating the birth and death of Christ, was an octogenarian priest allowed in to celebrate the service.

Through winding galleries, with cells on either side and caves of varying sizes, Supramati and her companion entered the church of the small community where the nuns gathered, if one could call them that. It was a large cavern with stalactite walls and a very high dome that was lost in the gloom. Inside, on an elevation of a few steps, stood the altar and on it the statue of the Blessed Virgin, larger than a human being; in her open arms she held the infant Jesus, as if showing him to the faithful; around her were grouped figures of saints much venerated in antiquity. On the altar, covered with a silver brocade cloth, was an ancient golden chalice. On each side of the steps were twenty women, dressed in white, with long veils over their heads, singing a hymn to the glory of the Blessed Virgin and the Saviour.

They were all young and beautiful. The harmonious chanting of young voices spread through the temple like the sounds of an organ. However, Supramati was attracted to one of them, also dressed in white, with a transparent veil on her head; only a golden cross hanging from her chest distinguished her from the others. She was genuflecting on the top step, with her hands folded and her gaze fixed on the image; her wonderful, sonorous, strong, velvety voice stood out from all the others.

She was a young woman of about eighteen or nineteen, so fragile, white and transparent that she seemed lifeless; her long, blonde, slightly wavy hair reached to the floor and her large blue eyes were clear and limpid like a child's.

When the prayer was over, Supramati's companion approached her sister and informed her of the arrival of the extraordinary visitor. They all hurried towards him, but Taíssa, coming within two paces of Supramati, stopped suddenly, shuddered, and her eyes widened when she stared at the image. On an impulse she fell to her knees, put her hands to her head and muttered.

"I know you. You're the envoy of the higher forces and you appear in my visions, but... I don't remember your name..."

Supramati put his hand on her head, lifted it and said affectionately.

"Your heart has recognised me. I have come to tell you that your final test is near. When you face it with dignity and overcome the last barrier, then you will remember my name and the past. But now I have to say a few words to you and your companions."

He described the situation of the world, pointed out the proximity of the end and explained that the believers would face a great and decisive battle, whose purpose was to wrest from the forces of evil the souls that could still be saved.

"Until now, Sisters, you have preserved your souls from the filth that surrounds you," he added. "However, it's easier to preserve purity and faith in retirement, far from any temptation, than in the midst of profligate people, under the threat of infamy, persecution and, quite possibly, even life itself. And it's in this anthill, dear sisters, that I hope to see your pure, strong and invincible army, rescuing souls from diabolical plots."

The sisters, full of faith and submission, promised to use all their strength to live up to their vocation. Taíssa, on the other hand, looked transformed. An exalted faith and a great firmness lit up her beautiful face, slightly flushed with excitement, and her blue eyes stared at Supramati with an inexplicable expression.

I'll face the last test, I'll overcome the difficulties and God will support me and open my spiritual eyes," she murmured, and an unusual energy came into her voice.

Supramati's eyes burned with joy. As she blessed the sisters, he suggested to them to pray constantly and then he left.

The visit to the caves pleased Supramati very much. The air there was very different and similar to that of the palaces of the Himalayas. He felt good and spent much time in the caves where ancient talismans of martyred humanity were kept: relics of saints and miraculous icons, before which people had for centuries exposed the pure inclinations of the soul and obtained innumerable blessings. And the power of the great invisible benefactors did'nt weaken one little bit after they were expelled from the luxurious temples and forced to descend into the dark underground galleries: they continued to ask Heaven to forgive the sins and crimes of the blind, who rose up against the Supreme Power that controls the Universe.

Supramati prayed for hours and hours, asking those high spirits to support him, inspire him and send him the understanding to become a true and submissive preacher of the -divine word.

He was a mage, trained in the laboratory of his masters, armed with enormous knowledge. He knew how to rule over the elements of nature, to understand and direct the great cosmic engines of the planetary machine, but during the time of that long ascent, he became completely separated from the human whirlwind and, knowing the complicated mechanism of infinity, he unlearned to understand that microcosm which is called the human soul. He forgot what lurks in the human heart: the struggle and the storm, the high tide and the low tide, the fall and the groan of this poisonous little insect called -man. Individually, this rational particle represents nothing with its miserable vanity, pride, selfishness and rebellious spirit; already by billions, it reveals itself as a devastating cloud of locusts that corrodes the planet, swirling and leaping between Heaven and the abyss... And Supramati, in fervent prayer, asked all the afflicted benefactors, whose great mercy wasn't exhausted by contact with human wounds, to teach him to understand sinners, to condescend to their judgment, and to lead them with love to the Heavenly Father.

His mentors transformed poor Ralf Morgan into a magician of three rays of light: with love and patience they corrected, purified and inspired every nook and cranny of his soul. He went from being a crippled moralist with dulled senses to an elevated being, able to see, feel and understand the unknown. The time had come to repay this debt of love by returning to the mentors the gifts they had so lavishly bestowed upon him. In profound submission, the magician stood genuflecting before the high spirits full of divine mercy, who renounced the peace of their personal beatitude and voluntarily chained themselves to Earth, listening tirelessly to all the tears and bitterness with which the afflicted came to their presence, asking, like children, for all that life had deprived them of: health, earthly goods, forgiveness of sins and crimes.

Teach me, O supreme teachers, to love and understand them as you love and understand these criminal creatures who have denied God. Let me not forget that I'm weak and blind to the secret of the human heart, that the pride of knowledge may never obstruct my spiritual vision, and that I may fulfil, with dignity, the difficult mission of bringing the light of the Creator to the human generations who will be under my care in the new world.

And in the darkness of the caverns, great floodlights were lit; the beneficent spirits approached the mage, looked at him with love and condescension, taught him the difficult art of understanding the soul, and promised him help and support. In this atmosphere of light and warmth, Supramati's body was filled with new strength. Her whole being trembled with sacred love for humanity and her moral disorder seemed less repellent to her in spite of her vices, crimes, blindness and fratricidal hostility. Through all this filth he glimpsed the radiance of the "divine spark," the immortal breath of the Creator, which no sordidness could annihilate or extinguish, and which lurked in all its primal purity, fanned to the cruel heart of Satan. And this gift from Heaven no one had ever been able to take away from a being created by God.

After a few weeks of isolation, prayer and asceticism, Supramati left the underground city and, with renewed strength, returned to Czargrado.

This time he appeared in society, and the magnificent halls of his palace were filled with the most elegant, rich and famous representatives of society. The festive, frivolous and ignorant crowd examined with avaricious curiosity the valuable art treasures collected in great quantity in that luxuriously furnished house, with numerous servants, which was already absolutely unheard of and incredible in the age of general "equality", when services were performed by machines or animals.

Nevertheless, despite all the audacity and shamelessness of the ladies of the "end of the world", something in Supramati's stern gaze and enigmatic smile restrained them and kept them at a respectable distance.

But in addition to the great interest aroused by the personality of the charming Hindu prince, the city was full of curiosity and gossip on the occasion of Shelom Iezodot's return to the capital, accompanied by a large and illustrious court that he always brought with him.

On the location of the ancient temple of Hagia Sophia, later transformed into a mosque, the son of Satan built a huge palace, making full use of the ancient walls. One part of the palace, where the remains of the church were located, served as a private quarter for Shelom Iezodot and Iskhet Zemumam, a strange woman who had never abandoned him and who called herself unabashedly the mother and wife of the king of the universe. In the annexes of the building, residences were prepared for the court, satanic priests, women and other moral monsters who participated in the incredible orgies and disgusting sacrileges, scattered wherever Shelom and his repugnant staff took up residence. All that had been venerated by the ancient pagan and Christian world was defiled and profaned by these latter-day monsters.

The news, avidly transmitted, told how, one by one, the countries willingly submitted themselves to Shelom Iezodot, for no one possessed so much earthly goods as he did, nor did he distribute them with so much magnanimity. In all the houses where Supramati stayed, nothing else was spoken of, and they also said that in all the regions that submitted to him, Shelom left his satraps, whose duty it was to supervise the welfare of the region, distributing gold to the needy, promoting satanic parties and orgies, and exterminating, wherever he went, both the faithful and everything connected with the ancient faith. To assist in this useful work, a council with an unlimited number of members was appointed in each satrap. However, in order to receive the title of councillor, one had to explicitly commit the "seven deadly sins", at least one murder and some unheard-of and outrageous sacrilege. The city of Tsargrad, it was said, had been chosen by Shelom as his capital.

Finally, the day came when the terrible and mysterious man arrived in the city. Still the day before, the excited crowds began to fill the streets, and with the coming of night there appeared, surrounded by the fleet court area, the black yacht, inlaid with gold and illuminated by a brilliant blood-red light. It was the ship carrying Shelom. Like a spirit of darkness, it descended from space to take up residence in the chosen capital.

Shelom's arrival was celebrated with satanic processions and sacrifices, the massacre of some people publicly recognised as faithful, and orgies that exceeded, in their shamelessness and unprecedented sacrilege, anything that had gone before. But Shelom didn't confine himself to celebrations and decorations; he also initiated economic reforms, the first of which caused general satisfaction. The population was exempted from paying for train tickets; in return, a small annual tax was introduced, allowing free travel around the world.

This was because, the new patriarch of the Earth explained in his law, you could not restrict people's freedom by forcing them to stay in one place, because they might want to move elsewhere, and air travel belonged to everyone, like the air itself.

CHAPTER XI

Two weeks after his arrival, we found Shelom sitting in his room. It was a room of medium proportions; the walls were lined with black cloth with red patterns; the furniture was of black wood, the backs decorated with carved goat's heads and upholstered with red silk cloth. Red electric lamps flooded the room with a light the colour of blood. Shelom sat at the table in a wide, high-backed armchair, listening intently to the words of one of the councillors, who, standing and gesticulating loudly, made a report with unusual ardor. A black star on his collar indicated the high rank of his satanic hierarchy.

The wicked Tsar was a young man, very tall, and so slender, slim, and supple that the movements of his physique, covered with black mesh, resembled those of a snake. The features of the face, though angular, were regular; the eyes - large, grey, with a strong greenish tinge, surmounted by eyebrows that almost joined at the interciliary - were so phosphorescent that they resembled those of a wild beast.

Behind the blood-red, full lips there were sharp, white teeth; his thick, curly, black hair and goatee further accentuated the pale, grey complexion of his face.

In fact, he might even be called beautiful, if his physiognomy did n't reflect all the vices and impious aspirations, and if his gaze weren't so icy and at the same time so savage and cruel. Next to Shelom, in a lower chair, sat a woman of fascinating beauty. The cloth that clothed her, contouring her wonderful forms, exposed her neck and arms of ivory whiteness. Her features resembled an ancient cameo; large dark black eyes glittered behind immense lashes, as if illuminated by an inner light; the small red mouth denoted voluptuousness; the elegant black hair, exceptionally thick, descended below her knees; a wide gold hoop, decorated with a goat's head with emerald eyes, supported her immense black wig. The woman was, in the literal sense of the word, devilishly beautiful and the very embodiment of sensuality, as if she'd been created to provoke passions and seduce people into the maelstrom from which she herself had sprung.

"So, Madim, do you think the Hindu is dangerous?" Shelom asked, stroking his goatee and looking with a smirk at the man who had just appeared before him.

"Yes, I consider it my duty to draw your special attention to him. This man has probably come out of a secret den of former Christians and is surrounded by such a nauseating atmosphere that when he passes our shrines with his secretary, a storm seems to break out. His house is full of servants, but none of them has shown any interest in our house or in taking part in our ceremonies. As I had already reported, Prince Supramati appears in society and organises lavish receptions, but it is known that his relationship with everyone is very discreet and what is more extraordinary: he has no lover."

"We need to fix it," scoffed Shelom.

"That won't be easy" worried Madim. "All the more so because Maslot, our great seer and astrologer, told me that this person, along with some others, was sent by our enemies and will cause us trouble. I have already been told that the Hindu has talked to Doctor Chamanov, telling him that the end of the world is near and that there will be terrible catastrophes, famine, earthquakes and who knows what else."

Shelom burst into a loud laugh.

We'll have to take away from Maslot his clairvoyant title, for he's beginning to go blind. And you, Madim, who I thought was more intelligent! Do you think I don't know what I should do? Iam on my way to the revelation and mastery of a mysterious substance, or blood of the planet or also the "elixir of life", as it is called by the despicable egotists who hide in the Himalayas. Clever was he who manages to destroy us after we take the primal essence, which will assure us planetary life. How can there be hunger if the same substance everywhere produces abundant vegetation and an abundance of all products? Well, let us wait until the catastrophe strikes! It will only take me one step to get in touch with the neighbouring worlds, to which we shall move; and then let the old Earth collapse with all its hidden fools, its idiotic faith and all its -velharia‖, carefully hidden by them in caves and underground galleries.

Shelom straightened up, his eyes shining and all of him breathing with unbridled pride and awareness of his power. Madim and that woman, along with a few other people in the room, stared at him dazzled and filled with superstitious fear.

"By the way, you are right about one thing," Shelom continued. "It will be good to disarm Prince Supramati and render him harmless. That will be your task, Iskhet. You'll tempt and seduce this man who won't be able to resist your charms."

Goosebumps ran through the young woman's body, and she, frightened, closed herself inside the red cloak that was on her shoulders.

"Sir, your order is cruel! That man must possess immense power, for just his approach causes our shrines to tremble. How, then, do you want me to approach him?"

An icy, implacable smile crept across Shelom's face.

"That's up to you. That's what you're in Iskhet Zemumam for. By the way, I'll make it easy for you and arrange a banquet that he will attend. I think that will be enough to lure him into your arms. Tomorrow Im going to visit Supramati. make sure everything is ready," he said to Madim.

The next day we found Supramati with Nivara in the laboratory attached to the room. The mage was pale and thoughtful, but meeting Nivara's somewhat concerned gaze he smiled at her.

"And so, you're worried about the future visit of His Excellency, the Tsar of blasphemy. I too cannot admit that it brings me pleasure. But since the encounter is inevitable, we have to get used to it. For now, let's take advantage of the fact that we're in the laboratory and make some preparations to welcome him."

Instructed by Supramati. Nivara activated a large electrical apparatus which began to release long beams of light, enveloping them and forming a kind of reticule. A short time later, everything dissipated.

"Welcome now!" Nivara cheered, stopping the machine. "It's a pity that the time hasn't yet come for us to show this diabolical monster who he is dealing with. It isn't advisable for an adept to be happy about the misfortune of others, but I cannot shake off the feeling of deep satisfaction at the thought of the impending punishment that will befall this miserable being."

Supramati shook his head.

"What awaits them is so horrible that we must be condescending and merciful."

An hour later, the room was suddenly swept by a gust of icy wind, and from outside a noise was heard that was obviously only perceptible to the initiated.

"Our visit is coming. I have ordered him to be taken to the blue hall," Supramati said, getting up. "Come with me, Nivara, he is also with his secretary Madim. The rest of his retinue will be detained by our friends at the gate," he added, seeing that the spirits of the elements, commanded by him, had gathered and surrounded him to protect him.

In fact, at the entrance to the palace a battle began - invisible, of course, to mortal eyes - of the spirits of the elements against the maggots, vampires and other sordid beings from hell that made up Shelom's entourage. The magician's army, however, was victorious and none of the impure ones managed to penetrate the palace. For those looking on from the outside, the battle between the warring parties was reflected in the formation of black clouds that covered the sky, the heavy air and the deafening rumble of thunder. When Supramati entered, the Blue Hall, which led into the garden, was shrouded in a whitish glow, and through a large window one could see how lightning streaked the sky and a scorching wind lifted columns of dust.

Shelom was alone, standing in the middle of the room. A nervous convulsion disfigured his face with cadaverous lividity. Madim, by the way, had remained behind the door, so Nivara, out of modesty, also withdrew from the room.

The two mighty adversaries stood alone and looked at each other measuring each other. They knew the importance of atmospheric disturbances. Supramati's gaze remained calm and translucent as before, while in Shelom's greenish eyes shone hatred and envy, as if all the hell of chaotic feelings lurked in his dark soul. As if by magic, his gaze could not tear itself away from the tall, slender figure of the mage, which seemed to glow in May in the bluish light that concentrated above his head in the form of a radiant aura.

To a slight bow from Supramati, Shelom reciprocated by tilting his head well below the usual, it should be said in passing. In that palace environment, the light seemed to crush him like a lead weight and an icy shiver ran through his body. They did not hold hands, since the custom had been abolished long ago. This practice was in vogue at the time when the laws of occultism were practically ignored and no one was aware of the power of the direct contact of two opposing forces. Satanists knew this law and avoided reaching out to the infidels.

"I greet you, Prince Supramati! I have come to offer you peace," Shelom began a minute later. "I know that you and your brothers have abandoned your Himalayan refuge to come and fight me. It is obvious, too, that in this world there is only room for one. The earth, with its delights and riches, is my area, and you, here, have nothing to do, for your kingdom -is not of this world‖. The confrontation will be terrible, because, as you know, my power is identical to yours. Like you, I govern the elements of nature, I know the secrets of healing and legions of spirits are submissive to me. I resurrect the dead and transform stones into gold. But, before we start this decisive combat, I propose you an advantageous deal. You want to save souls? All right, all right! Tell me how many souls you value your stay here and I'll gladly give them to you. You want five thousand... ten thousand... fifty thousand... Just take them and go. Don't get in my way."

Your proposal is brilliant, but unacceptable, because I cannot simply take the souls. They will have to come to me. Only a fight can purify and liberate them completely, when they can then choose good or evil.

Shelom's eyes sparked with anger.

"I know what you are counting on: the miraculous power of the original essence that you "immortals" consider as your exclusive property. Well, then you are mistaken, for I have discovered what you hide with such zeal and I will work more miracles than your foxes, unworthy custodians of tradition, who have deprived the people of this treasure. Before your eyes, it can be said, countless human generations have perished; yet you haven't even moved, while I have given everyone the opportunity to enjoy the precious gift, life.

You have predicted the imminent end of the world, whose destruction nothing can prevent? Here I am!" Shelom straightened up haughtily and continued. "I'll stop the decay of the planet and cover it with vegetation and the fertility will be inexhaustible; the always healthy and young people, endowed with planetary life, will enjoy all the blessings and will deify me as their benefactor."

"Take care, Shelom Iezodot, that the remedy doesn't turn out worse than the disease. Take care that instead of reigning over the cosmic laws established by God, they don't turn against you."

When he heard the name of the Eternal, a tremor of disgust marred Shelom's face, and in a fit of rage he cried out:

"I know only one supreme master, to whose laws I submit: Satan, my father! The last word has not yet been spoken, no one knows whether this or that will triumph."

"You ignorant, blind fool! - said Supramati. - Intoxicated by your hatreds and vices, you forget that Satan himself, whatever he may be, is also a son of God. No rebellion, no vainglory, no hatred can take away from him the essence of his Father; it will remain in him till the end of time, for that which is created by God is indestructible, and you are an unworthy offspring of Divinity. Beneath the shell of sordidness, crimes and rebellion, there, in the depths of your being, stirs the flame that gave you life. And this flame is sacred, it is the breath of the Eternal of your Father and mine, and this sacred spark you are not in a position to tarnish or destroy."

As Supramati spoke, Shelom crouched down, trembling nervously. His figure was disgusting, his face disfigured and a bloody drool appeared on his lips. The storm seemed to be increasing. In the gusts of wind, moans and groans seemed to be heard; was not hell weeping for its impotence in the struggle against the heavenly light?

Suddenly, Shelom straightened up and with clenched fists threatened Supramati, who remained calm and straight as before.

"Stop your exhortations, Himalayan hermit. I didn't come here to listen to your sermons. You didn't want peace, so let us fight and see who gives way. We'll prove our strength before the people and let them decide to whom the kingship shall belong."

"I have no intention of governing a dying world, but neither do I have any reason to refuse your challenge. I only warn you that you arent sufficiently armed against the catastrophe you think you can avert. You say you possess the primal essence? That's fine. But you don't know how to use it, so be careful. Otherwise, I repeat once again, the remedy may turn out to be worse than the disease," Supramati advised calmly.

"I don't worry about that; I answer for my actions. However, if you accept my "challenge", as you call it, also accept my invitation, Prince Supramati, and come to the party I'm organising."

An enigmatic smile pervaded Supramati's lips.

"If you, Shelom Iezodot, don't fear my presence in your house, I'll come without fail."

"And you'll go alone, as I came to yours?"

"Didn't you come with your secretary Madim? I can see him trembling from behind the door. So, I'll also come with my assistant Nivara."

"Which I see full of pride behind the other door," Shelom rebutted mockingly. - Thank you for your promise, prince. I'll be waiting for you at the party and without any confrontation, I'll give you the gift of a few hundred souls that you can save at your leisure in your comfortable refuges.

"I thank you for that. You are very condescending, but I am not used to receiving anything without effort, not even criminal souls. Only what comes from work has value."

Shelom let out a dry laugh.

"As you wish. For now, order the elements to calm down and tell your staff to stop fighting my people, so I can leave your palace freely and without embarrassment."

Supramati turned to the window and, raising his hand, drew phosphorescent signs in the air. Almost at the same time, a deafening noise was heard, the gusts of a strong wind swept the black clouds, the sky opened, from afar, a surprisingly soft music, and behind the great window light, transparent beings gathered, swaying like fluids in the wind.

A smile of infinite happiness lit up the beautiful cheeks of the magician, while Shelom, pale as a corpse, left the palace like a hurricane in the company of Madim. A strange anguish seized the heart of the evil tsar, and he held his breath. An oppressive feeling of hatred, bitterness and envy tore at him; from whence had this feeling arisen; was it stirring, forcing him to suffer in his own flesh that accursed thing, hidden in the depths of my being - that divine heritage of the Heavenly Father, which could not be destroyed, and constrained Satan's triumph by withholding the ascent of souls to the light?

With barely noticing Shelom's departure, Supramati's exalted gaze was fixed on a wondrous sight. In the distance, in a vast golden halo, he saw the reflection of his beloved leader. Ebramar, and pleasantly inhaling the scents of pure light, which illuminated him in golden cascades, felt the life-giving warmth of the mighty currents of good sweeping through his soul, and an indescribable feeling of happiness and gratitude came over him:

"Oh, what a pleasure it's to be conscious of the power of goodness and of sustaining the harmony of the spheres! Struggle, suffering and toil for centuries are rewarded, for thousands of years, by this one minute of indescribable bliss. Forward, without stopping, towards the light."

As Shelom left, Nivara entered slowly and paused at the sight of his master and friend in deep concentration. Supramati had never seemed so beautiful and enchanting to him as in that moment of exalted detachment. At the words he murmured, Nivara knelt down and, with tears in his eyes, pressed the magician's hands to his lips. Supramati shuddered and placed his hand affectionately on the disciple's head.

"Nivara, we're happy, and infinite is the mercy of the Creator, who has granted us the gift of beholding and attaining great secrets of creation. What a glorious destiny this force of good, acquired through our work, promises hereafter. At first we shall have to fight hard, but I hope to wrest from the enemy more than a thousand souls. In this way we shall have the opportunity to preach the word of God and lay the foundation of the laws of the Lord in a new world. Let us go forward, Nivara! The road to the goal of total knowledge is a long one, but we have already felt our wings. We must submit to the grandeur of the infinite and be unwavering in faith. These wings will carry us from rung to rung on the ladder of perfection. Our world is not great, our deeds are even less important, but God, in His mercy, only evaluates the dimensions of our efforts, judging us with love and measuring our strength and the knowledge we have acquired. "

Supramati fell silent, and both of them, deeply moved, returned to the laboratory.

The next day, working with his disciple in his office, Supramati asked him unexpectedly:

"Are you, Nivara, ready enough to face Shelom's feast? There we'll be tempted in all possible ways. "

"Oh, I fear nothing in their company, and we'll have Ebramar's help too! - replied Nivara fearlessly. - Have you not told me countless times, dear master, that with a torch in hand no darkness is to be feared, for the light reveals every pitfall and illuminates every abyss? Thanks to your teachings and my efforts, my spiritual eyes have been opened. I see the invisible and hear the harmony of the spheres, the contagious odours of vice and worldly feelings are repulsive to me. Can I, after all this, be vulnerable to bland temptations?"

"Well done Nivara! I sense that your eyes are truly open and that you will be careful. But, my friend, never underestimate the enemy however insignificant he may seem;

he can become dangerous the very moment we fall asleep lulled by the conviction of our invulnerability. It is best to believe that your armour is flawed and to be on your guard so that no arrow hits the unprotected spot."

Noticing a slight blush from the young adept, Supramati added affably:

There's no need to blush. I know you've always stood your ground and so have they. And as Shelom will probably want to - rest after your visit, before organising the beautiful banquet and preparing all the insidiousness in our honour, I think we'll have time to visit Dakhir with Narayana. We will tell him what has happened and Shelom's invitation, and we will take the opportunity to see there what strategy they have developed for their actions and how the preparations are going.

Some hours later, Supramati's spacecraft was taking them to the former Moscow, as Dakhir and Narayana had chosen Russia and its surroundings for the field of their work.

Flying at breakneck speed, within a few hours they could see a vast Russian plain below them. Always uniform in appearance, it was now taking on a very dull and pitiful aspect. The vast, sandy, barren fields were pure desert; the great green forests had disappeared, and among the few places of low vegetation there were no longer to be seen the green or blue church towers with the golden crucifixes that had once enlivened the vast countryside. Near the town, out of sight, stretched vast greenhouses, in which all agriculture was now concentrated. Meanwhile, the general picture was indescribably cadaverous and monotonous.

"And here once was -Holy Russia," Supramati lamented, sighing and casting a penalised glance at the city they were flying over.

"Yes," replied Nivara to the master's complaint, "the crucifixes and domes have long since been removed and everything that reminded us of the religion of our ancestors has been ruthlessly eliminated. The bells that called the faithful to the divine office are no longer heard; under the old domes the sacred chants are no longer intoned; any religious feeling is gone... But no other place shocks as much as this one, for the Russian people were once animated by ardent and moving faith."

"I know. I have been here with Ebramar and watched the astonishing lines of devotees congregating at various holy sites. Poor, dressed in rags, with only a penny in their pockets at best, these pilgrims came from the ends of the country, exhausted by the long journey and hungry, but full of such faith that all fatigues and misfortunes were forgotten as soon as they fell at the feet of the holy relics or the miraculous icon; and when, then, they lit a fine candle or held a Eucharistic bread, everything was a real feast. How pure and strong was the prayer that flowed from the hearts of these disinherited people! And how many graces they received from those to whom they went to pray! Purified and invigorated, they set out again on their difficult earthly pilgrimage."

"Master, is there a punishment severe enough for those diabolical deviants who through weakness, frivolity, ambition or perversion tore from this people the faith that sustained them, broke their ties with the Divine and transformed the good and pious people into a people full of bandits and apostates?"

"Yes, they took on a painful responsibility. Not for nothing did Jesus Christ say: "Woe to the one who causes seduction", referring to what would happen to the one who "seduces one of those children", Supramati observed. - How can a deeply pious people decay so quickly and, if they fight back, abandon all that they have worshipped and revered for centuries?"

It was like a moral gangrene. However, there were cases of resistance. One of our brothers, who was here during the last revolution, told me how the monastery - Trinity of Sergiy - was destroyed. Indignation gripped everyone, people were possessed by a sacrilegious insanity of hatred of God. Churches were desecrated and burned, priests murdered here and there. Next to the church of Iversk a bloody battle took place. The prince of a centuries-old Russian family came out with sword in hand in defence of an ancient shrine, but he was killed and his blood splashed on an icon; corpses piled up all over the chapel. What the end of the icon was... no one knows. At that time, danger constantly surrounded the monastery, as well as the icons that were there. The most jealous, preparing to die, prayed day and night at the tomb of the saint. In Moscow, however, the violence went beyond the limits, and our brother told us that what happened there went beyond the unimaginable. It is clear that the rascals decided to destroy the monastery as well, even if they had not set a day for it. However, they did not have time to carry out their vile plan.

One night an unprecedented storm occurred there; the lightning caused fires on an unprecedented scale; the hail killed people and animals; the hurricane uprooted trees, destroyed houses, toppled towers and, to make matters worse, the rivers overflowed their banks. The storm raged for twenty-four hours and thousands of people perished and many went mad with fear. When the storm finally passed, the city of Moscow and its surroundings looked like the scene of a bloody war. People and heavy objects were lifted by the wind and thrown, like chaff, incredible distances. The ancient monastery also became a ruin. The storm concentrated on it and lightning set it on fire. From the well, dug by St. Sérguiy, foaming water gushed out, which, together with other waters, collapsed and in its place the water brought mountains of sand, all piled up with the corpses of monks and neighbouring inhabitants. What was the fate of the saint's tomb? Nobody knows, but the relic had disappeared. The monks were supposed to have removed it by secret routes. No one dared to look for it, as superstitious fear scared people away from the place.

Supramati listened in silence to Nivara's narration, and then sentenced: " Crazy fools! What hell they must have in their souls that they have thrown themselves so fiercely upon everything that could remind them of God; and does this blind mob that covers the wretched earth with crime and discord, condemning it to death, imagine that with this planetary atom the Creator's domains end? "

CHAPTER XII

"We're coming, master. You see, this is Moscow, and there, where a whitish cloud hovers over the building, live our friends," Nivara explained cheerfully.

Minutes later, the spacecraft stopped next to a small tower and, as soon as the travellers stepped onto the platform, Narayana's sonorous voice was heard from the stairway:

"They're here! What a good idea to visit us!"

And with his usual impetuosity, he embraced Supramati and Nivara. Behind him appeared Dakhir, who also greeted them warmly, and, after the welcome, they all went to the dining room, where Narayana immediately began to prepare the meal.

"Do you know where you are now?" he asked, placing a silver jar of wine and a huge basket of fruit on the table. "You're inside the old Kremlin, or actually, the remains of it. When it became national property, it was auctioned off and a certain Goldenbliuk bought the Grand Palace and turned it into a furnished residence for rich people who could afford to pay a fortune. His grandson is our landlord, and as I'm an appreciator of antique objects, I've rented the whole house for Dakhir and myself. So, the rooms, which once housed great emperors, now modestly accommodate two Hindu princes and missionaries from the end of the world," Narayana concluded, with his jovial humour."

"Dear friends, I advise you that the meal is frugal, because the food is no longer as tasty and succulent as it was in the past; only the wine is good. It comes from our old wineries, where Narayana keeps the so-called "unnegotiable reserves," Dakhir added, laughing.

"It's true, everything has lost its flavour, as if mother earth wanted us to be disgusted by it so as not to mourn its loss. What is the use of money if it no longer has the same value? Nature seems to have gone mad; the temperature changes are unbearable; sometimes it's polar cold, sometimes tropical heat; and everything so abrupt, without a break. Spring and autumn have practically disappeared; the transition from summer to winter is unbelievably rapid. Added to this are terrible hurricanes, earthquakes and poisonous miasmas arising from the sea or from the land, suffocating people. In the plant kingdom, everything is also reversed. Greenhouse farming got so bad that they tried to go back to gardening in the open air, but these attempts were unsuccessful; everything freezes or burns, or is eaten by worms. So we have had to drink wine that tastes like wax and eat fruit with no juice or flavour that reminds us of trees; in short, rubbish like this."

He took a fruit from the basket and threw it angrily into the corner of the room. The apple split open, exposing a dry and shrivelled flesh. Everyone laughed about the exalted mood of the incorrigible glutton.

"So it is. Heaven has sent warnings to criminal humanity," Dakhir commented, "but unfortunately, it doesn't want to understand them and remains indifferent to the clamour of cosmic forces that have lost their balance."

"The whole earth is a desert," Narayana said.

"You forget one little corner of our dying Earth that has stayed as it was," replied Supramati. - India, the cradle of humanity, where one day "the immortals" landed from another world in extinction, great legislators and introducers of the first age of enlightenment. There they taught the alphabet of the great laws to inexperienced peoples, laws that sustained social and moral order, wisely opening to these peoples as much light as they were able to assimilate. There, their spirit seems to protect the places where they lived and where they built the archive of the world. And atmospheric disorder and poisonous miasmas, all, finally, were removed from the places where the will of those "great spirits" burns like eternal fire and acts as a protective shield for that fantastic kingdom. Never has a mere mortal, an infidel, who could count on his sacrileges to tarnish those joyous valleys, been able to approach the palaces of the mages and no curious eye has been able to vulgarise the havens of the wise, where nature itself breathes harmony. And only the last and final blow will embrace them in fire, invariably pure and chaste.

"You're right, Supramati. In our magical Hindu palaces, we still live well; but here it's horrible, we feel like we're in a nightmare. It makes me cold just to see others freezing; the people here are miserable. Some live in a constant lethargy of orgies and crimes; others wander around like gloomy misanthropes, unable to find peace, as if they have lost something, unable to find it," sighed Narayana.

"It's true. They've lost and are searching for their old faith, their God and holy protectors, everything that nourished their soul. And now, sick with addictions, without moral support and feeling that something abnormal is happening around them, they're terrified and the future looks to them as a dark abyss," Dakhir observed.

"And I estimate that it's precisely these misanthropes who will be most easily attracted to our preaching," Narayana added, raising his glass and pouring more wine into the visitors' glasses.

The conversation became animated and Supramati spoke about his meeting with Shelom, remembering his defiance and invitation to the armistice.

"Ah, so he's already noticed that you're dangerous!" exclaimed Dakhir.

"Exactly. He even tried to bribe me, offering me a thousand souls so that we could leave, but I declined - and Supramati laughed. - However, I accepted the second offer, a duel of nobles, and we'll measure our hidden strengths. He claims that whatever I can do with pure power, received from God, he can do with diabolical power."

"Well, I guess there must be some difference between those two powers, and when will this magnificent duel of magical powers take place? I hope you will allow Dakhir and me to be present."

"Without a doubt. I insist on the presence of both. Obviously, a large crowd will gather and I intend to start the conversion from that duel. But I don't yet know when it will happen. I think it will be after the infamous banquet, during which they hope to weaken or kill me."

"Ah! What a joke! But anyway, be careful, Supramati! If there is any of the old Adão left in you, Mrs. Iskhet may wake him up," exclaimed Narayana, laughing.

"The thing is," he added modestly, "my attraction to the fair sex hasn't completely died out yet. So I did a little reconnaissance to have a look at the "antichrist's" female friend and convinced myself that she's dangerous."

"I hope that I resist her charms and that the old Adão continues sleeping deep inside me," Supramati argued, smiling.

In the evening, when the mages gathered to talk in Dakhir's chambers, Supramati said, taking a deep breath:

"I feel like there's a church around here."

"Your sense doesn't deceive you. Actually there's a small chapel here, whose entrance was camouflaged by some faithful, but we found it and opened it. The entrance is behind that bar," Narayana agreed, laughing.

He pushed aside the heavy bar and behind it emerged a door that led to a small chapel filled with various sacred objects. They lit the candles and their light illuminated the stern faces of the ancient icons. The mages knelt and prayed fervently. When they left and put the bar back in place, Narayana recounted that the entrance had been so well camouflaged that a mere mortal would never have found it.

"In general," he added, "this shameful time the Earth is going through has generated many curious events from our point of view, of course. For example, the Petersburg catastrophe, the details of which I learned here."

"Oh, tell me, tell me. I knew that the old capital no more existed. I just didn't know the details, and even probably Noivara doesn't know anything about it, because he never told me."

"My pleasure," Narayana agreed. "First of all, I must remind you that here, as in all the places where the faithful have stayed, there are underground places where they hide. Obviously, Dakhir and I have been there and met an old man who told me what I'm going to tell you. The catastrophe occurred just after the overthrow of the great monastery of the "Trinity of Sérguiy". But many years before, Petersburg's climate was increasingly inclement. The polar glaciers came so close that northern Sweden, Norway and Russia became uninhabitable. In Petersburg it was still possible to survive, although the summer was getting shorter and shorter and the winter longer and colder. So the creative spirit of humankind invented a palliative: whole blocks were covered with glass domes and heated with electricity. In sum: they managed to survive at a high cost. In the meantime, sacrilege and all the vices that always accompany it were increasing faster than the cold; since the government of the time was usurping everything from the governed, a law was passed ordering all churches to be closed and sold at auction. In spite of this, there still remained, especially among the people, people who preserved the old customs and the old faith. Then, a gang of fraudulent businessmen bought all the temples wholesale and started selling subscriptions with the right to visit the churches, attend mass and receive communion, and the priests hired by the company celebrated the Divine Office. said the businessmen: - "Why not take advantage of the ignorance of the people?" But as the subscriptions cost too much, and a large number of poor people couldn't afford them, people began to lose the habit of going to church, and eventually the company went bankrupt. The anger of these intelligent people was indescribable, and as they had a great influence on the Government, they succeeded in getting the Government to pass a decree which, you see, was to put an end once and for all to all "old and stupid prejudices". To this end, it was ordered to gather together everything connected with the old faith and burn it in a public square.

I forgot to tell you that before that, when there was some faith, they bought the remains of São Nicolau, which were for sale in Bari by the Italians. That relic was placed in a church, specially built near the city... And then these relics, as well as all other shrines, were condemned to the stake. The day of this act of faith was postponed until spring, due to the particularly harsh winter. For the last time, the people were indignant and their hearts trembled at the thought that all that had been venerated by their ancestors, together with the miraculously preserved relics of their benefactors and protectors, would be destroyed. Protests began to arise among the population, but as the insurgents were in the minority, nobody paid any attention to them, and Heaven seemed deaf and blind to all these crimes, blasphemies and sacrileges. And to put an end once and for all to all this "annoying" and "uncomfortable" agitation, they decided to accelerate the " act of faith ".

However, spring was late, and after a few warm days, which melted some of the ice crust that chained the sea, the cold returned again. And once, at night, a terrible storm arose. With noises that sounded like cannon fire, the ice broke up and the angry wind pushed waves and large chunks of ice over the city. The city flooded with incredible speed, but the disaster wasn't yet over. That same terrible night, a volcanic shock slightly raised the bottom of Lake Ladoca; the water overflowed and the churning, foaming waves swept over everything in their path and, rushing like larvae, reached Petersburg, flooding it.

What happened was indescribable. Some hundreds of thousands of people died immediately, and when the water receded, the rest of the city was covered by a crust of ice that wouldn't melt. The same volcanic shock that overflowed Lake Ladoca brought the polar glaciers that moved along the coast of Sweden and closed the Baltic Sea. Today, in all these places, the climate is worse than that of the Eskimos, and Petersburg is a sui generis image of the city of Pompeii under the ice, for, it's said, whole blocks of the city, with its palaces and great buildings, have been left intact. It is said that before the catastrophe, mystical prophets appeared in the streets and announced that criminality had exhausted all the patience of Heaven and that the sacrilegious, who dared to burn all the holy relics along with the other shrines, would die before they could carry out their intentions. In trying to convince the faithful to leave the doomed city, many of them were branded as dangerous madmen and killed en masse. But in their place others arose, and the faithful, profoundly shocked, left the city, while the freethinkers and Satanists remained and all died. Later, when the elements of nature calmed down, some of the faithful visited the site of the catastrophe and found some churches and houses still intact. As the persecution of the faith became more and more insistent and fierce, they decided to settle permanently in that uninhabitable place, and there, little by little, a small community was formed, which lives in the old Neva monastery. The believers gather there to pray, while the Satanists have escaped from the razed city and, as a result, Christ's little flock lives there in peace and security.

This story interested Supramati and his friends so much that they decided to leave the next day to visit the wreck of Petersburg.

As they neared the dead city, the cold increased and the image of desolation provoked a deep sadness. They landed near the Neva monastery, where traces of human activity could still be seen, and a sand-speckled path led to the temple, from the entrance to which the ice had been removed, and from the chimneys of the dwellings little fumes were rising.

Two barrels of pitch were burning at the entrance to the temple, and small mobile ovens were lit inside them. In this way, the temperature inside, compared to the outside, was sufficiently warm and pleasant. The sanctuary was very clean and the damage caused by the flood was repaired as far as possible.

Next to the intact tomb of the saint were some lighted candles and about fifteen men and women. At the end of the Gospel reading, they began to sing and the wise men joined the faithful.

When the prayers were over, the travellers introduced themselves and were affectionately accepted as brothers and taken to the residence to be warmed and fed. Some families had moved into the rooms formerly inhabited by the metropolitans. The other members of the community moved into other buildings. It was warm there; a bright flame burned in the big oven and the hostesses served the visitors mulled wine, bread and a plate of rice.

After the meal, the conversation became lively and Supramati asked about the size of the community and the difficulty of living in that icy desert, among the rubble and death. A smile of satisfaction lit up the faces of the hosts.

"Oh, no!" they replied with one voice. "It's so nice and quiet here, away from the cruel sacrilegious people. Work and prayer don't allow them to realise that time is passing and, besides, we have spaceships that we use to fetch supplies, fuel and other things. And the cold, in fact, is still bearable. Those who come from other cities get very cold, and some of them freeze for good, so almost everyone runs away from here. We and the other residents don't suffer from the cold and we're fine. No one forbids us to hold services; a sanctuary has been preserved which we revere and enjoy the seclusion. We have renounced worldly life and consider ourselves happier than all the millionaires with their palaces."

But there are predictions of a great famine, how will you survive? - Dakhir asked curiously.

The flame of the Lord burns within us and will sustain us," replied one of the elders with resolute faith.

After this conversation, the mages deliberated among themselves, and then Supramati asked whether near the boundaries of the community there might not be a garden or land of some kind that had once been a garden or an orchard.

"How could there not be? There is still a place that used to be the Metropolitan's garden, and beyond that, behind the monastery, there used to be some orchards, but they are all covered with ice and snow."

At the request of the visitors, the mages were led to the place, and the members of the community watched them pour the contents of the small jars that they had brought with them into buckets of water, which they poured copiously on the ground. The mages then bade farewell to their hospitable hosts, intending to visit the dead city on their return.

The spaceship passed in silence along the street that had once been the main artery of the old capital. The sight was bleak and desolate.

In some places, garbage and debris from collapsed houses littered the streets, making them impassable. Other buildings were destroyed and appeared to be tottering; but there were also skeletons or seemingly intact bodies, which seemed to be grimacing under the layer of ice. Wherever they went, the picture was much the same, the mages turned their craft upwards and, deeply shocked, left the criminal city in the direction of 'divine wrath'.

A pleasant surprise awaited the hermits of glacial Pompeii. In the evening, after the departure of the mages, the snow and ice that covered the garden and the orchards disappeared without a trace. After a few days, fresh and abundant vegetation began to grow, and a few weeks later the trees revived, stretched their leafy branches towards the sky and were covered with fruit. Everywhere flowers bloomed and vegetables ripened in the orchards. This little corner of paradise bloomed and gave off pleasant aromas despite the freezing winds and the icy desert that surrounded it. Incredulous at what they saw, the inhabitants delighted in the sight of the miracle, and inwardly began to believe that they were being visited by saints, or perhaps angels, sent from on high to ease their burden and reward them for their faith in God.

The visit to the dead city made a deep impression on the magicians. Before leaving Moscow, Supramati wanted to visit the underground caves where the faithful were hiding. One night, they descended into the underground galleries beneath one of the ancient monasteries. The population was small, but different. In a small chapel, evening mass was being celebrated, officiated with seriousness and concentration by elderly priests in white robes. Weakened by fasting and a life of asceticism, their faces were of a transparent pallor, and the mage's eyes caught a bluish light emanating from them and a glowing aura enveloping their heads. Absorbed in deep prayer, the crowd of kneeling worshippers also gave off pure radiations which, like a golden cloud, hovered beneath the vault. All the people gathered there were from "another world"; their souls opened the way to Heaven, in which they believed. The magicians and Nivara were on their knees, merging in one prayer with the faithful, and their eyes wandered worriedly around this haven of banished faith.

Along the walls were the tombs of the saints and each one looked like a fire emitting rays of golden light.

At the solemn moment, when the priest left the altar carrying the Eucharist, a deep silence fell over the room. Suddenly, the cave was illuminated with a fantastic light and under the dome a heavenly chant - a powerful hymn of faith - rang out and clear and transparent images floated in the air like a white mist. At that moment, the head of Christ with the crown of thorns appeared above the chalice enveloped in rays of blinding light. The divine face wore an expression of deep sadness. A moment later, the vision began to fade and only the chalice continued to burn with a golden flame which then disappeared into the sacred vessel.

A fervent prayer of thanksgiving arose from the hearts of the Magi and those present; all were happy as never before that there were still places on earth where the Lord was revealing his mercy and where the contact between the Creator and his work had not yet been broken. After the mass, the Magi joined the faithful and visited the underground city. Narayana introduced Supramati to the aforementioned old man, who invited the magi to his cell, a tiny room with a table, a chair, a bed and an image of the Mother of God.

Offering the visitor, the only chair, he began to ask Supramati what was happening in the world from which he had completely retired. The approaching end of the world didn't surprise him in the least, and he, in turn, told him that strange things were happening in Moscow, indicating that Heaven was finally fed up with the offences committed on Earth by decadent humanity. One of his relatives, who lived in the city, told him that on the date when Easter was formerly celebrated, the demons were totally hallucinated, and among Satanists there were many suspicious murders and sudden deaths. Some said that on Easter night screams, moans and howls could be heard in the satanic temples, and herds of loathsome beasts ran through the streets. While in the ancient churches, on the contrary, the sound of bells that no longer existed could be heard, under the vaults songs were heard, praising the Resurrection of Christ, and thousands of sparks fell from the sky. During these celestial phenomena, the Satanists were completely stunned, went into hiding and suffered convulsions.

The next day, after visiting the underground city, Supramati travelled, instructing Dakhir and Narayana to visit him after the banquet with Shelom.

"You'll certainly find many interesting things in the house, because the beautiful Iskhet wants to seduce me," he joked.

"It's a good thing Olga knows nothing of the claims of such a dangerous competitor. This could spoil her whole calvary," Narayana observed mischievously.

Everyone laughed and, after shaking hands again, parted.

CHAPTER XIII

A few days after his return to Czargrado, Supramati received an invitation to go, together with Nivara, to the banquet at Shelom's palace. The invitation was brought by Madim himself. This time, however, the Satanist wasn't with his usual air of self-confidence: he was pale and his obstinate gaze denoted fear, mistrust and restrained hatred. Supramati received him kindly and promised to come. On the day of the banquet, long before the time of their departure for Shelom's house, Supramati called Nivara to the laboratory and they both took the usual electric bath. The mage then opened a metal chest and placed several objects on the table.

"We're going to need a very special toilet today," he said, smiling and holding out a phosphorescent blue knitted fabric to Nivara, who hurried to put it on.

The thin and extraordinarily fluffy fabric clung to his body and, to Nivara's surprise, seemed to radiate warmth. On the back, chest and also on the flanks were golden inscriptions of cabalistic signs and formulas. Over this mesh Nivara wore an ordinary blue party dress, with a silver belt, over which he placed a velvet jacket, also blue, sleeveless, embroidered in silver.

"Don't forget your magic stick and hide this dagger in your belt; it may come in useful. Be prepared for anything,

Nivara. And be careful, because they'll try to liquidate us by all means: poison, snakes, jail and who knows? But all that will lead to nothing. Take this magic ring, which can light up the darkest of cells and open any lock, no matter how complex. You certainly know how to use it."

"Yes, master. But what perplexes me is how this so-called Shelom, possessed of such infernal power, can ignore that neither poison nor animal can kill an "immortal".

"You're right. Despite his great evil power, he knows very little of the good. The secret of the primal essence is carefully guarded and, although it will be revealed, he doesn't know all the properties and methods of utilisation of this mysterious substance. In any case, if he has no hope of killing me, then he calculates to weaken me with poison or through temptation."

As they spoke, Supramati wore a fine, brilliant mesh that glittered as if woven with diamonds, reflecting all the colours of the rainbow. On his back, hips and also on his arms and legs were flaming kabalistic formulae and signs. On the chest, right in the centre of the mage's star, the chalice of the Grail Knights seemed to burn, crowned by a cross. The strange garment clung to the mage's slender body like a second skin. He then stood in the centre of a large circular metal disc and drawn with cabalistic signs, and Nivara knelt at his feet. Supramati drew a circle with the magic sword, bowed on all four sides and drew luminescent symbols in the air with the sword, reciting formulas to invoke the spirits of the elements. The herbs placed in three triptychs next to the disc suddenly caught fire and, for an instant, the laboratory was filled with fire and smoke. With each movement of the sword, a multitude of misty beings appeared, violet, red, greenish and bluish in colour. Their bodies had no distinct contours; only their heads were clearly visible, their glowing eyes denoting intelligence and great power. They stood around the mage, forming four concentric circles, resembling rings. Below them all were the violet ones, then the greenish ones, then the red ones, and finally the blue air spirits.

"Spirits of the elements under my command, I order you to surround and protect me and my disciple," said Supramati authoritatively.

There was a deafening rustle, like the rustling of tree leaves, and the misty figures paled and melted into the air.

"Now our noble guard has been warned and won't abandon us," said the mage, stepping out of the disc and continuing his grooming.

He was in white. He wore a knitted suit with a wide silver belt, encrusted with diamonds, a sleeveless, silver velvet coat with diamond embroidered lapels, and a tie of a type of lace that no longer existed.

"My God! How handsome you are, master! " admired Nivara, staring at him. Supramati was fixing his hair in front of the mirror and couldn't contain his laughter:

"Don't fall in love with me instead of Madame Iskhet. The sight of two adepts in love would be more curious than Shelom's banquet," he joked, continuing: "And now, to conclude the preparations, it only remains for us to drink the essence that will tenfold our physical and astral strength."

Supramati took from the cabinet a carved box containing two jars, one red and one blue, and two goblets, one of silver and one of gold. He filled the silver cup with the contents of the red jar: a red, thick, steaming liquid resembling fresh blood.

"This one is for you," and he offered the cup to Nivara, who drained it in one gulp. - And this one is for me. He filled the other cup with a bluish, phosphorescent liquid.

"Phew! now I feel like I could uproot an oak tree!" exclaimed Nivara, taking a deep breath of air.

"Instead of the oak, test your strength with this," suggested Supramati, handing him an iron bar which he took from the corner of the room.

Without any apparent effort, Nivara turned it into a spiral and commented with satisfaction.

"Not bad, but I would be more pleased to make a spiral of Shelom himself."

✳ ✳ ✳

Shelom's palace was magically illuminated. The large front square and the surrounding streets were crowded with people awaiting the arrival of the Hindu prince. The huge and well-lit hall was also filled with well-dressed and curious people. As the mage approached, the crowd opened up and, seized by an uneasy feeling, instinctively backed away.

Supramati went calmly and haughtily up the wide staircase covered by a catwalk and surrounded by statues of satyrs and demons. Suddenly, a beautiful little black marble devil, probably not properly supported, rolled down the stairs and wounded some Satanists who had gathered in a group and were whispering, following the adepts with malevolent glances. At the entrance to the great hall, Shelom greeted the mage with restraint:

"We have been expecting you, prince. All the guests have arrived," he said respectfully, inviting him in and leading him directly to a landing of a few steps at the back of the hall.

There were three golden armchairs; on the backs of two of them were goat's heads, with ruby eyes that shone as if they were alive, and on the middle armchair was an inverted pentagram. Beside one of the armchairs was Iskhet, and her great black eyes scanned the slender white figure of the approaching mage.

The strange garment of the young woman suited her beautifully. Instead of the knitted garments so fashionable at the time, Iskhet wore a sort of skirt of black pearls and rubies, reaching down to her feet and ending in a wide fringe of the same stones. Her waist, slender and slender, was girded by a wide belt of gold and adorned with diamonds; from the belt came a half-corset of purple gauze, cut in the shape of a crescent moon, which exposed the six slightly covered with diamond pendants. At the neck shone a multi-strand necklace which ran at an angle down the centre of the neck and joined the corset. Iskhet's immense hair was loose and wrapped around her like a cloak of blue-black silk. A thin gold ring gathered the unruly locks, and on her forehead stood out a small bat with wings outspread, a miracle of world art; the little bat's body and wings were made of black diamonds, grey pearls and filigree, and the eyes were made of rubies. The demure beauty of the young woman had certainly never been more dazzling: she was the very embodiment of voluptuousness in its most seductive form. When Supramati greeted her respectfully, his eyes, black as night, glowed with a blazing fire, and she, with a charming smile, nodded her head.

Supramati sat down and began to examine the room, whose furnishings, lighting and magnificent, heavy, gold-embroidered curtains formed a strange and magical atmosphere. By contrast, the crowd that had gathered there, from the bestial expression of the faces, the general indecency of the decadent race, and the unprecedented immorality of the dress, seemed repellent to the mage. Near him sat Nivara and Madim.

At Shelom's signal the first number of the show began. A strange and wild singing was heard, and from two side entrances appeared groups of dancers. All were naked, adorned only with necklaces, belts and tiaras of precious stones; the women wore wide gauze scarves and the men silk fans. The exuberance of the dance they performed was unimaginable. A shiver of disgust ran through Supramati's body, but his neighbour caused him an even greater sense of pain. They say that opposites attract, and in this case, with the confirmation of this paradox, maximum virtue attracted maximum voluptuousness.

Without paying attention to the spectacle, Iskhet devoured with her eyes the calm, handsome face of the mage, whose light, soft scent intoxicated her. She felt she had never met a more attractive being, and Shelom seemed repellent and dirty in comparison. She no longer needed any order to use her diabolical art to seduce this man who pleased her like no other; his bearing aroused all her impure desire.

Supramati sensed the inordinate influence of the storm of animal feelings that raged beside him, but the limpid serenity of his face didn't reveal his thoughts. It was even entertaining to him to observe the expression of awe on Iskhet's face, who tried to conceal from Shelom the comparison he was making between the two, fearing, probably, some merciless punishment in consequence, The dour look of the terrible host passed him by, trying to guess the guest's impression of the spectacle and the burning glances of his neighbour. The dances exalted the spirits of the guests; passionate whispers, laughter and hysterical shouts sounded from different parts of the hall, faces flushed and eyes sparkled.

When the dancers had left, a large carpet was spread out in front of the landing and a middle-aged man entered, dressed in black, wearing a long scarf on his head in the form of a turban. Standing in the centre of the carpet, two men placed before him an instrument similar to a harp of different design. It began to play, accompanying a strange song, with vibrant, strident modulations, like hisses cutting through the air. Gradually, a reddish mist enveloped the whole place. Suddenly, there was a hissing sound, accompanied by a snapping noise, and snakes of different sizes appeared on all sides, crawling among the rows of startled guests. But the vipers paid no attention to the confusion, moving directly towards the carpet, where they surrounded the musician and, rising on their tails, began a characteristic and terrible dance; their eyes glowed with phosphorescent light and from their open mouths dripped a greenish foam. The excitement of the reptiles was excessive, but the vapour floating in the air quickly condensed and poured on the carpet another numerous number of snakes. Those that appeared first, on seeing the new arrivals, became enraged and attacked them. Their slender bodies coiled, their pointed tongues appeared and disappeared. At that moment, something dreadful happened. The heads of the snakes that emerged from the air transformed into human heads and began hissing the harrowing melody that merged with the shrill hissing of the land snakes. Then some men dragged a terrified young boy and girl there, throwing them into the pile of vipers. The reptiles quickly uncoiled and attacked the offered prey.

At that moment, Supramati raised his hand. From his magic ring, as he turned the stone upwards, sparks flew; and short incantations, uttered in a sonorous voice, drowned out the noise of the hall. The vipers fell to the floor as if struck by lightning, and remained immobilised for a few moments; then the two species of reptiles attacked the stupefied sorcerer, knocked him down, and began to suck his blood; unlike the land snakes, which crawled out of the carpet and headed for Supramati. Ahead came a huge greenish scaled snake, which, as it approached the landing, swung up on its tail and placed a glowing blue stone in the mage's mouth at his feet. The mage waved his hand in a friendly gesture and, in a half-voice, uttered some strange words, apparently understood by the animal, which began to crawl backwards, emitting a high-pitched hissing sound. The other snakes, as if obeying this signal, turned and, scattering to all sides, disappeared. In the meantime, a whirlwind of smoke arose on the carpet. Then a deafening noise of wind was heard in the hall and all was silent. On the floor lay the corpse of the sorcerer and his two victims had disappeared.

All this, which would take too long to describe, happened in a few minutes, and the whole mass of guests fell silent with terror. The host himself was stunned and choked with hatred; only Iskhet looked at Supramati with passionate admiration.

"It's not right, prince, to disturb the order of someone else's house with tricks out of order," Shelom pronounced in a hoarse voice a minute later, his eyes flashing angrily.

"Forgive me, Mr Shelom, I wouldn't interfere with this if all the participants in the show were your subjects; but I consider it my duty to defend the members of my flock always and everywhere," Supramati replied with splendid calmness.

Shelom bit his lips, but, dominating himself, retorted with contempt:

"From this point of view, you're right, and so, Prince, let us continue with the festivity programme and listen to the concert I have prepared in your honour."

While they were talking, the carpet and the corpse had been quickly removed, and the place was occupied by an orchestra of sixty musicians and twenty singers. The musicians carried violins, cellos, and some flutes; all were repulsive, and their faces carried the marks of all the vices and animal passions.

"You're looking before you at an archaic orchestra, for these instruments were long ago discarded by our musical art.

But since you 'immortals' count the centuries as people count the years, I thought I might indulge you with an old-fashioned concert," Shelom revealed, his cold, ironic gaze boring into the mage's blue eyes.

He, in agreement, merely nodded, at which point the singers sang a bacchante song, at the end of which the orchestra began its truly infernal music. It was known that the strings of the instruments were made of human intestines, more precisely of women and children tortured to death with the utmost cruelty. Even Supramati's unshaken, armoured soul trembled as he heard the sounds and met the spiritual vision that opened before him. There, among clouds of reddish mist, swirled the slender bodies of worms and various creatures with lustful eyes and bloody lips, and amidst them, with impotent indignation, writhed the bodies of martyred victims. The infernal music continued, the sounds moaned, screamed and cried. In these terrible but expressive melodies - performed, without doubt, by great artists - the full range of human suffering could be heard, from angry blasphemy to the grim despair of the dead end. Nivara was tinged with a cadaverous pallor, sweating dripped from her forehead, and even Supramati's clear, serene gaze became sombre. Truly, everything that was happening was becoming more and more repulsive and revolting. The animal servants poured the guests bowls full of fresh blood. Shelom and Iskhet also gleefully emptied their cups of the hideous drink, greedily inhaling the tainted miasma that filled the air and allowing themselves to be penetrated by the intoxicating aromas intended to excite erotic feelings. A reddish vapour began to rise in the room.

The human herd, gathered in that palace, went wild then, and what happened next in the midst of those present - was indescribable. The burning eyes of animal desire also turned towards the landing. Supramati provoked lustful desires and the decadent beings, who submitted to every form of lechery, couldn't understand how he could remain unmoved amidst so many temptations of the flesh: a handsome man and a young one at that, the embodiment of virile strength and exuberant health. It was also surprising that Iskhet and Shelom, who usually participated in all the orgy's acts, stayed only as spectators. But there was no stopping this bloodthirsty, wanton mob, and soon a group of women - increasingly thirsty for both evil and good - made their way to the landing and, after a moment's hesitation, began to climb the steps with feline dexterity. Little was human in their inflamed faces, their burning eyes, and their gasping breaths. One of the bacchantes fell like an arrow at Shelom's feet, starting to kiss his knees, and another prepared to embrace him.

Breathing hard in the dense, contagious atmosphere and shuddering with disgust, Supramati sank into the armchair, staring at the floor. The other perverts were ready to pounce on him, but Iskhet leapt to his feet, a stiletto in his hand, and unloaded a blow into the chest of one of the women, sending the others stampeding away. Without paying attention to her blood-soaked victim, Iskhet rushed towards Supramati, beside herself with passion and jealousy, snuggled against him like a snake and tried to press her lips to his. The mage didn't move, but in the same instant Iskhet was repulsed, as if she had received an electric shock, and collapsed on the steps. Shelom rose to his feet and, uttering repulsive curses, violently pushed the two women away like snakes. Then, bending over Iskhet, he held a flask to her nose, which he took from his belt. With her marble face, her cameo features and her marvellous forms, she looked like a fantastic statue.

A few minutes later, she started to move and moaned softly. Shelom made a sign and some women took her away.

There was a momentary silence. Gloomy, like a storm cloud, Shelom stood thoughtfully, grasping with his trembling hand the handle of the dagger he wore on his belt. In the hall, the orgy continued to be excited by the violins of the infernal orchestra.

Supramati looked at Nivara and saw that he could hardly free himself from the women and men surrounding him, trying to force him to drink a bowl of blood and participate in the orgy. Supramati concentrated and a ray of light shot out of his eyes like a rocket and flew to the rescue of the faithful disciple, knocking down the semi-animals besieging Nivara. Shelom shuddered with hatred, and if Supramati had not been "immortal and a mage", the scorching glare he gave him would have struck him dead. A moment later, Shelom stood up and assessed, hoarsely.

"I observe, Prince, that your presence disturbs the entertainment of my guests, so I propose that you accompany me to the adjoining room, where we can converse freely."

Supramati stood up without replying. They passed through the exasperated crowd and entered a small room prepared, it seemed, for an intimate dinner, for the table was set for only ten persons, but with the refinement of royalty: the little buffets were filled with fruit, sweets and wine. Through the wide carved arches were a series of rooms with tables set for the banquet with which the feast was to close, after the sacrifice to Satan. Shelom led Supramati to the couch, sat down opposite it and held out a plate of roast meat.

"I thank you," Supramati refused, "but don't try to entertain me, Shelom. A mage's lips can no more touch your unclean food than your eyes can admire the hideous orgy you have prepared for me. I could stop this vile spectacle and destroy the despicable beings you call guests, but I won't use my weapons against you in your own house. Besides, the time hasn't yet come for our battle. By the way, don't destroy Iskhet, your horrible companion; her attempts to possess me are futile and you must know that voluptuous and racy feminine attractions no longer have power over me. I can only love spiritual beauty."

Shelom measured him with a dark gaze.

"You're a man of flesh and blood, and human things aren't alien to you; you must feel all human weaknesses; how can beauty and love be powerless before you, when your ever-young organism is full of life and strength?"

At that moment Madim arrived, carrying on a small tray a cup of wine which was offered to Supramati. He took the glass, but when he placed it on the table, the liquid began to smoke, caught fire and burst into coloured flames.

"I was served poison; therefore, my dear host, let me answer you with the same words you have just uttered: It's not nice to offer poison to a guest, and attempted murder wasn't on the agenda of your invitation."

Shelom roared in fury and his face contorted in a spasm. Instantly, there was a slight clatter and Supramati's chair began to fall with dizzying speed, leaving him surprised, for he didn't know whether he was falling into an abyss or a pit. When he stopped falling, Supramati realised that he was in a large circular room, dimly lit by red lamps. As soon as she rose from the couch, he flew back up. He paid no attention and surveyed his surroundings.

In the centre of the room there was only a couch, an armchair and a table on which was placed a large silver basin of blood; on the walls, in twelve niches, were statues of demons in indecent poses, while on the supports burned herbs that exhaled a caustic and heavy odour that provoked an erotic frenzy. Everywhere were the repulsive faces of materialised worms, smooth, swollen with consumed blood, overpowered by animal passion and ready to attack the magician, only to be restrained by the spirits of the elements. These, however, were greatly weakened by the contagious emanations from the house, and yet they fought bravely. Supramati, moreover, also defended himself. With his powerful will, capable of breaking off granite rocks, he quickly emptied the niches by throwing the statues to the ground, which broke into small pieces. Then, from his raised hand, flames of fire burst forth, wiping the blood from the basin and extinguishing the pillars with herbs. Finally, a shower of sparks fell on the worms, making them scream and moan, and quickly melted them. The consumed blood poured out of their guts in a foul-smelling red vapour.

Finally, they disappeared, as if they had entered the wall, and for a few minutes the underground was completely silent. But Supramati knew it was only a brief respite.

A door hidden in the wall opened silently and Iskhet, the mage's latest temptress, appeared. She was naked, and only her luxuriant mane of black hair covered her like a cloak. She stood two paces away from Supramati, devouring him with her eyes, and her magnificently shaped body was trembling with passion.

"Wretch, what do you want from me? Beware when you come near me, because my pure inner flame may burn your body poisoned with vices," pronounced Supramati sternly.

"What do I want? I want you. You're wonderful, like an enchanting illusion. I love and desire you as much as any man in my life, and you must belong to me! No mortal has ever resisted my charms and you won't be the first."

She quickly opened a flask in her hand and poured the contents around her. The air seemed to catch fire and the walls of the underground shook as if in a dynamite explosion. The spirits of the elements, affected by the shock, paled and faded from the action of the poisonous miasma, leaving Supramati unarmed.

Iskhet, watching him with eyes burning with passion, taking advantage of this moment, threw himself upon him, embraced him and, in a fit of madness, drove his sharp teeth into his hand. At that instant, the worms appeared again and tackled Iskhet, enveloping Supramati and trying to pull him down. However, they underestimated the strength of the mage, who, with lightning speed, concentrated his mighty will and quickly disposed of all the vipers, hurling them from all sides. Raising his hands, Supramati uttered an incantation, and Iskhet, clinging to him, rose into the air and fell to the tiles.

At this moment Supramati looked marvellous and tremendous. Pure and limpid, his gaze luminous, he stood still as a ray of light, for from every pore of his body an inner fire came forth, and in this pure flame the spirits of the elements appeared again and gained renewed strength, surrounding him anew. A zigzag of fire shot through the underground and collapsed upon Iskhet, who was still lying on the ground.

"Useless creature," roared the voice of Supramati. "As punishment for your audacity, you'll remain blind and mute until the day you wish to see for yourself the light of truth and repentance. And no lord of hell will be able to restore your sight and speech."

An instant later, the rumble of thunder shook the building. A gust of gusty wind swept through the underground, carried by the spirit of the elements, Supramati rose to the surface, and within minutes was in his laboratory. Soon after, Nivara arrived, pale, bruised all over, his clothes torn, but looking triumphant.

"Oh, master!" he exclaimed. "Now I can say that I have escaped from hell. Only one thing worries me: I seem to have finished off a score of Satanists; finally, I miscalculated and the electric shocks were too strong."

"You acted in your right to self-defence. Anyone who touches an electrical device must suffer the consequences. But don't worry, Shelom will bring them back to life. But I did something crueler. To punish Iskhet, I took away her sight and speech, and even Shelom won't be able to heal her, because she dared to touch a mage. But that's enough. We need to take a quick bath to clean ourselves and wash our clothes, because we smell like carrion."

An hour later, the two adepts sat down to a frugal dinner.

"Master, what to do with the two victims saved by you? Although they're without my palace, they aren't Christians."

"No, they're indifferent to any creed. However, today's events have undoubtedly cured them of Satanism, so we will try to convert them. In the coming great battle, it will be precisely these "indifferent ones" who will be the easiest to convert. As you know, Shelom is preparing an occult duel with me; similar struggles will take place everywhere, for the satanists will begin to challenge our brethren and this is very good. The pride of the sons of satan compels them to this daring combat, in which they will surely be defeated. We count on this defeat to bring about countless conversions."

"It's going to be a curious spectacle!" - said Nivara.

"Too curious and too instructive. All the evil accumulated over the centuries will enter the arena to test its power. And woe to those who pervert the multitude and push them towards evil. They will all be assembled here and their first punishment will be the total annihilation of their pride before the power of the Creator and the revelation of all the weakness of their supposed power. Blind men! They imagine that all the interest of the universe is concentrated in this one particle wandering among billions of similar particles and planetary giants of this infinity, where all hail the glory and wisdom of the Creator." If they could only realise all their insignificance and how extremely ridiculous their storms are before a drop of water, then they would be ashamed and ashamed of themselves. It is always one of the "great" and infamous sacrilegious and apostate apostates from God, who in an impotent rage declare war upon Him and undo His laws. And this apostate, full of pride, pretending to be wiser than God and envying the glory of Christ, was he ever in a position to oppose the cosmic laws? Could he stop a storm or avert death? And when this rebel, overcome by the terrible and unknown power, is laid on his deathbed, his lips that uttered so many sacrilegious words are silenced by divine command, and his body is but a piece of flesh destined to decay, then all will realise how weak, insignificant and pitiful was all that they considered great."

CHAPTER XIV

As soon as Shelom and Supramati left the hall, the banquet quickly took a new turn.

Satanic priests entered, bringing in a group of men. Women and children were tied up. Under the hysterical screams of the enraged crowd, the prisoners were dragged to the statue of Satan at the back of the room and bled, their blood collected in huge metal buckets. When Shelom returned to the hall, seated on the throne, the satanic priests began to recite magical incantations gathering and materialising maggots of both sexes for the orgy. Shelom, however, wanted nothing to do with it, for he had long since grown weary of anything that could be invented by the most unbridled depravity. With a pitiless and indifferent gaze, he watched the victims in their last gasps, spewing curses and offences; the infernal dance that unfolded before him did not appeal to him either. He only took pleasure in emptying the cups of blood that were served, without being able to quench the thirst that tormented him.

Suddenly, something unexpected happened. A terrible clap of thunder shook the palace, the support of the statue cracked and the idol fell to the ground with a crash, crushing those at its feet. At the same instant, a blinding light flashed like lightning and a blast of pure wind - the current of the four elements - swept through the hall, knocking Shelom and the satanic summoners to the ground. Instantly, all the torches went out and from all around came roars, groans and cries of despair: the worms were attacking the crowd as their summoners temporarily lost power over the monsters they conjured from the darkness.

Shelom was the first to come out of his stupefaction. He rose quickly, foaming with hatred, recited most powerful magical incantations and, with his undeniable power, the demons came to his call and rekindled the fire. He then dispersed the worms with electric shocks, and only then did he survey the battlefield that the room had become. Many people were torn to pieces and their bloodied remains littered the ground; many of the Luciferian priests were also slain and lay on the ground with deep neck wounds. Shouting, roaring and pushing, the frightened mob ran for the exit, but Shelom's threatening call stopped them. He choked at the thought that the guests put to flight by the mage's power, convinced of their defeat, were trying to save themselves by fleeing the palace. He had barely had time to recover and make a speech befitting the situation, when women burst into the room with Madim, horror stamped on their faces. Pale and upset, Madim informed his master that Iskhet had been found slumped underground, but more terrifyingly, she was shrouded in a blue mist that would not allow anyone to approach her.

"It's the damned magician's fluid," whispered Madim.

Shelom was stunned for a moment, but struggling to regain control of himself, he shouted hoarsely:

"Blood! I need blood for a bath!"

They ran to the tanks, but they were empty and the blood collected in the jars wasn't enough. Shelom was startled with fury, but unexpectedly, seeing a strong young man near him, he grabbed the dagger and plunged it into his throat. With the blood that flowed in abundance they filled some large vessels, but nothing more could contain the fleeing crowd. It was known that in moments of fury, no one, not even the most intimate, was safe from Shelom's dagger, and though murder had become a commonplace that attracted no one's attention, everyone wanted to save their own skin. Shelom paid no attention to the rapid disappearance of his guests.

Accompanied by Madim and the bloodbearers, he descended into the basement, where Iskhet still lay motionless. When she was sprinkled with warm blood, the bluish mist disappeared completely and she could be touched. So they took her to her quarters. Shelom had a bath prepared, poured some strong-smelling preparations into the tub, and there lay Iskhet, still paralysed. The women left and Shelom was left alone with the secretary. Iskhet's body was full of burns and, strangely, two bands of white light covered her eyes and mouth like bandages.

"I warned and begged you not to challenge the mage. He possesses terrible power. See Iskhet's wounds!"

"I'll cure her immediately," Shelom replied, with a hint of pride. Madim shook his head.

"Youre forgetting that these burns aren't ordinary. They were caused by the heavenly fire that the Himalayan hermit possesses."

Madim was right. Neither incantations nor magical remedies helped, and instead only increased the wounds. Finally, Iskhet's moans and spasms indicated that she was regaining consciousness. Straightening with an effort, he gestured that he wanted to write. Madim immediately brought pencil and paper, and Iskhet, with trembling hand, scribbled: "He has made me blind and mute; I can neither see nor utter a word. Save me, Shelom; if you are as powerful as he, restore my sight and speech.

She was seized by new convulsions and fainted again.

✳ ✳ ✳

From that day on, a fierce conflict between the forces of hell and the will of the magician began. Shelom employed all his efforts and knowledge in vain, invoking the most powerful demons and calling upon the most distinguished sages of Satanism; all his efforts were dissolved against the unbreakable will of Supramati.

Discouraged, indifferent to everything and suffering tortuous pains, Iskhet lay there, more and more alone every day. Shelom's visits to his queen became increasingly rare; in her presence, a strange, dark, antagonistic irritation and a torturous awareness of his own impotence overcame him. And while Iskhet could no longer take part in the festivities, her beauty faded, her body lost suppleness, and her chamber, in the sepulchral silence of the empty hall, lit only by a red lamp before the statue of Satan, Iskhet's soul passed through all the phases of impotent rage, indignation and despair: she began to doubt Shelom's absolute power. The "other" closed his indecent eyes and shut his blasphemous lips, and Satan himself couldn't open them. Once he thought he saw in the distance a luminescent cloud billowing around the head of Supramati, gazing at her with sternness and sadness. He punished her cruelly, and still his memory haunted her, and little by little, somewhere deep within her, something began to awaken, fluttering like a little bird against the bars of its cage. Perhaps it was the inheritance of Heaven, that indestructible and divine reality with which the soul is created, and which, tired of darkness, longs for freedom and light, longs for something that is terrible and unknown to the criminal creature who has spent his whole life immersed in moral filth.

Once, at night, when Iskhet was meditating on her own life spent in crime and intoxicated by libertinism, she felt revulsion for the first time for this past, and immediately the darkness that enveloped her was illuminated with a soft, bluish light, and in this blinding background the beautiful face of the mage was clearly outlined; his luminous gaze seemed to fall upon her like a warm, fragrant dew, relieving the tortuous pain. Admiring this image, the sick woman was distracted, and when the vision disappeared, two burning tears ran down Iskhet's thin face. At that instant it seemed to her that before her stood the demon, whose statue adorned her chambers, and whose eyes watched her doomed soul. Now those red eyes looked at her angrily and maliciously, but strangely enough! - she felt no fear. The vision vanished after an infernal gravitation of the defeated demon.

As Iskhet went deeper and deeper into her inner world, even Shelom's rare visits became less bearable. Once, when she was served fresh blood but she refused it, saying that it tasted bad and smelled rotten; instead she asked for milk and fruit. The women who served her, astonished and angry, complained to Shelom about his antics, saying that the blood served was fresh, from a freshly slaughtered child. And that it was very unpleasant for them to enter the patients' rooms, because, after what had happened, there was often an unbearable smell of flowers or perfume which made them nauseous. Shelom listened sullenly to this story and clenched his fists; in reply he curtly ordered that, if she didn't want blood, she might be given fruit and water. But from that day on he practically ceased to visit the patient, and her former friends deserted her entirely. Not infrequently, for days at a time, she wasn't fed and often went thirsty, but Iskhet made no demands, and the absence of her satanic court brought her indescribable well-being. Iskhet absorbed the silence and meditation with increasing warmth; exploring her inner self, she questioned herself and could not find the answers she so desperately wanted. Sometimes she seemed to hear a piece of sweet and harmonious music that couldn't be heard, or felt a soft, reviving scent. At such times Iskhet felt sad and troubled, and her whole being longed for something she didn't understand, but which she longed for more and more, and which seemed to her like a haven, a safe harbour, quiet and peaceful. One night, when these thoughts again assaulted her, she had the impression of seeing a blinding light shining, and a short distance away, Supramati appeared as if he were real. In his raised hand shone that symbol against which her Luciferian brethren fought so fiercely: the shining cross. At the sight of it, Iskhet felt a terrible pain; it seemed to her that her body was burning and that everything in her was shattering into pieces. Suddenly, she got off the bed, fell to her knees, and a flood of tears streamed down her face.

"Oh! " she heard herself yearning from the depths of her torn soul. "Who can tell me where the truth is: in the darkness or in the light? "

The mage's luminous gaze seemed to denote sadness and compassion.

"Return to the light in which you were conceived, divine spark and breath of the Creator. Mercy and forgiveness await you at the Heavenly Father's side. Knock at the ever-open door of repentance and the pure servants of the Creator will draw near to you, and bring you out of your filth, cleanse you from dishonour and exchange your rags for white garments. "

Iskhet listened with delight to that harmonious and indescribably serene voice and its sound seemed to envelop her aching body with a life-giving breath. Meanwhile, a veritable storm was raging all around her. Loathsome beings appeared from all sides, monsters, half human, half animal, their mouths covered with fetid foam.

There were roars and hisses in the air, and the whole mob surrounded Iskhet, threatening her and ready to attack, but held back by an invisible force. She seemed to see and hear nothing; her whole soul huddled in the cross the mage held out to her.

Suddenly, the door opened noisily and Shelom came bursting into the room like a hurricane. He was truly terrible, his face distorted and distorted by ferocity, foaming at the mouth, his eyes bloodshot and roaring like an animal.

"Ah, the despicable renegade! Thou hast resolved to worship here the Himalayan hermit, to worship him whom thou must curse and trample under foot. Wretched, worthless... And don't even think of running away from me. For your treachery and blasphemy against Lucifer, you shall pay with your life!"

Quickly he drew his dagger, knocked her down and wounded her in the chest. Then, lifting Iskhet with the lightness of a feather, he carried her to the window, opened it and threw Iskhet out, laughing fiendishly and screaming:

"This is for you! Frost on the street with broken bones and be the first martyr of the wretched Hindu."

But, amazingly, a current of wind caught Iskhet in the air, lifted her up and threw her to the ground some distance from the palace. Blood gushed from the wound, but Iskhet was still alive; she even had the strength to get up and grope around. Taking a few staggering steps, she groped for a wall and leaned against it.

"Damn you son of Satan, I'll forsake you and begin to adore the one you hate and insult," she said inwardly.

Feeling weak again, he knelt down and from her aching soul poured forth a fervent prayer to the Eternal.

"Almighty God, whose name Ive cursed and whose laws I have profaned, forgive me my sins. And You Jesus, heavenly Son of God, have mercy on me and save me by the power of Your cross!"

Tears ran down her face in torrents, and suddenly someone grabbed her hand, helped her up and held her gently. Iskhet thought she was dying. The wound burned and the strength left her; she weakened but didn't lose consciousness. A strong arm held her and practically carried her, carrying her quickly somewhere. She went up a few steps and finally they entered a room filled with a life-giving aroma. Her guide stopped and a melodic voice was heard that she recognised immediately, though she had only heard it once before.

"Do you want to renounce all your illusions, cut ties with hell, purify your soul with prayers of regret and adore the cross, symbol of eternity and salvation?"

Iskhet made an effort to reply, but at that moment she felt as if her tongue was loosening and she exclaimed happily.

"Yes, I want to! I want to!"

She extended her hands and, feeling a support, leaned her head back. Suddenly a stream of fire shot through her and, opening her eyes wide, she realised that she had regained her sight. She was standing at the foot of a large crucifix, and beside her was Supramati looking happily at her.

"I greet you, dear daughtet," he said, placing his hand on her bowed head, "because you have recovered your soul. You have worshipped God, your Creator, and His Divine Son; from this moment the Holy Spirit will bless your path. Once again I greet you, prodigal daughter, with the return to the paternal home. And we're extremely happy."

Outside, moaning, howling and roaring with impotent fury, the infernal pack suffered a severe setback; the mage's power wrenched his queen, Satan's chief priestess, from the middle of his flock, proving to the self-styled "king of hell" that he's not invincible.

From the small group at the back of the room came Nivara and a young woman of incomparable beauty, carrying a white robe on a golden tray; it was Edith, Dakhir's wife.

She took Iskhet amicably by the hand and, with Nivara's help, led her to an adjoining room: a small chapel in the centre of which was a large tank, built at ground level. Together with another woman from the community, Edith led Iskhet into an adjoining room, where they washed off the blood that covered her but had already stagnated, and dressed her in a white camisole. Iskhet was then taken back to the chapel, where Edith and Nivara helped her into the pool.

"We're your godparents," said Edith. - And now, kneel in the water so that the sacred incantations may be recited and your ties to hell severed.

Then Supramati came forward and with a golden cup poured water three times over Iskhet's head. Then he stretched out his hands and recited mystical words that introduced her to the Christian community.

Then he added:

"I take away your old name, which served as a symbol of dishonour, I baptise you with the pure and holy name of Maria. Use it with dignity."

But the enormous force that had descended on Iskhet was too much for the woman's suffering body, recently plucked from the very crater of hell, and she fell unconscious. Nivara carried her to her room, where Edith and another sister of the community cared for her and anointed her body with an ointment that almost immediately reduced the burn marks and closed the wound on her chest. They combed her long hair into plaits and, when Iskhet came to her senses, dressed her in a white robe brought by Edith and took her to the chapel where Supramati was praying fervently. Iskhet knelt before the altar, and the mage, ascending the steps, took the golden cup adorned with a cross and brought it to the lips of the new convert.

"Take and purify yourselves with the divine blood of the Son of God. You have experienced his power and mercy. He has saved your soul with a miracle and from this moment he receives you into the group of his faithful."

Then he took a small crucifix that hung on a chain from the altar and put it around his neck.

"This is your protection against demons who want to attack you."

He made her stand up and kissed her on the forehead. Edith and Nivara repeated his gesture and together they passed into the next room, where a group of men and women were gathered to welcome her as a new sister.

Iskhet, or Maria, as she was to be called from now on, did everything obediently but the terrible shock through which she had passed still made her tremble; for a moment her thoughts interrupted, and her sad gaze was fixed on Supramati with an expression of fear and love. He noticed this, took her by the hand and put her in Edith's hand.

"Accept your spiritual sister, I make you responsible for her so watch over her and protect her from enemies who might attack her."

"Be assured, brother, that I'll support her. I'll watch over her and pray with her like a mother with her newborn child. But now she needs rest; Sister Maria is tired physically and spiritually."

In the satanic village, Iskhet's disappearance caused astonishment: everyone was convinced that Shelom had killed her, but they didn't know how or why. Upon hearing what had happened, Shelom and his followers felt an indescribable fury. Not only had they suffered a terrible defeat, but they had lost one of their most important supporters: the Sabbat Queen, who was difficult to replace. At first, Shelom tried to bring back the fugitive while he burned with a thirst for vengeance and Sá imagined new tortures as punishment for her. And though he called upon his science, summoned legions of demons and consumed himself with incantations and sorcery, Iskhet was still missing. She wouldn't leave the walls of Supramati's palace, forbidden to Shelom's men. Finally, one fine day, the traitor disappeared from Czargrado, and by the time Shelom managed to follow her trail, she was safe at Dakhir's house, where she was taken by Edith.

Still seething with impotent fury, Shelom decided to postpone temporarily the pursuit of his victim in order to save all his strength for the terrible duel to which he was daring Supramati. He now knew that the struggle with the Himalayan hermit would be terrible and dangerous and that the outcome of the fight was doubtful even for him, and even among his staunchest defenders there was apparent fear and doubt as to victory. Some voices even urged Shelom to desist and not to risk this confrontation, not to tempt the terrible forces of Heaven, but all in vain. In his satanic vanity, Shelom was deaf and blind as the thirst for revenge and the hope of humiliating the enemy blunted all other reasoning. He wanted to prove to Supramati that evil was his inheritance and that on this ground he was and would remain the master, breaking any reaction. Moreover, he reckoned that the atmosphere was permeated with evil miasmas, blood and crime; moreover, in view of the large number of Luciferians, for every believer there were at least a thousand unbelievers. All these motives, taken together, should consume and destroy the light, which would weaken or perhaps even paralyse the magician, even if he had the help of the Himalayan brethren, whose numbers would be greatly reduced. Shelom's supporters had never seen him so grim, cruel and furious, and his hatred for the mighty adversary and the God he worshipped took on such an incredible dimension that he prepared for combat with fury and energy. He called upon the most powerful black magicians from all over the world, with whom he spent days and nights summoning demons and legions of shadow spirits, and rehearsing the "miracles" he would use in the duel. And as he had so far achieved everything without difficulty, the pride and certainty of victory took hold of him more and more, filling his heart with a triumph filled with hatred. His defeat could only happen by chance. However, many blasphemies he uttered, however many crimes he committed and however many obscenities he triumphantly committed, the earth did not swallow him up, the wind did not sweep him away, the water did not drown him, and the fire of heaven did not devour him. Positively, the Divinity remained mute. He,

Shelom Iezodot, was and would remain the invulnerable lord of this doomed land and the peoples would fall at his feet, worshipping him as a beneficent god, squandering goods.

Finally, it was ordered to all the leaders of the regions to announce in every corner, by advertisements, telephones and all available means, the date when Shelom Iezodot, son of Satan and lord of the world, would measure his forces in a magical duel with the Hindu prince Supramati, a magician of the Himalayas. Citizens of all countries were invited to this strange tournament, so that they could see for themselves that the power of hell is equal and even superior to the power of Heaven. Scientists and agnostics were specially invited to this spectacle, the programme of which was extremely attractive and offered the two contestants every opportunity to demonstrate their powers. Shelom proposed to transform stones and sand into gold, which would then be distributed among those present and, at his command, several trees should grow to blossom and be covered with fruit; he would raise the dead and, finally, force the magician to worship Lucifer and offer him sacrifices.

A large field on the outskirts of the city was chosen as the stage for this original spectacle, where more than two hundred thousand people could easily be accommodated. Huge stands were built, boxes for authorities and celebrities, scientists, regional leaders and, above all, two large boxes for the opponents and their friends. Next to them, gigantic buffets were built to serve meat, fruit, sweets and drinks. The interest of the public was enormous, and as the seats were distributed free of charge, many tickets and seats were lacking, more seats were added whenever possible, and the number of interested people grew more and more. Obviously, everyone wanted to be present at such a peculiar spectacle, a special "end of the world" type of sport, when Heaven and Hell would be measured in the arena. Supramati simply accepted the challenge, without announcing any kind of schedule.

He prepared silently and prayerfully for this difficult moment, not because of his own power, but because of the infected environment in which he had to operate. Nivara was very excited, not because he doubted the master's victory, but because he was irritated and indignant at the current situation, which made possible such a tournament and defiance of God. One evening, a few days before the great event, the mage was dining with his disciples and sipping wine, and he looked smilingly into Nivara's dark face, so absorbed in his thoughts that he didn't notice what was going on around him.

"You look like a storm cloud. What troubles you, my friend," asked the mage kindly.

"Ah, Master, I wonder if the impious mob is right when it says that there's nothing, since Heaven is silent, however unworthy the offences directed against it may be. Why doesn't the mighty heavenly army come out in defence of its altars and of truth? Why did they allow the destruction of the earth, instead of interceding and stopping at its beginning the sarabande of the deniers of God, who preach against every law of morality, against every feeling of ideals and announce, for example, that true goodness is not to react to evil, or that property is theft, and a hundred other identical absurd, harmful and even criminal paradoxes? And so it is with us: we shall also present ourselves in the arena to demonstrate our power, while the world is dying."

Supramati straightened up and observed sternly:

"My friend, our Lord and Creator has given us the key that opens the door to Heaven: it's nobody's fault that men don't want to take it or don't understand the Divine law. Nothing comes without a struggle; we see it in every being, even in the tiniest micro-organisms; everywhere two principles clash. Jesus said it clearly: the kingdom of heaven is taken by force and we have to admire the efforts made. He also said: "Ask and it will be given to you; knock and it will be opened to you". And he explained that faith moves mountains. The blame for the abandonment of the church and the weakening of faith falls on those who, having been initiated into the services of God, should stoically defend the altar, preventing its profanation. They, who celebrated the great sacraments and were intermediaries between men and heaven, were compelled, by fervent prayers, to invoke heavenly power, to call for higher help, to draw believers to themselves, and, in joyful united prayer, to ask the aid of unseen forces to defend the sanctuaries. There are many proofs that such prayers are heard. I am no speaking of Moses, who called down heavenly fire on the wicked and the fire obeyed his will; he was an initiate of the Egyptian temples, whose colossal science hasn't yet been unravelled. But even mere mortals achieved identical results during epidemics and floods. Once, an avalanche of lava retreated before a procession carrying the image of the Blessed Virgin; the fear of death provoked in the crowd that powerful breath of faith which gave life to the collective prayer and activated the cosmic forces. Thousands of miraculous healings, in all ages, have resulted from this very motive, as have the pleas of the innocent condemned, demanding that their enemies and persecutors be brought to divine judgement. The impassioned appeal to the Divine is heard and Heaven responds; it is like the matchstick which, when rubbed in the matchbox, causes fire.

When, at the beginning of the 20th century, revolution and anarchism began to spread like a contagious insanity, bringing down the social fabric, morals, suicides, sacrileges and other mass psychopathological phenomena, it was clear to anyone who wanted to see that there was something unnatural, and that these people were seized by the evil forces swarming in space. The known and proved remedies were available: joint prayers, processions, preaching, and here I don't mean idle chatter or scholastic altercations, but that fervent and convinced word which electrifies the crowd, invokes the sacred fire and creates martyrs and heroes.

You know Nivara that the lower atmospheric layer surrounding the Earth is populated by those who have returned to the invisible dimension as spirits, whose crimes and evils prevent them from ascending to the higher level because of their leaden astral body, full of carnal excretions. It's not by chance that in the prayer to the Lord, left by Christ, it is said: Deliver us from evil. All these evil spirits are trying to invade the world and the greater their number entering the planet, the more the poisonous contagion will be amplified. These savage hordes fill the air and destroy everything in their path to satisfy their animal instincts and in search of food: they feed on blood and on the dense, heavy, foul-smelling vapours of debauchery, alcoholism and all animal pleasures. Like poisonous vibrions, the vapours of these monsters of the invisible world fill the air and men breathe them in, subjecting themselves to a fluidic epidemic.

Faith, prayer, mercy and good works are the heavenly guard that protects the earthly world from the invasion of the enemies of the unseen world.

The law is unique. In the same way that material disinfection is effected by light, sunlight and the right aromas, contagion is prevented by cleanliness and good nourishment. And so it's that prayer and faith, sources of light and warmth, purify the spiritual atmosphere, and wholesome spiritual food guards the purity of the soul from moral contagion. That's why the science of the soul has always been despised and persecuted; it has been muddied and mocked. However, this renegade science has never harmed anyone; on the contrary, it has taught mankind much, illuminating the darkness that surrounded them and arming the living against dangerous and imperceptible enemies, revealing the existence of these creatures, who would prefer that no one ever knew of their existence so that they could take advantage, unhindered, of blind and ignorant mankind. This great and pure science that studies the invisible world is a terrible weapon against evil spirits and has already saved countless souls from their treacherous clutches.

In conclusion, I repeat that the responsibility for the events lies with the indifference of the Church and society, especially the believers. Unity is strength, but this strength hasn't been activated and the invasion of the spirits of darkness hasn't been repelled. Men don't know and don't want to understand the colossal lever of power which is for the astral world the reflection of the pure fluid of a fervent prayer or a surge of will. And the fire that this fluid provokes, burning with the purifying fire horrible miasmas, innumerable larvae, infamous invisible beings, poisonous bacilli and much astral rubbish. The air becomes healthier and people recover their senses. If hospices, in addition to showers, used incantations, introduced sacred, serious and elevated music, introduced uninterrupted prayers, and applied holy or magnetised water, the results would be astounding. Even now, poor humanity could be rallied to give a single impulse to Heaven and it would respond; we could save the planet for a few hundred thousand years. But no! Men won't do it, and the fate of the unhappy Earth will be fulfilled," Supramati concluded, sighing.

A few hours later, Dakhir, Narayana and Niebo arrived to witness their friend's fight with Shelom. It was decided that the three days remaining before that terrible duel would be spent in the laboratory, praying and gathering strength for the fight that would be the prelude to the future tragic events of the end of the world.

CHAPTER XV

The expectation in the city grew and the number of curious was so great that, when there were no more places left on the ground, it was decided to use the airspace, with ships gliding over the arena, providing a good view for the passengers. This spectacle, exceptional for its kind and still unprecedented, promised to give enormous satisfaction and bets were already being placed, with the majority obviously betting on Shelom's victory. It was an unheard-of impudence that this totally unknown Hindu wanted to fight the most powerful man of the age, the son of Lucifer himself. It was clear that Prince Supramati was a very handsome young man, immensely wealthy and eccentric to the point of ridiculousness. However, it was foolish to suppose that he could compete with such an extraordinary person as Shelom Iezodot.

Finally, the decisive day arrived and nature itself seemed to cooperate. The weather was excellent and it had been a long time since the sun shone so brightly and the sky was so blue.

The large circle that would serve as the arena for the competition had been divided in half by a red line and the opponents' boxes were facing each other.

Shelom Iezodot was the first to arrive, carried on his throne by famous black mages and accompanied by a large court that filled the cabin. As he took his place of prominence, he cast a triumphant and proud glance at the innumerable crowd. For the first time he wore his ceremonial costume of "great invocations" in public. He wore black chain mail and a short tunic of a grey, metallic-veined material, which from a distance looked like steel. On his chest was an image of a goat's head with ruby eyes, and from his belt hung a magic sword with a black hilt, entirely set with diamonds. On his head was a broad golden band with enamelled cabalistic symbols, crowned by two huge twisted horns.

On his shoulders were two sharp-pointed wings, made of a thin, malleable metal - a rare work of art - and tied with ribbons of the same grey material. The costume, grim but original, matched well with Shelom's demonic beauty, and impressed the crowd that greeted him with much noise, while the sorcerers traced circles on the ground, prepared candelabras with herbs and resin, or erected the altar where Lucifer was to appear.

The Hindu prince's cabin was still empty and the crowd grew increasingly impatient. Someone even shouted:

He got scared... He gave up and ran away!

As soon as this phrase ran through the crowd, the mage's cabin was illuminated with a soft but bright bluish light and, by the balustrade, five men in white appeared. From where they appeared. No one saw them enter and no ground or air vehicle had approached the cabin. This caused great astonishment, provoked a profound silence, and the eyes of all present were gazing at these mysterious people:

young, handsome, with serious faces and flaming eyes. Almost immediately, all attention was focused on Supramati, who was slowly descending the steps of the arena. He was also wearing his mage costume for the first time in public: a long white robe, tied by a silk belt, and a muslin turban. The symbol on his chest glowed with a blinding light, and in his hand he carried the magic sword, whose broad, glowing blade seemed to burn. The crowd looked at him with involuntary respect, and never had Supramati seemed so beautiful and charming as at that moment, walking calm and dignified. His large and luminous eyes shone with that powerful will to which everything seemed to submit. The basket, some distance from the cabin, stopped, raised its sword, and traced in the air a phosphorescent sign which, flashing and hissing, cut through the air like a flash of lightning and disappeared into space. A few moments later, the deep silence was broken by the rumble of thunder, as if a storm was approaching, and a huge incandescent object appeared in the sky, flying at great speed. It soon became apparent that a meteorite of unusual proportions was falling.

The crowd went silent with terror and even screams were heard as the bolide fell to the ground a few feet away from the mage, burying itself deep in the earth. Supramati calmly climbed up the still glowing stone and paused, leaning on the handle of the magic sword as if waiting for his opponent.

A sudden blush came over Shelom's face. He stood up and addressed the crowd in a loud voice, announcing in a few words that he'd decided to take part in this competition with the Hindu magician, who had dared to challenge the King of

Darkness, to prove to all the world the power of my father, Lucifer, and that he was therefore convinced of his victory over the Himalayan braggart.

Indifferent to his words, Supramati remained impassive, Shelom descended into the arena and began his invocations. The veins in his forehead swelled, the black wings were injected with a fiery blush and the magic sword flickered in the air, tracing cabalistic signs. Black clouds gathered, descended to the ground and tongues of flame licked the air and earth. When the clouds cleared, everyone saw that the sand and stones, previously prepared, glittered in the sun like gold. The spectators shouted in admiration and the crowd devoured with their eyes the piles of the coveted metal, which the experts confirmed on the spot to be truly pure. Shelom cast a triumphant glance at Supramati and gestured to the prepared mounds of sand.

Supramati raised his sword, its tip lit up with a blinding light, cabalistic signs appeared in the air and a shower of sparks fell on the stones and sand. Immediately set on fire, they reflected all the colours of the rainbow and, when they were gone, they too had turned golden. But at the same instant, from Supramati's raised hand flickered a bolt of lightning that struck Shelom's piles of gold. These were covered with black smoke, crackled and turned into a grey mass that crumbled into ashes.

"Try to destroy my work as I did yours." Supramati calmly proposed.

Shelom and his advisors screamed in hatred, but despite all their attempts they were incapable of destroying the mage's gold, which the experts recognised as being of extreme purity, without any additives. The black mages quickly gave up their attempts, since the fluids emanating from Supramati's gold made them weak and dizzy. A murmur of amazement rippled through the audience, but Shelom's fierce glares and his face deformed by infernal rage frightened the spectators and the crowd fell silent.

"You're a stronger mage than I imagined, but this is still a pittance," Shelom sneered, sizing Supramati up with a hostile glare. And turning his back, he began new incantations.

Soon, a dense smoke appeared from the ground and, swirling swiftly in spirals, curled up. When the smoke cleared, everyone could clearly see a tree trunk slowly emerging from the earth, covered in foliage and green fruit that was rapidly ripening to a golden colour. The mages plucked the fruit and tossed it to the crowd, who gave a satisfied shout of thanks when they saw that they were top quality oranges.

Curious glances now turned to Supramati. Silently, he raised his sword, swung it above his head and then, reverencing the four cardinal points, pronounced formulae and traced signs that dominated the elements. A moment later, the daylight was transformed into a violet gloom through which objects could barely be distinguished. The wind raised clouds of dust and lightning lined the sky. The whole atmosphere seemed to crackle and boil with a dizzying roar and different scents, sometimes caustic, sometimes mild, changing with dizzying speed. In the midst of this chaos, the tall figure of the mage stood out clearly in the gloom, surrounded by beams of sparks. The stunned crowd fell silent in amazement, but when the violet gloom lifted, shouts of admiration were heard from all around. In a large area of the arena, reserved for Supramati, a small forest of fruit trees and flowering bushes was greening up. Among the foliage, several fruits were visible, and a large apple tree was in blossom as if covered by a blanket of snow.

Everything you see here," Supramati addressed the fascinated crowd, "is the work of the purifying flame of the ether. Whereas that," and he pointed to Shelom's orange tree, "is a manifestation of the devil, who creates things out of the debris of chaos. Therefore, may the delusive illusion of hell vanish and be shattered!

He reached out, swinging the cruciform handle of his sword towards his opponent's handiwork. Immediately, the cross released a flame that set the tree ablaze. The leaves curled with a snap and the fruit burned like incandescent balls, taking on a greenish appearance and spewing out yellow, foul-smelling smoke. Then, before the eyes of the spectators, the oranges turned into snakes that silently disappeared into the earth. Almost at the same time, screams were heard from the crowd: those who had eaten the oranges fell into convulsions and Niebo and Nivara immediately ran helplessly away.

With his eyes bloodshot and his arms folded across his chest, Shelom could barely contain his rage. Foaming at the mouth, he bellowed curses, while the mages and mages assisting him trembled with fear and stood pale as shadows. They knew that if Shelom did not resist the mage's power they would all risk a horrible death. The excitement of the fascinated crowd was growing. No doubt Shelom's prestige was shaken. The son of Satan sensed this and turned to his own insolence for help. Straightening up proudly, he shouted in a hoarse voice:

"What happened here proves nothing. This is child's play. I want to see if you can raise a dead man, a real dead man," he roared.

And before his pretensions could be perceived, Shelom hurried to one of the stands, near which the crowd was crowded, seized a pretty young woman, and struck her in the breast with his dagger. The unfortunate girl fell without a whimper, covering the assassin and the arena floor with blood. But Shelom ignored it. He picked up the corpse and threw it on a black carpet with cabalistic symbols, which one of the mages had hastily laid out. Then he tore the clothes from the corpse, exposing the naked body to an astonished crowd, but generally accustomed to the bloody spectacles and arbitrary cruelties of their lord. Shelom's excitement reached the verge of madness; he drew cabalistic signs with his sword and in an enraged voice shouted incantations. His attendants, gloomy and clearly depressed, meanwhile covered the chest of the dead woman with a red cloth, burnt resinous herbs on it, and expelled a dense caustic smoke, so profuse that it disturbed everyone, for it spread over the whole arena. The crowd began to become horribly disturbed, for the aromas diffused by the sorcerers were causing an erotic madness. And while Shelom, totally crazed, committed a perfidious desecration on the corpse, the crowd around him would have undoubtedly started a collective orgy if the mages hadn't acted quickly and spread some vials of essences on the ground, whose potent aroma absorbed the toxic smell of the sorcerers, restoring a certain calm. When the spectators regained full consciousness, enough to be able to watch the show, they ended up seeing something strange and horrible. The body of the murdered young woman moved. She stood up and glared wildly at the surrounding crowd. Then, standing up with incredible lightness, the young woman ran to Shelom, fell to her knees and, kissing his hands, exclaimed in a passionate rush of gratitude:

"Lord of life and death, I'm grateful to you for giving me back my life."

Triumphant, Shelom showed it to the people. Some of the spectators cheered him, but many remained in an apprehensive silence. Shelom paid no heed and said with disdain:

"Bring the Hindu any carrion so he can show his power."

"It's not necessary," replied Supramati in a clear and sonorous voice. And with the point of his sword he traced a circle in the air that flew around the -resurrected one. "I want to prove to the people here that the life you gave to this body is fictitious. You haven't restored the soul of this unfortunate one, but you have introduced into her body one of those ignoble creatures of the unseen world which are dominated by your science of darkness. And as for you, wretched worm, animated only by blood and putrefaction, get out of this body which doesn't belong to you!"

From the point of Supramati's sword a flame shot out and flew with the speed of thought towards the woman and struck her in the chest, exactly where the wound was. There was a pitiful, piercing scream, the woman fell as if struck by lightning, and before the stupefied crowd something terrible and revolting happened.

From the open mouth of the body emerged a kind of snake, whose head, with bloodshot eyes, had something of a human shape. As soon as the loathsome creature emerged from inside its victim, it attacked Shelom and instantly wrapped itself around him, trying to suffocate him. If Shelom had been a mere mortal, his bones would have broken immediately. Now he was fighting a beast that he himself had summoned from the depths of darkness and, with the help of the mighty sorcerer Nadim, managed to subdue. The creature's flexible body weakened, falling to the ground, dead or disfigured. As this scene took place, many of the black mages rolled on the ground in convulsions. The body of the deceased once again took on the appearance of a corpse. Lifted by an invisible force, it was carried across the red line and deposited on the ground a few feet away from Supramati. Immediately, Niebo and Nivara approached and poured two bowls of a silvery, frothy liquid over the corpse, still covered in a black, frothy, sticky, fetid mass. Immediately the liquid began to crackle and sizzle like water poured on a hot iron; then a thick vapour rose and enveloped the corpse for a minute. When the whitish cloud dissipated, the body regained its original whiteness, and the features of the face took on a serene beauty. The foam that stained it disappeared completely and only a red stain indicated the place of the mortal wound. Then Supramati knelt down, took the two hands of the deceased and, raising his eyes to heaven, pronounced with feeling:

"Let my Heavenly Father, through my pure power, allow the soul criminally and forcibly banished from this body to return to its earthly abode. Lord Jesus Christ, support me and help me by making your servant worthy to overcome hell. He bent over the deceased and said imperiously: - Give back the divine breath, to this new life, granted anew by the Almighty and consecrate yourself to the praise of His name and His laws."

The young woman's body began to tremble. Taking a deep breath, her eyes opened and, as if awakening from a long sleep, she looked around her with a mixture of fear and amazement. Nivara covered her nakedness with a wide-jawed white robe and helped her to stand up.

"Worship your God and kiss the sacred symbol of eternity and salvation," said Supramati, holding out to her the cruciform hilt of his sword, which she kissed respectfully and piously. "Now go back to your parents and tell them that they must seek the light and not the darkness. Show your gratitude to the Creator by living according to His laws."

Staggering, but happy, the young girl ran to her parents. Filled with happiness, they ran to her, covering her with tears and affection.

It would be difficult to describe what was happening in the crowd. The nerves of the people, weakened by depravity and anomalies, could no longer bear so much emotions. The horrible silence that had hitherto remained was suddenly broken. The people shouted, laughed, roared, cried, and, oscillating between fear and doubt, wondered whether it was really possible that Shelom Iezodot, the lord of the world, was a demon, while the Hindu magician, who had impressed them with his beauty and power, was an envoy of that ancient God long since forgotten and disowned.

Calmly and impassively, Supramati climbed back onto his stone and looked down at the pale and lost Shelom, who was panting to recover from the terrible struggle. Minutes later, the mage's sonorous voice was heard.

"I propose to you Shelom Iezodot, to start the final act of our duel. The sun is already setting and the spectators, just like us, are waiting for an outcome."

"I didn't have any idea that you were in such a hurry to venerate Lucifer and his greatness. Wait a while, while I make the final preparations," Shelom replied with an evil smile. Turning around, he went into his dressing room, which had a private room.

Supramati also took advantage of the break and, anticipating that it would be quite a long one, went up to the cabin to rest and talk with his friends. At the back of Shelom's part of the arena were the ruins of an ancient church destroyed by the Satanists, its crumbling walls and steeple forming a large escarpment. The spectators were surprised that the ruins had not been removed. However, it was here that they erected the altar to Lucifer: a massive, recessed, cubic block of black marble, beneath which rose what was left of the church's vault. Gradually, reddish-grey clouds covered the sky and a strong wind lifted the sand from the arena and stirred the green of the forest created by Supramati. The darkness increased rapidly and in the distance they heard thunder approaching. Tongues of flame flickered under the vaulted ruins, and finally a violet, ominous glow illuminated the arena and the ruins. In some places, in great bronze piles, tar was burning, whose smoky light gave the scene a fantastic and archaic air. Suddenly there were cries and howls, and from behind the stones hyenas, tigers, leopards and other wild animals began to emerge like shadows. With fur cocked to one side and eyes gleaming with hatred, they stood in a semicircle before the black rock, roaring softly and wagging their tails nervously. Seeing this, Supramati stood up, resumed his place on the aerolith and this time was followed by four friends who stood close behind him.

Soon Shelom Iezodot appeared, accompanied by twelve sorcerers. He was naked and carried, instead of a sword, a red-hot pitchfork. The horns on his forehead also seemed to burn. Lining up on either side of the black rock, the twelve sorcerers fell on their stomachs, Shelom stood before the stone where their terrible lord was to appear, tracing cabalistic signs with his trident and chanting a strange song of sharp, lacerating notes. Gradually the song became a stormy recitative in which he told Lucifer of all his services to hell, of all the crimes and sacrileges, in short, of all the enormous work carried out by the servants of darkness for the purpose of wiping out mankind. The trick had been a success, for mankind had been stripped of faith and of any moral support, bound to their own passions and fallen at Lucifer's bidding; and now he, Shelom Iezodot, his faithful servant, demanded his reward. With sacrilegious, hate-filled words, he insisted that Lucifer should appear and destroy the impudent Hindu who had dared to compete with him and bluster. Increasingly concentrated and foaming at the mouth, he insisted that Lucifer avenge him and destroy the enemy, sending the earth to swallow him up and fire to burn him, first depriving him of power and then breaking him and prostrating him at his feet.

A mighty clap of thunder burst in response to this terrible call, the earth shook and the ruins were illuminated like a flash of lightning. Under the vault, multi-coloured fires were lit and suddenly, on the rock, a titanic and horrible figure appeared. Against the fiery sanguine background was clearly outlined the typical head of ominous beauty, whose face bore the mark of all crimes, passions and spiritual sufferings. The huge, pointed wings grew from its shoulders, and on its forehead were the twisted horns, the symbol of the beast.

"Kneel down, damned Hindu, despicable worm! Kneel down and revere our lord and your lord, for your power cannot affect him," roared Shelom.

The spirit of darkness released swirls of smoke that the wind carried towards the mage. When Supramati felt the contact with the noxious fluids he turned pale, the colour of his own robe, but his eyes burned as ever with a powerful will and his voice rang serene and sure:

"I only have one Lord whom I revere: God. And I have only one weapon: my faith and the symbol of salvation, blessed with the blood of the Son of God.

And drawing from his robes the mage's cross, which emitted torrents of blinding light, he rushed towards the mighty demon, bravely crossing the line of demarcation. As he spoke, Dakhir and Narayana drew their swords and Niebo and Nivara brandished their magic staffs in support of their friend with the full force of their powers. Supramati, as if carried by the wind, rushed up to the satanic altar and struck menacingly, his cross raised over his head:

"Back, negative demon, author of evil and misfortune. Be gone, return to the abyss from which you emerged to the perdition of mankind, I conjure you and smite you with this weapon of light!" thundered the voice of the mage, bravely attacking the evil spirit.

Suddenly, the demon's face paled, a great trembling shook the earth, and where the wicked altar had been, the earth opened up, forming a great crack, as deep as a precipice, and swallowed Lucifer. Supramati paused, breathed a sigh of relief and with the glowing cross traced a sign of redemption over the abyss. Immediately, above the place of the dethroned demon, a luminous cross of enormous proportions shone in the air, illuminating the farthest surroundings with its soft, bluish light.} Shelom and his companions were astonished, because everything happened with unbelievable speed. And when the glowing cross shone, the black mages began to shout and howl, some fell dead and the rest fled. Shelom, caught by a strong wind, was hurled away from the arena, the place of his terrible defeat.

Clearly, to people of past centuries, for example of the 20th century, such events in the open air, in broad daylight and before the eyes of thousands of spectators would seem incredible, but the general rule is this: the more power develops, the greater its manifestation. The same was true of occult power. The more power the invisible one acquired, the more frequently and with greater intensity he revealed his presence. Unfortunately, Hell became more manifest; Heaven and the number of the faithful diminished. Apathetic, indifferent and disunited, they squandered their strength and power, they buried the gifts they had received, while the headquarters of darkness, energetic and threatening, opened its way.

What happened to the audience was indescribable. The crowd, stunned and motionless, watched the appearance and disappearance of the demon. However, the sight of the cross had the effect of lightning. Some began to run like maniacs, others, deeply shocked, stared at that desecrated and forgotten symbol, once worshipped by their ancestors. At that instant, harmonious sounds were heard in the air, which muffled the general shouting and acted to calm the excited nerves of those present, keeping them in their seats. When the strange music ended, Supramati began to speak:

"Come near, children of God, and worship your Creator. Repent and return to your forgotten faith. Blinded by the enchantment of the spirits of darkness, you have insulted the Divine. And what have you gained by such wickedness and sacrilege? You have upset the balance of cosmic forces that will destroy the planet. I am a missionary of the last days and I tell you: the hour of Judgement announced by the prophets is nearer than you imagine. And you, along with your earth, are condemned to a death from which hell cannot save you. Take advantage of this very short delay, repent and purify yourselves to escape the terrible punishment. Reopen the empty temples, these centres of prayer and collective strength, re-energise the altar of the Lord, sing the sacred hymns whose sounds will drive away the impure forces. Exorcise the demons who have taken possession of your souls, destroyed and defiled your bodies. Everything dies and is transformed in the divine breath of the Creator. Save this celestial spark so that it may rise towards the light and not fall into the abyss of darkness."

When Supramati fell silent, an unusual agitation seized some of the spectators and, while the raving Satanists fled, suffering excruciating pain and foaming at the mouth, a crowd of humble people, with joy and tears in their eyes, denoting superstitious fear, approached and prostrated themselves before the glowing cross, a symbol worshipped of old, a sacred talisman of their ancestors.

In those ancient times the joy of life was greater; on earth there was still faith, when the symbol of salvation received the new-born, purified him and separated him from invisible enemies, or stood over the grave, protecting the deceased from the attacks of impure creatures. And behold, this symbol, so long persecuted, stands before them, pure, resplendent, visible to all, and mercifully calls to itself the wretched humanity which, denying God, has given itself over to the power of the dark forces and has been bound hand and foot. In a sudden ecstasy, these people who had not learned to pray would fall face down, raise their hands towards the Cross and with tears in their eyes repeat the words that the Magi had taught them:

"Have mercy on us, O Lord, and forgive us our crimes!"

In response to this appeal, where the supplicant completely unburdened his soul, miracles occurred: the deaf could hear again, the mute could speak again, and the paraplegic could move freely.

Supramati, leaving the crowd adoring the Cross, returned to his part of the arena accompanied by his friends, and as he approached the box he saw near the entrance a dozen persons whose heads were enveloped by broad auras. In front of them stood Ebramar. With eyes wet with tears, he held out his hands to him and said, pressing him to his chest.

"Congratulations on your victory, my dear son and disciple!"

The other magicians also embraced him. The crowd, seeing the group of strangers dressed in silver robes and surrounded by an aura of light, took them for saints descended from Heaven to appear to men.

"And now, friends, let us spend a few days in our Himalayan shelter, because a tempest is about to rage. The spirits of chaos, Lucifer's army of darkness intend to avenge defeat through destruction."

Later, another spacecraft, of a construction unknown to mere mortals, brought the mages, at breathtaking speed, to one of their inaccessible safe havens.

CHAPTER XVI

Ebramar's prediction came true. The next day, a terrible hurricane, the most powerful hurricane ever seen, raged for three days straight and caused a lot of damage. When the storm finally subsided, the land was devastated for hundreds of kilometres. In the fields, everything was destroyed by a fearsome wind or blown down by hail; greenhouses shattered; houses roofed over and countless people crushed under the ruins of collapsed buildings. Following this disaster, another disaster began. The heat was so fierce that the earth cracked, the water dried up in the lakes and rivers, and the fish perished. Trees that survived the hurricane burned, lost their leaves and looked like burnt poles. Domestic animals died like flies; famine gradually increased and terrible epidemics broke out. Even people immersed in gold, inside their palaces, succumbed to starvation and suffocation because the air was permeated with the smoke of the burning peat. These cosmic phenomena were certainly contagious, for from every corner came terrible news of hurricanes and unprecedented tropical heat that turned the earth into a desert.

By a strange coincidence, only the forest created by Supramati during his duel with Shelom resisted the bad weather with ease: the radiant crude floated peacefully in the air, illuminating that little piece of land with mysterious light; from its entrails gushed a spring of cold, crystalline water. Gradually, the whole place became covered with fruit-laden trees, to which hungry crowds flocked to quench their thirst and hunger. Only Satanists avoided the place without benefiting from it, claiming that the water caused them internal pains and the fruits were indigestible.

The moral state of the people was no less deplorable. Sick and hungry, they cried in vain for Lucifer's help, for hell seemed deaf and dumb to their entreaties. He had given them gold to acquire anything they wanted, including divine souls. Now in possession of all goods, they were annihilated and outraged. God was banished from human hearts, and terrible misfortunes befell men. There remained for criminal humanity only gold, which could no longer buy anything to stock granaries and larders. Everything had been sold by mankind to the demon of gold: natural riches, the sap of the earth, green forests crumbling under the axe of the dealer, oil, coal and electricity. All was consumed without the prudent thrift of a wise rich man, but with the insane carelessness of a spendthrift who thinks neither of the present nor of the future, and who with savage barbarism sacrifices the legacies of his ancestors for the ephemeral delights of the present. Ruined physically and morally, the people reached the edge of the precipice that would swallow up the world - which might well survive a while longer, fertile and green, serving countless generations as a school of improvement and purification. The discontent of the masses began to grow more vehement and dangerous, for the depraved mob, unaccustomed to obedience, knew no restraint. The people gathered before Shelom's palace, insistently shouting and threateningly demanding an end to the scorching heat of the earth.

You're the son of Satan, equivalent to God and you subjugate the elements of nature. Put an end to the drought, give us bread and water. Or, - threatening him with clenched fists, the people shouted wildly: - We no longer want your gold, we want air, bread and water. Show that you're powerful, that you're not a pretender or a braggart, for you were defeated by the Hindu. It's you Satanists who have brought down the wrath of God upon us! - shouted others. - There, where the cross hangs in the air, there's a great abundance of fruit and water. Give us back the old God, give us back our old faith, otherwise there won't be a stone left of your palace and we'll destroy all your temples.

The indignation was growing day by day, and the beginning of an internal war was already perceptible in the face of the terrible hunger and thirst that plagued the earth and mankind. The rebels attacked Satanists wherever they were found, armed with iron or wooden crucifixes. They invaded satanic temples, tore down altars and broke the statue of Lucifer. There was senseless murder, rebellion and despair; the angry mob searched for Shelom to annihilate him, but he seemed to have disappeared and was nowhere to be found. Information from all quarters indicated that the picture of hatred and poverty was general, while unperturbed nature continued in her destructive zeal. The sun burned implacably, illuminating the arid desert and the rotting corpses of men and animals. Never had contempt for gold taken on such dimensions. It would gladly be exchanged in handfuls for a cup of water, a piece of bread and a breath of fresh and pure air. For the first time, probably, the vile metal became dead and useless in the hands of its owners.

The tumult and clamour of this fratricidal war, without truce or mercy, didn't reach Shelom, hidden underground. It was a large room, furnished in imperial luxury: the walls were covered with a red cloth embroidered in gold; the furniture was of inlaid black wood, and the floor was covered with a carpet as soft as leather. In a deep niche stood a large statue of Lucifer, indifferent to the sufferings and struggles caused by him, the sullen figure of the demon stood out against the surroundings, and on his petrified countenance was a mocking smile. In front of the statue, black wax candles burned in a seven-branched candelabra. In the centre of the room was a large table, on which stood a huge jug of wine, a goblet and an old open book.

Shelom was alone. Sitting in a high-backed armchair, resting his head on a red cushion, he pondered impatiently with the magic dagger he held at his waist. His face was grim, marred by inner rage and wounded pride; after confronting the mage, he felt weak and his strength returned too slowly.

He trembled with hatred at the thought that he, Shelom, was forced to hide like a thief from those people who adored him as a divinity. In the long hours of solitude in the underground, he was suddenly assailed by doubt - that terrible force, created by hell to suggest to people disbelief in the existence of God, And this monster that tears human hearts apart, was now standing beside Shelom's couch; its serpentine head was bent towards his ear, its emerald eyes stared at him, full of indescribable mockery, and the diabolical voice was murmuring: - Where is your power? What can you do against laws that are stronger than your knowledge? The Hindu and the facts show clearly that, in a vast whole, you're a diminutive creature? Who knows? Perhaps the Lord you serve is no match for that other Lord and you can never win Heaven, for your cause may be ignoble.

A shiver of violent bitterness ran through him at the thought that perhaps he was but a mere pawn in the hands of the cruel lord who was drunk with his spilt blood, abandoning him in that trying hour, with no strength to quell the rebellion, a direct threat to him, for unbridled passions know no bounds. His soul contorted, overcome by the painful sensation that hell was not as powerful as he thought it was.

But Shelom was different from the clumsy and indecisive rabble who believed in neither good nor evil. He straightened up and with his hand pushed back the strands of hair that had stuck to his sweaty forehead.

"Get out of here, you cowardly monster of doubt. You can't beat me," he thought. He greedily drank his glass of wine and then rang a metallic bell. Madim answered his call.

"I want to call Lucifer and ask for his help," cried Shelom. "It's time to put an end to all this misery. He may have the means to show me the way out, revealing to me the promised secret of the essence, the source of life. The law is one: Ask and you will receive, knock and the door will open. No matter which door you knock, the door of Heaven or the door of Hell. If you know how to demand, one will open somewhere."

Concerned and absorbed, Madim helped him with the preparations, which began immediately. In front of the statue of Lucifer, they lit the candelabras with resinous herbs, smoked them and turned off the lights. Now only the black wax candles and the smouldering flame of the candelabras illuminated the room. Shelom picked up a trident and took off his shoes, while Madim prostrated himself on his knees before him with an open book on his head. In a shrill voice, Shelom began to read magical formulae aloud, making cabalistic signs with a trident that he beat on the floor in specific places, and increasing the speed at which he recited the formulas. Soon the entire underground room was filled with multicoloured smoke that seemed to dissipate, giving way to a veritable legion of devils of all colours and sizes, flying around the summoner. At the same instant, on the black background of the book, cabalistic signs were drawn in fiery lines and the goblins disappeared as if swept by the wind; then they returned carrying, with visible difficulty, a large dagger with several cabalistic signs that glowed on the black sheet. Shelom picked up the magic weapon and signalled with the trident: the imps disappeared and the triptychs were extinguished. In a hoarse voice, he ordered Madim to light the lamps and, after carefully examining the signs on the blade, said with a sigh of relief:

"It's necessary to prepare the sacrifice demanded by Lucifer, and then it will lead us to the place where the primal essence flows, which restores the forces of nature."

Two days later, we found Shelom far from Czargrado, in the mountains of Lebanon. A vast underground cavern was adapted for invocations at Lucifer's request. The torches, stuck between the stones, smoked and with a reddish light illuminated a diabolical and repulsive picture. In the centre of the cave, a huge cauldron hung from three long, huge iron rods, filled to the brim with a steaming red liquid. Beneath the cauldron, in a brick chimney, was the fuel: a pile of corpses, arranged like firewood and impregnated with pitch and other resinous substances. A nauseating smell of burning flesh pervaded the cave and the thick smoke rose to the top and disappeared there, probably rising through the cracks. Shelom and Madim, both naked and with iron hooks in their hands tended the fire, but as soon as the disgusting stew began to boil, they dropped their tools. Shelom picked up the magic pitchfork and Madim the black book, which he placed on his head, kneeling before his master. While Shelom read the formulas and drew cabalistic signs, a multitude of black dots began to emerge from the smoke, taking the form of a legion of capets. The cavern was filled with groans and agonised cries; the earth shook with a mighty explosion, and from the cauldron appeared the hideous figure of the demon, defeated by Supramati during the magic duel. An infernal cruelty deformed sinisterly his handsome features; his bloodshot eyes glittered, and between his ruddy lips gleamed the pointed teeth of a beast. The hideous being arose, and his dull voice was heard:

"I came to your call, Shelom Yezodot, and I'll give you the means to win back the land. The first time, I gave you gold, which perverted the world. The second time, You took advantage of the art of printing, invented by men for the purpose of bringing light, but which in my hands and in those of my servants served for the black imps to roam the universe, spreading darkness, licentiousness and sacrilege and penetrating with the same ease into palaces and humble houses, poisoning every child and every old man. Now I give you my third gift: eternal life, harvest without labour, pleasures without limit or illness. I give into your hands the sap, the blood of the planet, and I'll see what you can make of it all. Reclaiming the realm, create fertility and thriving, become like God? And now, let Madim take over the fire and follow me."

Jumping quietly out of the cauldron, he went to the crevice that led deep into the earth. The way was terribly difficult, through narrow passages that hardly permitted the passage of a person but with his fearsome companion, Shelom feared nothing. Fearless and tireless, he crawled through the caves, climbed the chasms, scaled the cliffs, and passed into the caves of suffocating sulphuric fumes. Finally, they arrived at a vast cave, filled with silvery vapour and blinding light that reflected off multi-coloured stalactites, giving them the appearance of a fabric embroidered with precious stones. In the centre, gushing up from within the earth, rising a few feet, was a thin golden stream resembling a liquid flame, which then descended into a natural reservoir, where the liquid seemed to lose itself at the bottom in golden fillets.

"Here is the source of life! And I thought we would have to face the hermits of the Himalayas, who jealously guard their secrets; but apparently they're more worried about protecting the main source, or maybe they've already given up fighting," the demon mocked, and added in a joking tone, "In any case, we're here, the source of life is in your hands, and I just have to open an easier way for you to come here. For now, let's take that container. Fill it up."

He pointed Shelom to a depression where there was a large crystal jar, and when it was filled to the brim, he took it and the two of them went to the cave of invocations. When they arrived there, Lucifer showed his disciple the method of using the terrible substance and completed:

"When the liquid is ready for use, order the gardens and fields to be sprayed with it, provide for all regional governors to be watered everywhere. It's also convenient that the air be sprayed with the liquid for its purification. What we have for now is enough, but we must find an easier way to get the elixir."

Indicating the best means of bringing the primal essence into the cave, the terrible demon slowly slipped into the cauldron and seemed to dissipate into the boiling blood. Left alone again with Madim, Shelom straightened up, proud of his triumph and his appeased rage.

"What wrong Madim? you're a great fool to dare to doubt me and tremble before the Hindu! Do you understand now what powers I hold in my hand? When I restore life on this planet, the insolent Supramati will have no option but to hide with all his hermits in the redoubts where they remain to this day," exulted Shelom in a contemptuous tone, stretching his slender feline body."

"Oh, you're the true lord of the universe and your power is unequalled! - exclaimed Madim, rising to his feet and kissing his nefarious lord's hands respectfully."

Some time later a rumour spread, which then reached the whole world; not as fast as in the past, because telephones only worked here and there and the wireless telegraph was even worse. Spaceships couldn't take off in a dense and scorching atmosphere, they flew too low and disasters were frequent. Nevertheless, the information became public, in a fanatical tone, that Shelom Iezodot possessed the secret of restoring to the planet the pure air, the abundant water, and the fertility of olden times. -The golden age has returned," he announced. There will be no more death and disease, and every being who now lives on earth and recognises the power of Shelom, the son of Satan, will be eternal, beautiful and healthy, and will enjoy all earthly blessings. Soon after, an advertisement appeared offering those interested to try the elixir of eternal life, and that they should come to the large square in front of Shelom's palace the next day, when the first distribution would take place.

As dawn broke as an experience, the owners of the primordial essence sprinkled the air with it and, Indeed, the atmosphere took on a bluish tinge, in which everyone felt a pleasant freshness. The crowds that had come in the morning and filled the square and the adjacent streets soon sensed the change in temperature and concluded in amazement that Shelom's promises were being fulfilled. In front of the palace, on a long platform, a barrel with a pink liquid emitting luminous vapours was placed, and a huge number of small glasses filled with the mysterious drink. With crazed eagerness, the human crowd rushed onto the platform, draining the contents of the cups. But then something unexpected happened. As soon as the first ones finished swallowing the offered drink, they fell down dead and those behind them fell back in terror. At first, panic spread through the crowd, but then the enraged crowd began to shout:

He wants to poison us to get rid of us!

The enraged people threw themselves against Shelom and Madim with the intention of destroying them. They had a hard time saving their skins by fleeing to the palace, closing behind them a huge gate. Then the crowd pounced on the supposed poison, broke the glasses and overturned the barrel. As a result of the contact with the liquid, burns and wounds appeared on many, which increased the fury even more. Nevertheless, Shelom was feared and no one dared to storm the palace. Cursing and shouting insults, the crowd dispersed, carrying their dead and wounded. Hiding behind the curtain, Shelom watched through the window the end of the spectacle. On the other hand, pale and dejected, Madim stood beside him. And when at last Shelom turned grim and frowning, the secretary asked him timidly:

"Master, isn't that another trick of the damned Hindu?"

"Nonsense, maybe the dosage is a bit strong. I don't know how to handle the substance yet and I haven't even had time to study it. And how much precious liquid those damned animals destroyed! " He thought for a while and added: "In the evening, dear Madim, we're going to make a new experiment. We're going to water the palace gardens, some public gardens and, above all, the trees on the boulevard that look like burnt posts. Let's see how it will look."

As the evening fell, they armed with pneumatic pumps - the kind used for watering the streets - and large buckets of prepared liquid, they went out into the garden and watered trees, lawns and flowerbeds. As the fine splashes fell to the ground, a reddish mist rose and a strange crackle could be heard coming from the dry tree. Then they watered the neighbouring public garden, a part of the boulevard, and what was left of the liquid was thrown back home into the lake of the public park, which was practically dry. Although the amount of the mysterious liquid was very small, in contact with the water it caused a strange phenomenon for both researchers. Something like an explosion was heard, the water began to boil, the surface rippled in waves and its level rose, as if the bottom was pushing the water upwards. Because of the loud roar, the "researchers" were thrown far away and, when they recovered from the shock, they were convinced that the lake had acquired its normal shape; they calmed down and returned to the palace, surprised and happy, curiously awaiting the results of their work. And these proved to be surprising beyond the most promising expectations. All over the place where the enigmatic liquid had fallen, in a few hours lush vegetation appeared, the trees of the boulevard that had been dry were covered with dense foliage, forming leafy canopies, the lake filled with water and bubbled with fish, the air became pleasant and cool and the suffocating heat ceased.

Extraordinary surprise and fascination gripped the inhabitants. Above all, they were stunned by the news, which came as fast as lightning, that those thought to be dead were still alive. And as if the fact that they were alive wasn't enough, they were transformed. All were rejuvenated and in perfect health: the deaf could hear, the blind could see, the deaf and dumb could speak and the paraplegic could walk. Only the burned remained sick. The city was in an uproar.

All were bitterly sorry for the thoughtless rage of the previous day, while those who hadn't had time to drink despaired at the thought that only yesterday they had unthinkingly destroyed such a quantity of the renewing elixir. Shelom was indeed an extraordinary being, endowed with supernatural powers and knowledge. Would he not be a benefactor of mankind if, by chance, he restored fertility, abundance of everything, temperature, and - most important of all - cured all human diseases and preserved them from death? And instead, they wounded him and even wanted to kill him. What would happen if he now turned his back on the ungrateful, abandoning them to their fate? And the frivolous and exalted mob, who only yesterday wanted to do him in, came again to Shelom's palace, but this time to glorify, thank and revere him. With loud cries, the people called out to him, but he kept them waiting for a long time, and when at last he appeared on the terrace, his face was grim and his gaze cold and stern.

It should be added that in all the places where, the day before, the liquid had been poured from the barrel and the cups, and where the mysterious substance came into contact with the ground, a strange vegetation appeared during the night: a small grove of intertwined, cactus-like bushes with huge leaves about twenty centimetres thick, covered with long, sharp, razor-like thorns, full of thick, bloody veins. In some places, through the dark foliage and low, thick, reddish-purple trunks, melon-shaped flower bulbs, strikingly resembling chunks of flesh, dangled, lightly shrouded in a purplish-grey mist. The force with which these monstrous bushes sprouted from the earth broke or tore up the asphalt slabs that lined the streets.

When Shelom appeared on the terrace, the crowd opened their arms, shouting: forgive us, forgive us. Shelom at first delivered a severe sermon, reproaching them for their ingratitude and stupidity in destroying the precious liquid that could have provided eternal life to thousands of people; then, pointing to the thorny grove that filled half the square, he added:

"The essence discovered by me, as you see, possesses so much power that even when criminally poured out it can give life. The difference is that when it is handled wisely by an experienced hand, it brings fertility and abundance, whereas if it is poured irrationally and without measure, it creates monstrosities such as the one before you."

The crowd, frightened and silent, fell back sharply, and again there were cries, weeping and pleas for forgiveness. Shelom seemed moved and in his speech announced that Lucifer, the merciful lord he served, forgave his subjects, afflicted by hunger, thirst and fear.

"He forgives your sacrileges," Shelom continued, "but you must correct your faults. Go, then, and rebuild Satan's temples, light the candelabras, and sacrifice to him the evil ones who have dared to insult his name and underestimate his power. Has there ever been a God who rewarded his loyal servants with so many gifts as Satan, who spares them nothing? He has put an end to death, famine and disease, and those who worship Him will enjoy an eternal life and will reap without sowing. The infidels, those who deny Satan, will all be eliminated because there's no place for them among us. And since they won't be able to drink the vital essence, they'll remain mortals who will perish in the fire. Or rather, on the cross. As they worship that symbol, they'll enjoy dying crucified. We only have to lure them out of those crevices and undergrounds where they hide without letting any of them escape. And while we'll apply to them the deserved penalty, may the One. To whom they pray, descend from heaven to defend and save them."

The speech provoked immense enthusiasm. But as the crowd dispersed to invade the remaining temples, a terrible and unexpected event occurred. A middle-aged woman passing near the bushes caught her skirt on the thorn of a leaf. To the astonishment of those present, when the leaf straightened, it grabbed the woman and threw her into the centre of the forest as if she were a feather. At the same instant, long, slender, previously unnoticed stalks emerged from the leaves, thick as arms; at their tips were curved acorns, like a clawed hand. Instantly, this living cordage enveloped and felled its victim, thus concealing the end of a fatal drama, for the screams of the unfortunate had ceased. The crowd was stunned, but the ingenious Shelom shouted aloud:

"This torture is the equivalent of a bonfire and the Himalayan hermits will be the first to experience this kind of death."

Some expressions of support were heard in response, but the impression left by the event was too depressing to rekindle enthusiasm, and the crowd dispersed hastily, trying to leave the square as quickly as possible. From that day on, however, febrile activity began in every corner of the earth. Shelom continually sent large quantities of the mysterious liquid to all the regional governors, under whose direction the irrigations were carried out, producing astonishing effects. Most impressive was the speed with which vegetation appeared and developed, wherever this extraordinary dew touched, barren soil was transformed into green gardens, and with such rapidity, as if the years were counted in days. The agitation among the scientists was enormous, and in vain they tried to analyse the new substance, for it did not decompose and its elements remained unknown. Unable to know why, they merely observed the facts. And the earth was transformed into a paradise. The vegetation was luxuriant, the rivers filled with water and fish, springs of water sprang up everywhere, the old age ceased to come, and the rejuvenated and flourishing population seemed full of a vigour never seen before.

CHAPTER XVII

Waiting for the moment when their enemies would challenge them to the last and greatest battle, our friends retired to one of the Himalayan palaces, the very one where, as we saw before, Olga had died. Again Dakhir, Narayana and Supramati lived under the same roof, and because of the spaciousness of the palace each could imagine himself in his own house and alone to do his own tasks and reflections. One evening, Supramati sat alone on the terrace where Olga used to spend the agonising hours of her last days on earth. Memories flashed before him and the image of the lovely woman who loved him with all her being rose vividly in his memory. Suddenly, the image of the church in the cave monastery on Mount Sinai came to his mind and the young prioress of the community stood genuflecting before the altar, absorbed in fervent prayer. In her thoughts floated the image of Supramati, as she had known him on her visit to the cave, and her whole soul was given to prayer: -Divine Sender, reveal to me who you are and tell me your name. His whole being stirred when I saw you and went to meet you. I know you, I revere you and I love you as one sent by God, but I want to know your name.

A smile came over the mage's handsome countenance. He raised his hand and from his thin fingers flickered a streak of light that seemed to reach out and envelop the young woman kneeling in prayer; her eyes closed and her body dropped to the steps. Almost at the same instant, next to the sleeping woman, a clear and transparent shadow appeared, which, with the speed of thought, flew into space and stopped next to the magician, densified and took on a human aspect. It was Olga in her current incarnation. Her head was enveloped in a golden aura. Supramati stood up, took the vision's hand and kissed it. Her eyes lit up with indescribable joy.

"Supramati! Now I know his name and I recognise him. Your image has always lived, unconsciously, in my soul like an unapproachable ideal." he murmured in a weak but clear voice.

"Do you not forget me, faithful heart, in spite of the many centuries of our separation, the painful trials and the new forms your spirit has acquired? " asked Supramati, moved.

"Forget you? Would it be possible? No, don't ask such foolish questions. Tell me, instead, have I worked hard enough to remain with you and to be your disciple? There are no trials or sufferings that I cannot take on with joy to merit this sublime reward. But perhaps my love for you should be further purified?"

"No, my dear, love me as your heart suggests, since your love is as pure as your faith. The hour of our reunion draws near, but you must endure the last and difficult test, overcoming the obstacle that separates us. You left me by death and by death you must return to me."

A radiant light of joy lit up Olga's clear eyes and a powerful energy resonated in her voice.

"Do n't be afraid, my dear master. Don't think that I'll hesitate before death, all the more so now that I'm strong and purified. For even before, being ignorant, blind and an indecisive spirit, I faced death for the happiness of becoming your wife. No, Supramati, I'll not weaken. Fearing nothing, I'll spread the divine word, I'll save souls as an example of my unwavering faith and courageous death. Only the body will die, and it will fly to meet you. How grateful I'm to you that you have called me! Your appearance and your word have given me new strength."

"Go then my faithful friend, go back into your corporeal sheath and be assured that in all the difficult moments you'll face I'll be close to you."

"I know that you'll be my shield. Here is the weapon that will make me invincible and before which all the forces of hell will retreat," she replied, raising the hand that held a glittering cross. And with a farewell sign, the vision receded, paled and vanished into the night mist.

Supramati took a few steps across the terrace, leaned on the railing, contemplating thoughtfully the magical panorama of the gardens bathed in silvery moonlight. Suddenly, a feeling of pity came over him for the anticipated destruction of the Earth, still so beautiful. Unable to realise how much time had passed in his reflections, a soft sound roused him from his reverie. Trembling, he turned quickly and exclaimed with joy, holding out his hands to Ebramar.

"Master, how good to see you! I just thought of you, or did you hear my call?"

"Precisely. I heard your lament about the end of our planet and I have come to cheer you," Ebramar replied, laughing.

"You bet! I'm tormented by the thought that the Earth, our Earth, must die. Tell me, is there no way to save it? There are so many pure fluids rising, so many deaths that will be voluntary to the greatness of the divine ideal, and add to this the aid of our science? Could we not try to preserve it? I feel as if something near and dear is dying, while I do nothing."

"I understand, dear friend," Ebramar sighed. "Do you think we don't suffer at the thought of having to leave our home, where we have become what we are now? We are powerless in the face of the terrible cosmic laws that have been set in motion. How can we stop the dynamite explosion when the fuse is already lit? The chaos has gone on for too long, slowly corrupting and perverting the population. The servants of Evil maintained this downfall and contributed by all means to the destruction of the foci of faith, purity and light that, in a way, kept the balance. They maintained the balance. And now, the insane Shelom, distributing the primal essence without limit or measure, overflows the cup of death and accelerates the catastrophe. Under such circumstances, what can we do?"

"You're right, master, my hope was absurd and was suggested to me by weakness, a feeling of fear of a new world into which we 'll have to go, taking on this terrible responsibility. "

"It's true that the responsibility is enormous and at the same time more difficult because we will have to work alone, as our leaders move to a higher system. But if the task is great, the reward is also great. Is it not an immense joy to lead the nascent peoples on the path of Good, to establish wise laws, which in the course of infinite centuries will maintain harmony or direct the faltering humanity on its way of ascent? We were given the opportunity to create the golden centuries, to be scientists and legislators, legendary tsars, who in popular memory will be remembered as gods, personified in human bodies, tsars of divine dynasties. And, as a final reward, we will be freed from this putrescent body to return, purified and clear, to the eternal home." Ebramar became animated. The great black eyes seemed to admire a glowing vision in space, and Supramati's eyes also sparkled.

Where is that world in which the last act of our extraordinary existence will be played out? In which stage of development is it now, master?

"It's a world in our system, invisible to our eyes and pretty distant. As far as its level of development is concerned, it's fully formed, because there are human races, fauna and flora. However, all this is concentrated on a single continent. The remaining part of the planet, not covered by water, consists of vast inhospitable plains, poor in vegetation, with active volcanoes and an intensely profuse Kingdom of animals of gigantic dimensions. The human races are in the first stage of intellectual development and are, of course, half-savage, but they are very suitable material to work with. In the centre of the inhabited continent is the earthly paradise, the kingdom of the golden age, Shangrila, which will remain in popular memory until the end of time. And this paradise is near the main source of primordial matter, where nature profusely satiated with the vital essence has already revealed those riches of a new world, concentrating plant, mineral and animal resources. There we'll descend, seek a place for our archives, build temples and palaces, and from there we'll rule the world that has been entrusted to us. We shall no longer need to drink the elixir of life, since our organisms will have already acquired an extraordinary life force, our life span will be long, that of the patriarchs, and those whom we take will be the pioneers of civilisation, to whom we shall show the way. Will you go to your new home?" asked Ebramar smiling, noticing the interest with which Supramati listened to him. "I have to go there and I came with the intention of inviting you, Dakhir and Narayana to accompany me."

Supramati felt invigorated as if electrified.

"Ah, what a good master you are! I dreamed of this, but I didn't dare expect so much grace!" exclaimed Supramati, squeezing his leader's hand effusively.

"I see, my dear disciple," laughed Ebramar, tapping him on the shoulder, "that though you're a mage with three torches, the 'old Adam of curiosity' is still alive in you. Look, you don't want, being a mere tourist there, to taste the apple of the 'tree of the knowledge of good and evil'."

Supramati also laughed.

"Let's tell our friends. Pack your things, go to my house, and in the evening, we'll go on an excursion."

"Packing? Are you joking, master? Do we need to take anything else but ourselves? What for?"

"I suggest that we each take a travel bag with the objects we want to keep."

The news of the journey to the place of their future activities excited Dakhir and Narayana, who quickly packed their belongings. Supramati and Dakhir picked up a large metal divination box with various souvenirs and magical gems, while the most voluminous luggage was that of Narayana. He gathered numerous jewels, true treasures of the jewellery art, and even included a bunch of splendid lace "for the ladies", which provoked general laughter. Two hours later, they all made their way to Ebramar's house, and at sundown they climbed the mountain platform from which they had set out the other day to inspect the gigantic ship destined to emigrate from the dying Earth. With the same shape but reduced in size, the spaceship floated tethered to the platform. Ebramar led his disciples in, closed the door tightly and showed them the ship. They arranged their luggage in the long but narrow side cabins of the plane's lounge. On the table in the centre of the room was a jar and a basket of small dark breads that melted in the mouth.

"Drink to the success of our journey," Ebramar suggested cheerfully, filling the cups, which the disciples drank to his health.

Then they each ate a small loaf of bread and Ebramar told them to take a seat in the lounge. Cutting the straps with an electric shock, Ebramar activated the ship's engines, which began to take off rapidly.

"Now, sit still while I drive," said Ebramar.

The friends leaned quietly against the back of their seats and immediately fell into a heavy sleep. The cheerful and sonorous voice of their master finally woke them up:

Get up, sleepyheads! You've been snoring for ten days and I think you've had enough.

Surprised and embarrassed, the friends got up.

"My God, why did you leave us sleeping so shamelessly, master?" Supramati reproached him.

"It was better that way, calm down. I was only joking and it's not your fault that you slept so deeply," replied Ebramar. "I admit, I made you sleep on purpose, because it's my first trip there and I was afraid that with your chattering you would disturb me to keep the desired course. However, we're getting closer to our goal. Come closer to the windows."

In a hurry, the three of them lowered a metal plate that concealed a thick pane of glass and peered through the window. The craft was travelling at such a breakneck speed that it was difficult to make out objects. However, their experienced eyes could make out below them an infinite surface of water, separated by immense grey regions, sometimes sectioned by gigantic mountain ranges. Gradually the speed slowed, the craft descended into a depression covered with vegetation and surrounded by high mountains. A few minutes more and the nose wheel stopped spinning, throwing sparks. Finally, the plane came to a halt with a slight jolt. Ebramar opened the door and jumped to the floor. Excitedly, the disciples followed him and, involuntarily, they all fell to their knees. After a brief but moving prayer, they respectfully kissed the ground of their new home, that virgin land entrusted to them by the will of the Eternal to introduce His laws. They found themselves on an immense plateau, surrounded on one side by high mountains and on the other by terraces descending to a plain covered with lush vegetation. From their altitude, they could look out over a fascinating panorama. An almost imperceptible strip of water could be made out on the horizon, and the dark forest mass was hidden to the sides of the valleys until it was lost from sight. The plateau itself was a cheerful oasis. A soft blue-grey moss covered the earth, like a carpet; among the ivory-white pebbles ran a crystalline spring, reverberating in sapphire tones. From the gigantic trees. Covered with lush blue-green foliage fell a pleasant shade and the canyons, the ground and the bushes, all were decorated by marvellous flowers of shapes and colours never seen before. The air was pure, transparent, saturated with oxygen and pleasant aromas; the birds sang in the foliage and the sun's rays illuminated and warmed that picture full of total placidity.

"Oh, God! How beautiful it looks here!" exclaimed Dakhir, fascinated.

"It's indeed. Here one feels the plenitude of strength and the virgin beauty of the young earth. Here is the earthly paradise, the cradle of future civilizations. Savage humanity hasn't yet found its way here and everything here is the way it was created by generous nature. And now friends, let us unpack our baggage and put it in a safe place."

They immediately took the desks, baskets and various bundles out of the ship and carried them all into a cave that Ebramar had indicated nearby. It was a large place, difficult to access, illuminated, it's not known from where, by a soft pink light that ran magically through the stalactites of the vault and walls. Next to it was a second, smaller cave, with less light, screened by amethysts set in nooks and crannies. Here they left their belongings. Supramati proposed that they all descend into the valley, which was easy enough because the place was made up of terraces, the descent was downhill, forming a giant staircase. As the mages descended, nature became increasingly lush and diversified, and to a keen and subtle eye, those natural riches were no secret. Ebramar drew the companions' attention to the abundance and diversity of precious metals, marbles and other rocks.

"See, my friends, what abundance and beauty of materials will occupy the time and minds of our future painters, instead of idleness, depravity and sacrilege. Here is with what to fill the tastes and skills."

When they reached the plain, they saw that it was an immense plateau in the centre of a great mountain range, whose summits seemed to be bristling, the richness of the vegetation was astonishing. Trees bent under the weight of unseen fruit, unfamiliar flowers emanated a dizzying scent, and everywhere among the cliffs gurgled waterfalls and fountains. Crystalline springs meandered strangely through the trees and disappeared into the distance.

"What a magical place!" Supramati remarked.

"I like it! I'll build a palace here," exclaimed Narayana, "since I have to build a nest for my future family. Ebramar has mentioned a divine dynasty in this world, so of course I'll get married and have a child. It will be a minimal reward for the work I have done to become a mage."

"You'll need a lot of time for that. But that's not the point. If you have the first torch, maybe you'll become one day even a good husband," observed Ebramar.

"Oh, that's more difficult, but you can try anyway," and Narayana grimaced. "Women are very ungrateful and demanding. Since it's Nara, Supramati is not likely to concede Olga to me. And Nara? Oh! She is a demon of jealousy."

A general guffaw, including Narayana's own, burst out at the witticism of the funniest of the mages.

"Don't worry. I'm sure that Nara won't desire the happiness of being your wife a second time," said Ebramar, when the burst of laughter was over. And he added in a serious tone: "I hope that in addition to your conjugal duties you'll take on the noble task of directing and inspiring the artists who, under your guidance, will create the new art with their masterpieces. You're sons of the people in whom the perfect art has been incarnated; therefore, to you more than to anyone else, belongs the mission of training artists and workers, especially those we bring here, taking them out of the chaos of laziness and criminality, to teach them the arts and to fill their long life with useful and noble work."

"I promise you, dear master, to devote all my efforts to this noble cause," replied Narayana, and in his beautiful black eyes an energetic flame was lighted. "Here, in some secret haven, they will probably build the first shrines."

"No doubt," Ebramar replied. "I know we're reproached for hiding the shrines and called selfish for keeping the collection of our science secret. But have we not acted rightly in concealing dangerous secrets from ordinary mortals? The lamentable and premature end of our earth, which according to occult laws should exist for two more cycles, is it not a proof that men are incapable of using wisely the elements which have fallen into their inexperienced hands? Only fools can "play" with the cosmic giants and make light of their dynamic force. Only enlightened scientists have access to the laboratory of the Eternal".

The conversation continued on the same subject, then Narayana said that he was dying of hunger and thirst and that the heat was beginning to be unbearable, Ebramar agreed and took the disciples to a unique cave with a natural door, and a window completely interwoven with climbing plants. Inside, the ceiling and walls were all white, as if covered with snow. The temperature of the room was quite refreshing. Narayana and Dakhir quickly collected the most varied fruits and Supramati with Ebramar went in search of the honey which, according to the latter's words, must be in the vicinity. In fact, shortly afterwards they brought back in a broad leaf a piece of freshly gathered honeycomb, very dense, ruby coloured, but very tasty, though distinguishable from the earthy honey. After a lively feast, the mages returned to the plateau where the ship was parked and began a conversation about the future and the work that lay ahead. At the request of the disciples, Ebramar agreed to spend the night and leave at dawn. This first night in the new home was peaceful, the air soft and fragrant, the vault of heaven glittering with thousands of stars. In this mysterious twilight the snow-covered peaks of the high mountains were vaguely visible, and in the valley lurked the sea of immense forests - the refuge of nascent peoples who slept the sleep of the profane, without having tasted the poisonous fruit of "good" and "evil".

The conversation stopped. Immersed in contemplation of the gorgeous panorama, enveloped by the immense stillness of nature, the mages reflected on the past and the future. Suddenly, sounds from the upper level reached their acute hearing. Standing up quickly, they saw how in the dark blue of the starry night a broad beam of light shone out from the background as if opening up the sky. Then the genie of the planet appeared, surrounded by beams of blinding light, and around him fluttered the pleas of spirits, the workers of space, and sounds of wonderful harmony flowed in the air. With one of his hands the genie held an incandescent cross to his chest, and in the other he held such a force of flame that it illuminated space to its utmost limits. And there, in the immeasurable depths of that exuberance of light, shone, like an infinite flame, the Supreme Sanctuary - the abode of the perfect spirits, the last refuge of spirits free from all matter. There the last doubt of the pure divine spark returning to the Father's house would be overcome.

And beside that Flaming Obstacle, the shapes of the seven mysterious guardians of the great enigma were vaguely outlined, like clouds of diamonds. The Mages prostrated themselves, devoting their whole souls to contemplate the image of celestial beauty. And as if by a breath of divine harmony, the voice of the genie was heard:

"This is your way, children of truth, and the reward for all sufferings, for all victories over the flesh. Diligent children of science, keep in your hearts an unshakeable faith, and let your minds only create light. The arcana of perfect recognition has opened the gates for you, stubborn workers, conquerors of evil, fear not, in the infinite kingdom of the Eternal, there will always be a work for every particle of your breath."

The vision faded, the blue dome closed, and the souls of the mages burned with exaltation at the unforgettable moment. Calming down a little, Supramati took Ebramar's hand and kissed it:

"O master, what you have made of us wretched and wavering creatures, and what a debt of eternal gratitude rests upon us." Ebramar drew him to himself and embraced him.

"Bring me disciples like you and your debt will be paid," he replied gravely. "And now it's time to think about our return to our poor land. "Our new leaders have blessed us for the final battle, and so onward into the light!"

An hour later, the door behind the travellers closed and the spacecraft dissipated the ripples in the atmosphere with incredible speed. The mages took their seats again, this time without sleep. The memories of a moment ago still lingered in their souls, and each plunged in without my thinking about it.

Like stills from a film, memories of every phase of Supramati's strange existence flashed before him. Surprisingly vivid, there emerged in his memory his modest residence in London, where the young dying doctor Ralf Morgan, with anguish in his heart, suffered in the face of the unknown of death. And the sudden appearance of a stranger transformed him into an Hindu prince, the immortal Supramati, who had a fateful need to witness the death of the planet. He became not only an immortal, but also an initiate, endowed with immense knowledge and power, capable of migrating, like a bird, from one planet to another. A rough stone became a precious one in Ebramar's hands. And yet, the mere thought of how much he had yet to learn, of the path he had to tread to reach the mysterious threshold, behind which lies the ultimate enigma - to be or not to be - made him sweat and he wiped his hand across his forehead.

Narayana was also deeply shocked. All that he had seen turned his passionate soul upside down. His heart was anxious to follow the path of truth and from the depths of his soul flowed a mighty impetus towards the light, which transports men to the supreme step of ecstasy, raising their will to its apogee. A flame flickered in his black eyes and a broad aura illuminated his head. In the gaze of Ebramar, who watched him, there came an expression of joy and love. Narayana was his "prodigal son" and this moment of pure ecstasy, this light on his brow was a reward for long centuries of patience and labour devoted to educate this rebellious soul.

CHAPTER XVIII

To the palace of the Holy Grail were summoned all the members of the order and never had a gathering of brothers and sisters been so numerous because now, for the last time, they would meet in that fiery refuge where so much knowledge and toil, so many moral struggles and triumphs of the spirit over the body, had been bound together. Also present were Ebramar and other members who had already reached the higher echelons of the hierarchy. The divine office was celebrated in an atmosphere of deep veneration and emotion. Everyone's eyes watered as the members, one by one, approached the chalice and received the blessing of the superior of the brotherhood. Later a meeting was held in which the final decisions were discussed and the deadline for the definitive departure was set. After lunch and a farewell tour of the Grail temple and its service areas, the brothers and sisters retired to the places they had been assigned to carry out their activity.

So Supramati returned to Czargrado, but nowhere to be seen. From the outside, the magnificent palace seemed closed and empty, but inside, the work was hard. Every evening, in the courtyard or in the palace gardens, passengers descended with pale ascetic faces and looks expressing a powerful, exalted faith. Now, beside the mage was a whole cadre of young adepts. They were Supramati's assistants who, under Nivara's direction, made rounds in a predetermined region, gathered the faithful and conveyed to them the message of the great missionary. All those who remained loyal to Christ and served God obediently came out of hiding and made their way to the palace of the Hindu prince, which served as a meeting place. As the last warriors of good closed their ranks and prepared with fasting and continual prayer for the great battle, an unheard-of bacchanalia was taking place all over the world. The transformation of barren land into lush gardens took place at incredible speed.

It seemed as if the globe had really been transformed into a paradise; the abundance of everything was so patent that it didn't correspond to the needs of the population, whose numbers had greatly diminished. Moreover, all nature took on a certain abnormal character: fruits and vegetables of immense dimensions and brighter colours than before had a sour taste; the air, though pleasant and warm, was heavy as on the eve of a storm, and humid as in a sauna. The people were afflicted with a kind of lethargy and not infrequently with drowsiness, as if they were under the influence of narcotics; for this reason, the satanic festivities were attended by less people than expected. In fact, the diabolical ignorance in the use of the strange substance was already palpable, but enraptured and blinded by success, Shelom feared nothing and amused himself with that terrible force, as with a toy. Everywhere, at his command, satanic temples were erected, orgies were organised, and, with the help of the primal essence itself, armies of worms materialised. These repugnant and dangerous beings, invoked from invisible space, took part in feasts and processions. Yet despite his triumph, Shelom wasn't happy; a secret hatred gnawed at him. He couldn't accept the loss of Iskhet, who had disappeared without a trace, and his agents couldn't find her. He was oppressed and tormented by the realisation that the Hindu had dared and succeeded in taking the woman at the very centre of his power almost out of his hands. And for some time now, another new circumstance began to irritate him. The monstrous vegetation that appeared in front of his palace the day after the distribution of the elixir of life suddenly began to wither and dry up, which made Shelom feel possessed, for he enjoyed watching the faithful being devoured by the bloodthirsty vegetation. As an experiment, he condemned some suspected anti-Satanists to this death and threw some old or sick domestic animals into it as well. Convinced of the near end of his entertainment, he decided to animate the bushes with primordial matter. But what was his surprise and astonishment when he saw that as soon as a few drops of the vital essence reached the yellowing leaves, they began to burn like a bonfire. Within minutes, all that remained of the little thorn forest was a pile of ashes, which the wind soon scattered. Shelom had no doubt that this was another of the Hindu's tricks. His hatred grew even greater, if such a thing was still possible.

One night, after a feast in a remote satanic temple, Shelom, with his sumptuous retinue, returned to the palace. Sitting on a mobile throne, surrounded by a naked and dishevelled crowd singing a mind-boggling and shameless song, Shelom gazed contentedly at the bestial throng at his feet.

As they passed along a street, at the end of which the palace of Supramati was visible, the party paused in amazement, for a flash of reddish light seemed to envelop the mage's residence. Suddenly, the light thickened, rose, and in the dark blue of the sky above the palace shone a gigantic crucifix. At the sight of that invincible symbol, the Satanists were seized with terror; many fell into convulsions, others began to stampede. The porters dropped the mobile throne and fled. Only the closest and most loyal rushed to the aid of Shelom, lying on the ground. They lifted him up and carried him to the palace, while the crowd, with barely contained hatred, tried to disperse quickly, each one hiding like a dog in his den. It would be impossible to describe Shelom's fury. Foaming at the mouth, shaking his clenched fists, he roared that he would take his revenge and prove, once again, to the accursed Hindu that he would be condemned for having provoked Shelom Iezodot.

Meanwhile. At the scene of the event, as soon as the crowd had dispersed, the palace doors were thrown open and a procession came out. In a tight line came the men dressed in white, carrying crucifixes and lighted candles. Banners, tributes and saved icons, much venerated. Behind the men came the women, also in white, with long veils and candles in their hands. In front of them, carrying the banner with the image of the Blessed Virgin, was a young woman of angelic beauty. Clouds of incense ascended and the air was filled with a powerful and melodious hymn. The procession headed straight for the great city square, and from there, larger and smaller groups broke away from the main mass and made their way to the less important streets and squares, including the square in front of Shelom's palace. Speechless with astonishment, the remnants of the crowd and the few people standing on the street looked on in terror at these stern-faced people whose eyes were ablaze with exalted faith. Wherever the procession passed, altars were raised, crosses and icons of the Saviour were placed, and when, with the rising of the sun, pedestrians began to appear, pausing in curiosity and surprise, the preaching began. With the strength suggested by their unshakable conviction, they announced the approaching end of the world, saying that the days were numbered and that whoever didn't want to lose soul and body should reject the lord of darkness and venerate the only God, the Creator of the Universe.

In the intervals between sermons, the Gospel was read and prayers were chanted. Gradually, crowds began to gather at these altars. Hardened and convinced unbelievers turned away laughing, offended and scornful of the antediluvian "bullies" who came to spread their "idiocy". Fortunately, in his opinion, the world had long since rid itself of such ridiculous obscurantism.

Many, however, were intrigued and listened attentively. The wretched were born and grew up without knowing God and no one ever spoke to them of the mercy of the omnipresent Father, of the abode of the soul, of the power of goodness. Certainly, there was a legend that there was a time when God and the Saints were venerated, that is, people who by their virtues and exemplary life were worthy of special graces and used them among the living to perform miraculous cures, or to give moral help and alleviate suffering. But all this, they taught, was superstition, fairy tales, to deceive the foolish and the incredulous. And then people appeared who boldly proclaimed those same old convictions and said new things. Little by little the crowd began to stir; some ran away, others drew near, like moths to the light, timidly examining the stern and sorrowful countenance of Christ or the docile image of the Blessed Virgin, who seemed to look upon them with extraordinary kindness and mercy. Horrifying shivers would run through the bodies of the listeners when an old man with eyes full of fervent and exalted conviction, or an inspired woman full of enormous faith, would say aloud:

"Abandon your houses and perishable goods; nothing belongs to you anymore, for everything will be swallowed up by the unbridled elements. Save your souls. Seek refuge at the feet of your Creator."

Many who listened seemed to pass through the magic circle that separated them from evil and lit the flame of renewal in their darkened souls; they fell to their knees or crowded around the altars, asking to be taught how to pray. It was a strange day. Processions of the faithful went through all the streets of the city with their crosses; Satanists, disgusted by the fumes of incense, fled in anger, asking for help and advice from their priests, or went to Shelom with reports.

However, no one dared to attack the adventurers; these weren't the pseudo-faithful of old, who had shamelessly made concessions, had gone into hiding, had allowed their banishment, giving way to apostates and satanists. No, these, with all their fearless faith, involuntarily suggested respect;

one felt that there was a force there, and that no hand had dared to rise against them.

Shelom was agitated and furious at the unexpected news of events, both in Czargrado and in all the regions that told of the "attack" of Christians, coming out of their shelters, flooding the cities, preaching the end of the world and repentance.

"These animals that came out of their burrows are either mad or idiots! They found the time to propagate the end of the world! Are these clowns ignorant that we have primordial matter? Or are they blind and can't see that the planet will never experience such well-being? Nature provides it with all earthly goods in profusion, the climate is magnificent, humanity enjoys perfect health, is rich, happy, and yet all this is going to come to an end? Why should it all end? This is absurd! Don't be discouraged my loyal friends, let these idiots talk nonsense. The people will judge them."

"Master, in a few short hours they got followers," observed Madim, worried.

"So what? If they cause too much disorder, we'll declare war, we'll fall upon them, and it will be a good opportunity to wipe them out once and for all. Now, when eternal life and unlimited well-being await us, peace and tranquillity are desirable, though it is useful to know the cowards who have disowned God and who will no doubt disown Lucifer. We must purge the flock of all useless sheep and let the Hindu return to their impregnable Himalayan dens. We'll leave them alone, for they're harmless to us."

"So are you ordering that these idiots be given temporary freedom of action and not be arrested?" Madim asked.

"Precisely. But at the same time order the regional governors to keep an eye on these imbeciles and make a meticulous list of all those who have corrupted and disowned us. In the meantime, we'll remain in our fortresses safe from their contagious expansions. "

"As for fluid contagions, their focus is not far from his palace," Madim mocked. "I've seen these prophets and prophetesses come here. Among them is a woman as beautiful as a dream, and she will no doubt produce a strong discomfort among our young men, who will swarm to her like flies. To tell the truth, I don't remember ever seeing such a lovely being. Can you imagine her in Iskhet's place?"

No doubt, dear Madim, when the time comes. I will make her the Queen of the Sabbat and her great physical virtues will ensure fidelity to me - replied Shelom laughingly.

A few hours later, he withdrew with his entourage to one of the satanic strongholds, calling together there the most renowned members of Luciferianism for the great challenge and discussion of a detailed plan, which he had devised for the eradication of the apostates. According to the decision of the terrible leader of Satanism, the missionaries shouldn't be obstructed in their work.

Tirelessly travelling the cities and regions, they called the people to repentance and prayer, announcing that the hours of life on earth were numbered and that only souls could be saved. Among the most fervent preachers was

Taíssa. In the largest square of the city an altar had been built, so large that it could be seen from every corner. On its steps stood the young preacher, and her eloquent and convincing words attracted many listeners. At first, men were attracted by the rare beauty of the young woman, to which was added her melodious voice and clear, an innocent gaze; from her very beauty emanated a purity so powerful and clear that it subdued animal instincts. But Taíssa spoke above all to the women, telling them of their role as wives and mothers, of the great duty and the terrible responsibility that rested upon them. Women had fallen on this great and difficult battlefield, their offences contributed greatly to the impending cataclysms, they bore much guilt for the anticipated death of the world. Woman must be the guardian of the home, the protector of the divine altar, the mother who educates her child, inculcating in it, in the path of existence, faith in God, teaching it human and civil obligations. The moment a woman neglects her role as a mother to become a concubine or even turns with unheard-of cynicism against nature, denying motherhood, she signs the death warrant of humanity, which is engulfed by physical and moral decadence. Children stand up against their parents, parents hate their children, brother pits brother against brother, enmity takes the place of love. And just as woman repels the cradle, so she tears down the altar of the home and neglects the nuptial sacrament, which she has always distinguished from concubinage. And husbands become lovers, mother and wife - bacchante, priestess of voluptuousness. Oh, terrible is the crime of the woman who, instead of using her influence to elevate and ennoble the man, perverts him and transforms him into an animal.

Taíssa often described the images of the past, when under the protection of the cross the families flourished, geniuses and folk heroes grew up. She recalled the times of old, when divine laws curbed human passions, when moving festivals, such as Christmas and Easter, brought people together in prayer and awakened in their hearts feelings of piety, humility and brotherly love. Today, by contrast, the world is dominated by crime, violence and debauchery, broken laws no longer protect anything and everyone is at the mercy of the strongest? These speeches made a deep impression. Many men and women began to blush at their shameless nakedness, began to wear white robes with a red cross on their chests, came to pray before the altars and begged the missionaries to lead them to God. It was strange to see how, after fervent prayer and the sprinkling of holy water, the people were totally transformed; something gentle and humble emanated from them and in their enlightened eyes no longer burned the flame of animosity, greed and animalistic aspirations. Often a deep irritation arose in the hearts of the listeners, which expressed itself in talk and cries: "Lucifer, away! The antichrist Shelom Iezodot is gone!" And the angry crowd gathered menacingly in front of Shelom's palace, shouting: "Give us back our ancient belief in a just and merciful God, who had commanded everyone to love his neighbour and to forgive offences, to repay evil with good! Give us back the familiar joys and laws of our ancestors.

The same intense activity was developing in Moscow, once the heart of Holy Russia. Dakhir worked with his characteristic calmness, ehile Narayana was overflowing with work, in keeping with his enthusiastic nature. Dakhir preached, promoted cures, purified and soon acquired a mysterious aura that inspired a mixture of respect, gratitude and superstitious awe. Narayana was present in everything and under his guidance, the servants of the destroyed churches left their secret shelters and, together with other faithful, occupied the most important places. Their numbers were limited, but their faith was immense. Calm and fearless, they took possession of the abandoned temples, turned into museums or desecrated by Satanists, and purified them. Altars were raised and crosses set up, candles and lamps were lit. Under long-silenced vaults sacred chants were heard and clouds of incense ascended. Narayana preached his eloquent discourse in the squares and his surprisingly charming personality attracted huge crowds. The people, astonished, captivated and convinced by him, followed him to the church and the echoes of the past were awakened in their souls. Under the ancient vaults of the temples the invocative outpourings of the high prayers were engraved in the course of centuries, and like a harp of Zodo, which waits only for a breath of wind to sound, so began to speak the darkened soul of the unfortunate people, once so strong in faith, from whom all earthly and spiritual goods, including their understanding of God, were taken away, systematically corrupted by filthy and amoral literature. The preaching places and churches were, as we have said, crowded with people. Atavism awakened the past, sweeping away atheism and sacrilege like a mighty wave and installing new hopes in souls. Filled with faith, love and commotion they beheld the images of Christ, the Blessed Virgin, the patron saints, whom they had venerated for centuries, and the mighty guardians of Holy Russia weren't deaf to the frightened cry of their people, to their deep and sincere repentance; when from throbbing and vulnerable hearts the plea was heard: God have mercy on us and do not abandon us execrated! Out of the ether came streams of fire and light that illuminated the prostrate multitude and swept away the sordidness that brought the crimes and obscenities.

Just as before, on the first mission, God's wrath had not yet been unleashed. Dakhir had found support and cooperation in his faithful companion Edith. She was now guided not only by love, but also by knowledge, acquired through tenacious work and an ardent will to rise to the rank of the great mage that destiny had reserved as her husband. She went to live with her daughter in Moscow, and assumed the responsibility of seeing to the purification and religious education of women who, returning to God, were to prepare themselves for the trial of martyrdom. The new converts were certainly unaware that this terrible ordeal, bravely endured, would enable them to leave the planet sentenced to death, and so, those whom she judged unfit for so exalted a feat, she tried to convince that they must not touch the elixir of life, distributed by the generous hand of Shelom, for it would only increase their sufferings at the great final moment. Also, she clung to Iskhet in a special way. This young creature, perverted since the birth and miraculously plucked from hell, inspired in her a deep attachment. With patience and love, Edith guided and taught Iskhet, marvelling at how she, transformed into Maria, shook off all impurities, blossoming like a flower taken from a dark cave and placed in the sun. It wasn't too difficult to guess that at the bottom of this metamorphosis was hidden a deep love for Supramati, but a purely earthly feeling could only aggravate the young girl's ordeal. Edith tried by all means to ennoble her, trying to impress upon her the idea that any carnal feeling would drive her away from the mage with an insurmountable precipice, and that only by virtues, by the performance of her duty, and by a useful and pure life, could she prove to Supramati her love and recognition; her efforts weren't in vain. As Maria began to understand herself and Supramati, carnal passion gave way to an adoration of the superior being who had brought her out of the abyss.

Cases of conversion became more frequent. The powerful and exalted faith of old, with ever-increasing strength, awoke in human hearts. People abandoned their work and their affairs, substituting places of pleasure for the church. Such an event caused immense unrest. At all levels of society, people spoke only about the end of the world, desperately searching the earth and the sky for evidence of the terrible catastrophe, but nothing was to be seen. The sun's rays flooded the planet, everything was blooming magnificently, and in the midst of this restless society angry voices began to be heard, demanding the banishment of the "half-wits" who had come from who knows where and were confusing the people, restoring the old "obscurantism" and the old foolish superstitions; others merely laughed, saying that when individual liberty and freedom of thought reign, people should not be forbidden to be fools, if that is to their liking. However, astronomers began to notice some apprehension at the observatories. the apparatus indicated that a broad band of faint smoke began to form near the globe and gradually increased, forming a gaseous envelope around the planet, invisible to the naked eye, but making it difficult to observe the stellar firmament. At the same time, it was observed that igneous sparkles sometimes appeared in this haze, moving like zigzagging rays or coiling in spirals and disappearing into space. The causes of these strange phenomena remained unexplained, and the facts were not publicised, for fear of worrying the population with the missionaries' prophecies of the end of the world. At the Moscow observatory there was a young astronomer surnamed Kalitin, famous for some surprising discoveries. He was very impressed by the phenomena mentioned; moved by scientific interest, he began to perfect an instrument he had invented, which he kept secret from everyone. When at last he used his device, a combination of telescope and microscope, he was astonished, and for the first time in his life he felt a superstitious fear. The whole atmosphere was a faint igneous lattice, trembling and shaking as if driven by the wind, and between the great links of this strange lattice hovered dark clouds, whose outlines, though not sharp, resembled the fantastic figures of demons as they were represented in antiquity. The number of these magical creatures flying in all directions was legion. Convinced that he wasn't dreaming and that something strange and sinister was indeed happening in visible space, the scientist thought long and hard and decided to go to the Hindu prince who was openly announcing the end of the planet. If anyone in the world would know the truth, it was him.

Dakhir returned from the city in the evening and was getting changed for dinner with his friends, when Niebo announced the arrival of the scientist, whose name was known to be a person of great scientific merit. Dakhir ordered him to be introduced. The astronomer was a young, slim man of medium height, with a pleasant, serious face and a broad, thinking forehead. To the discerning eye of a mage, one glance was enough to understand that he was an honest person, much less depraved than his compatriots, and that he had in fact devoted his strength and his life to the pursuit of science. The only thing missing in his work was the living spark: faith.

"What can I do for you, sir? - Dakhir asked, pointing to a chair near the visitor."

"Prince, I came to ask you to answer a very important question. Please forgive my presumption, but... Strange things are happening in the streets and, apparently, also in the sky. They say that you're initiated into higher magic and openly announce the end of the world. So I ask you to tell me frankly if we are on the eve of a catastrophe. The end of the world was predicted a long time ago, but nobody knows the exact date. If you know more, tell me. If the catastrophe is partial, there may be a way to avoid it and save ourselves. It would certainly be unpleasant to have to put aside the most interesting research I'm doing. But it did come to my mind: could Shelom's dementia have affected some unknown force, unleashing the fire of atmospheric gases, leading to an inevitable catastrophe? This enigmatic personality calls himself the son of Satan, in whom I don't believe. I'm convinced that there are laws with which we must deal carefully, and, Shelom, being a vain illiterate, may have upset their balance."

Dakhir stared at the scientist's intelligent face and replied seriously:

"You're right, Professor. The phenomena you have observed, the gaseous envelope, the fiery flashes and the legions of dark creatures, are preludes of a final and not a partial catastrophe. We're on the eve of the end of the world and this is inevitable in view of the present state of cosmic forces. It's a great pity that the planet, which should continue to exist for a long time to come, serving as a school for the perfecting of an infinite number of generations, should come to such a horrible end as a result of unprecedented abuses, but... there's nothing we can do about it."

The scientist looked pale.

"Prince, you say the situation is serious and unavoidable and yet you remain calm?"

"And why shouldn't it be? We have long been preparing for this great moment, while humanity, in its vain blindness, dances on the edge of the abyss, unheeding the prophets and even the warnings of nature. And you scientists, also proud of your immediate knowledge, haven't been able to foresee the catastrophe, nor to understand that you are mere atoms in comparison with the great forces of the Universe, and that, for the balance of the world, a handful of grains of good is necessary to oppose evil. That balance has been broken and the unbridled and devastating elements will descend upon the globe, bringing about its end."

As if suffering from vertigo, the astronomer involuntarily clung to the arm of the armchair; but his weakness lasted less than a second and he got up calmly.

"I'm firmly convinced and I read in your eyes that you and other Himalayan inmates won't perish, preparing for you a means of salvation. Save me too. I'm a good person and can still be useful."

"Do you think it's that easy?" Dakhir asked, smiling. "Where we're going, we'll need humble people who believe in God."

"A true scientist is always ready to give up his misunderstandings when he understands them. Tell me the conditions of salvation, prove to me that I, beyond matter, possess an immortal soul, convince me that I'm but an innocent student on the ladder of knowledge, and I'll humbly renounce my misunderstandings and surrender to the supreme science."

"Do you want to know if you have a soul? Or, on the contrary, do spirits exist? Who do you think are the dark beings you invoke in your satanic temples?"

"I'm not a Satanist, I'm indifferent. As to the beings of which you speak, I consider them to be the animated thoughts of the invokers, because various experiences have shown that human thought creates living forms. For example: a poet creates the heroes of his poem or an artist the figures of his painting, animated by the concentration of his thoughts, giving them a real life, however temporary. It's quite natural for demon summoners to create demons, and as the quantity of human thoughts is immeasurable, space is full of different personalities that we can see and invoke but cannot verify their temporary existence."

"I'll give you the proof you desire," said Dakhir, rising and laying his hand on his visitor's shoulder. - In these great days, when the agony of the world begins, a pure and bold intelligence has a right to be convinced of the truth. Follow me to my laboratory."

Near an open window was a device unknown to the scientist. Dakhir placed the visitor in front of the device, told him to close his eye to the circular hole, which was closed by a blade, and then covered his head with a dark cloth. Pressing some springs, he pressed several electrical buttons. Shortly afterwards, under the moving cloth, a muffled scream was heard.

"Don't move, said Dakhir authoritatively."

Fifteen minutes later, the professor's head appeared under the cloth. He was livid as a cadaver and leaned against the wall to keep from falling.

"My God!" he murmured "The atmosphere is decomposing. I don't understand the elements unknown to me that appear there. So this is the real visible world. I couldn't imagine anything like that." he added a little later, closing his eyes and holding his head in his hands.

"You see, Professor," smiled Dakhir enigmatically, "our knowledge is superior to yours and we have more sophisticated equipment. But don't be disappointed, on the infinite ladder of knowledge we're also ignorant. Only in one sense are we superior to you. It's that we're aware of our insignificance and don't dismiss anything thoughtlessly, that is, we don't shout that such a thing is impossible just because we don't understand it. Now come, I'll show you that you have more than matter."

He led the professor to a large wall device, put his hand on his head and began to utter formulas in an unknown language in a half-voice. As he spoke, a reddish mist began to appear and concentrate on the scientist's chest and head. Then the red mist slid to one side, and was about a metre away, attached to the body by a luminous red band. Soon after, the misty mass thickened, widened and took on the exact shape of the professor, the only difference being that the astral figure seemed more alive, while the blue, glassy-eyed body looked like a corpse. Placing his hands on the shoulders of both figures, Dakhir said:

"You see, you're but a piece of matter; that, on the left side, is your fleshly sheath, temporarily abandoned by the vital principle, having acquired the form of a corpse; the double of the body is your individuality, that which thinks, works, and is the astral body. And there, in your double of ether, that bluish something with golden tints of flame, that which stirs between the heart and the brain, is your soul, an indestructible spark, obscured as yet by many imperfect fluids, but which by work and trials can be purified. The day will come when the pure divine flame, freed from all material bonds, will present itself before the altar of the Creator."

"You see professor, you're a great work of art from the hands of the Creator, the infinitely kind Father, who gave you a particle of his divine breath and gave you the opportunity to understand and realise everything."

Dakhir withdrew his hand and the astral double re-entered his body with lightning speed, but the professor had probably suffered from vertigo, for he staggered and would have fallen had he not been supported by Dakhir, who helped him to sit up in the armchair. A minute later, he straightened his body and muttered, clutching his head in his hands:

"In this minute I learned more than during all those years of hard work in the dark."

"Yes," replied Dakhir, "all those who work in darkness don't want to know that the focus of light is so close to them. It is within ourselves, we only have to want to invoke it. The inner flame must be ignited through contemplation and reflective work. It will illuminate our aura and tell us what we do not know. All the riches of knowledge are within us, if we want to use them. All the springs of intellectual work are to be found in our nervous system. We only have to know how to control these complex mechanisms."

"I want to study all this!" exclaimed the professor enthusiastically, rising to his feet. But suddenly he lowered his head and added in a sad tone: "But, maybe, it's too late to begin. The end is near, and I shall die forgetting this great moment; when the true light illuminates the darkness of my researches, I'll perish like a blind man, a rough atom who considers himself 'great' and was unable to comprehend the gigantic forces around him. Only one thing won't be denied me: before I die, tell me who you're, teach me to worship the one you worship. And who disposes the destinies of mankind?"

"Your question is a good and wise one," Dakhir replied, smiling. "Who am I? I'm the prophet of the end times.

Now look" he stepped back and was suddenly illuminated by a kind of stream of light, which seemed to radiate from his head and body. Enveloped in a bluish aura. As if transformed into a glowing vision, crowned by three beams of light, Dakhir stood before the astonished professor. "You have before you a mere mortal who, through work, has acquired astral strength. Anyone who's willing to exert himself can attain a similar state, concentrate in himself the flame of the ether and use it intelligently. And this is the one I revere," he raised his hand with an authoritative gesture and uttered a few words in a strange tongue. At the same instant a golden chalice with a cross topped by a crown of thorns lit up in the air. - It's faith in the enigmatic symbol of eternity, whose centre is God, the indescribable and inconceivable Being, whose idea shines in the whole universe created by Him. The crown of thorns are the sufferings through which the soul purifies itself and rises up the steps of infinite perfection. In the great effort of this ascent nothing is lost, nothing is useless, everything serves the spiritualisation and salvaion of our brothers and sisters for humanity."

As if moved by a higher power, the scientist fell to his knees and, for the first time in his life, his lips uttered, in a rush of faith and emotion

"Forgive me, heavenly Father, and have mercy on me."

As soon as he stood up, the vision disappeared, as well as the mage, and before him stood Dakhir, in his social robes with which he was known. The professor looked at him with a mixture of fear and curiosity, and gasped:

"I don't understand what has happened to me! It seems that a heavy burden has fallen from my shoulders and my brain works with incredible speed, my thoughts fly by, one after the other, with a speed and ease never before experienced; while before I used to work with great effort."

"You got rid of the prejudiced denial, the disbelief and the preconceived idea that hid the invisible from you, enslaving your thoughts."

"I've ceased to be an unbeliever and I want to work with my eyes open. How can I follow you?"

"To follow me it's necessary to die voluntarily and then be resurrected." Dakhir commented with a smile, casting a scrutinising glance at the master.

"I'm confused about the meaning of your words," replied the scientist, shaking his head sadly. - However, my faith is so strong that I accept, without question, whatever you tell me to do. I won't go back to the observatory, because now I know that I' am ignorant and that future work is useless in view of the coming catastrophe. For the same reason, I don't have to concern myself with the salvation of earthly goods, and, that being so, I beg you to allow me to stay here to die with you."

"Sir, are you afraid to die?"

"No," replied the young scientist firmly. "Give me a poison cup and I 'll take it as proof that I'm even capable of dying to reach at least one step higher. "

"And you don't have the slightest doubt that if the planet doesn't die you'll make a useless sacrifice, depriving yourself of a life that could be long in a strong and healthy body?"

"I haven't the slightest doubt about the inevitable end of the planet and I'm fully convinced that you'll support me and help me with my spiritual state."

"No doubt," replied Dakhir, approaching a cupboard and taking out two flasks, one large and one small. Half-filling a glass bowl, he poured a few drops from the little bottle, the liquid fizzed and turned a rosy colour. "In here is death and resurrection. Whoever drinks the liquid without a hint of fear will save his soul and rise to the light instead of fading into darkness." He held out the cup to Kalitin as he looked at him, pale and concentrated.

Still, he resolutely picked up the cup and commented:

"If I remember correctly, I read somewhere that Christians, when they died, said: Lord Jesus, I place my soul in your hands."

Dakhir nodded his head. Then the professor repeated the phrase respectfully, crossed himself and, without hesitation, took the liquid in one gulp. A second later he stood, enveloped in flames that seemed to rise from his body, and then fell to the ground. Dakhir propped him up, then carried his lifeless body to the couch and carefully covered him with a red blanket.

"Brave soul, you'll go with us, because in you the principles of a mage are fused," he said, gazing fondly at the prone Kalitin.

Then, putting away the essence and the cup, Dakhir went to the hall, where a modest lunch awaited him in the company of his family and friends. Dakhir passionately loved family life with its pure and quiet joys, but during his strange existence of many centuries, absorbed in constant intellectual work, he was always alone. That is why the few years he spent with Edith in Czargrad seemed to him an oasis in the midst of the rigorous, difficult and solitary life of an ascetic. All his love was concentrated on his daughter. The child awakened in him the feelings of a mere mortal, serving him as a living link to humanity. Urjane grew slowly like all mortal children; under the shadow of the sanctuary, under the watchful eye of Ebramar and the enlightened women, this strange human flower blossomed, coming into full bloom in all its virgin beauty. Truly, Urjane was beautiful as a dream. She resembled Dakhir: she had a pale complexion and curly black hair, but the slenderness of her tall frame and her large blue eyes reminded him of his mother. Her eyes expressed a deep and dreamy contemplation, characteristic of all enigmatic beings who live somehow outside the world.

Under Edith's watchful eye, Urjane took under her care the whole house, which soon acquired a homely appearance. Narayana, who, in spite of the mage's torch, always liked to eat, once said that even a seven flamed enlightened one is a poor wretch if he has no housekeeper like her, for even a body countless times spiritualised was endowed with a stomach. Dakhir and Edith laughed heartily at the mage's original mockery, surprised that even after so many centuries of struggle and vicissitudes, her soul retained purely human traits and an inexhaustible capacity for pleasure. Satisfied with the compliment as to her culinary knowledge, Urjane, from that day on - to the amusement of her parents - devoted herself to making her own at the modest table, inventing the most delicious dishes for her friend, uncle Narayana.

When Dakhir entered the dining room, Edith had not yet arrived and the friends were sitting at the table, busy as it turned out with a very interesting conversation. Narayana was talking warmly about something, illustrating his words with drawings on a large sheet of white paper. Flushed with emotion, Urjane listened, her eyes shining with curiosity. Seeing her father, she threw herself into his arms.

"Ah, if you only knew how many interesting things your uncle told me about your past life!"

"Which ones?" Dakhir smiled.

"For example, the chariot crash in Byzantium during the war between the greens and the blues, when they won that one; then the tournament during the crusades in which he took part. God! What interesting times those were; no better than now."

"And do you regret not having lived at that time?" Dakhir asked, sitting down.

"No, uncle has promised me the same entertainment on the new planet, and as I'm very fond of his palace in the Himalayas, where I once went with mother and our master Ebramar, he has given me his word to build one just like it on the new world. Around it he wants to found a city, giving it, in my honour, the name of Urjane," concluded the young woman happily and contentedly.

"I see that Narayana's colonising and civilising activity will be useful and diverse," Dakhir observed with a slightly mocking smile, looking mischievously at his friend of centuries. With that he embarrassed him visibly, for in Narayana's large eyes shone an expression of satisfaction and embarrassment. But the conversation was interrupted by the arrival of Edith with Iskhet, Niebo and Nivara.

Supramati's secretary brought a message and told him that persecutions would probably soon resume everywhere, for in Czargrado some believers would be arrested, and Madim, at the head of a gang, would attack the young preacher Taíssa, imprisoning her in the palace of Shelom.

"You know that spirit incarnate! The master will certainly protect her, but even so, it will be a difficult and terrible ordeal that will undoubtedly cost her life," Nivara added.

Iskhet, listening attentively, reflected deeply and, standing up suddenly, approached Dakhir.

"Master, let me go back to Czargrado. I know every nook and cranny in the palace. I'll help the girl Nivara speaks of to escape, and also all the prisoners, under the direction of the master."

"Your desire to be useful is commendable, my daughter. But have you ever considered what dangers await you when you decide to enter Shelom's palace or the satanic temple? You may fall into the hands of the wretches again," Dakhir commented, looking at her scrutinisingly."

"I hope my knowledge of the place will save me but, even if Shelom catches me, only my body will be tortured, for my soul has already been freed from him for ever. I fear neither death nor torture, the more so as my sufferings would be just and a deserved expiation for former offences," she redressed herself, and in her beautiful black eyes shone an energetic and exalted flame.

They all looked at her with affection and Dakhir put his hand on her bowed head.

"Make it as you wish. Nivara will leave you in Czargrado. Supramati's house will serve as your safe haven and you'll act on his advice."

Iskhet seemed satisfied with the authorisation, and a few hours later Nivara's plane was taking her out of Moscow.

CHAPTER XIX

As already described, Shelom Iezodot took refuge with his accomplices in a satanic stronghold. There they lived a life of orgies. Every day news came from all sides about the successes of the Christians and the alarming increase in the number of deserters, but Shelom took it all in jest, responding with contempt to the remarks of his advisors and friends.

"Let them! The more deserters, the better chance we have of wiping them out at once. You know our Lord likes the smell of blood and charred flesh. The screams and groans of these scoundrels, who will pay for all their slander with their own skin, will be pleasant music to his ears."

The invocation of the powerful demon seemed to confirm Shelom's opinion. The spirit of darkness gave an evasive answer and the leader of the Satanists continued his debauched life. Meanwhile, the disorder among the people increased to such an extent, and the casualties of the Satanists' party were of such magnitude. That at last Shelom became alarmed and considered that the time had come for energetic action. He began with the solemn invocation of Lucifer and assumed the role of high priest in the satanic cult celebration. The prince of hell came to the call and when questioned by Shelom to indicate to his faithful servants the programme of actions, he responded with a biting laugh, echoed by thousands of voices, Shelom shuddered without understanding. Why this laughter from the terrible leader of the dark forces? Was it happiness or mockery? When the funeral merriment ceased, the devil commanded that his be followed in the great squares of every city, and before every image of him a bonfire was to be lit and all who refused to bring sacrifices and worship Satan were to be burned. The sacrifices were to be repeated three times a day, and once this was done, Lucifer would agree to support his loyal followers. Shelom decided to act immediately and, on the spot, headed for Czargrado with his entire court. A dispatch was sent to each regional ruler with the express order to begin, without delay, the persecution of the faithful at the behest of Lucifer himself.

All night long a great commotion reigned in all the satanic temples, and at dawn a very convincing caravan departed from Shelom's palace. A statue of Satan was solemnly carried, and at the head of the procession was Shelom surrounded by councillors and chief priests of the satanic temples. By the time the procession reached the main square, it was already crowded. Around the altar, raised and decorated with a cross, there was a large crowd of kneeling women, men and children. All had already covered their nakedness with white robes and, with tears in their eyes, were listening to the preaching of a woman who was standing on a step to be seen better.

It was Taíssa, who attracted the masses with her captivating words and her ardent faith. The young woman's fascinating beauty was further accentuated at that moment, when her soul flickered outwardly in a harmonious voice and an inspired gaze. The soft folds of the white robe contoured her slender figure and, in the heat of preaching, the veil that covered her head had fallen from her shoulders and the immense hair enveloped her like a golden aura. Shelom stopped motionless and his lustful eyes fixed on the young preacher, who seemed to float, like a radiant vision, above the crowd.

"Madim" he murmured, squeezing his accomplice's hand, "This is the woman I want to possess. If you have a love of life, arrest her and bring her to me."

"We'll do your bidding," Madim replied with a cynical smile. "It was her I told you about that time, telling you that she might well deserve to replace Iskhet. Isn't that right? Ha ha!"

"I don't know if she'll replace Iskhet, but she'll be mine and she'll die in my caress, that's for sure!" Shelom replied, continuing on his way.

Those present in the square panicked at the appearance of the satanic procession. Shouting and jostling, the crowd dispersed around corners. Only a part of the crowd was spared, the rest were repelled by Lucifer's followers, who occupied all the adjacent streets. The cross was immediately knocked down and the statue of the spirit of darkness was placed on the altar table, before which the Satanists began to build a huge bonfire. In the midst of the uproar, Madim, assisted by some men, seized Taíssa, who was bound and taken to Shelom's palace. But the young preacher was too well known and loved for her disappearance to pass unnoticed. The news soon reached Nivara, who, concerned, rushed to Supramati. Supramati listened calmly.

My loyal friend, you're concerned about the news that she's in Shelom's possession, for you know the secret that binds me to her. You know that Taíssa is Olga. Rest assured, I'll certainly protect her with my astral force; moreover, her own faith will serve as a shield, and Shelom will never succeed in tarnishing it. And if he condemns you to death, that will be the great test of martyrdom you need to rise to me. I have no power to deliver her from it, but her love is so strong, her spirit so mighty, that she'll scarcely feel the horror of death.

Taíssa was locked in one of the underground rooms of Shelom's palace. It was a round room, furnished in gloomy luxury, for the curtains, tapestry, and furniture were all black. The lamp on the ceiling gave out a light as red as blood. The young prisoner had been thrown, tightly bound, on a broad black suede couch, and was without a crucifix and without clothes. Against that black background, her white and virginal body looked like a marble statue, her golden, wavy hair was strewn across the mosaic floor. Shame and fear gripped her heart, but praying fervently, she repeated with faith and emotion: "God, Almighty, protector of the weak and innocent, keep me, save me from the violence of the impure, do not allow me to defile myself! Let me die glorifying Your Most Holy Name". Sometimes he shivered as if he had a fever because of the subterranean cold and the toxic air.

Suddenly there was a noise, followed by a slight tinkling sound similar to that of a bell; her face felt a breath of warm, aromatic air. Minutes later, invisible hands cut the ropes that bound her, wiped her face with a damp, fragrant cloth and dressed her in a fine linen robe. Taíssa stood up, looking both delighted and startled, at a white cloud that hovered before her, rapidly thickening. Tall and slender, a man in white whom Taíssa immediately recognised Supramati and fell to his knees.

"Master! You have come to set me free!" he murmured, holding out his hands.

"No, not to free you, my daughter, but to comfort and encourage you. Here is the cross in place of the one taken from you. Take this cup of wine, a piece of bread and a cup of holy water. These provisions you'll receive from me daily. Don't touch anything here, any food contaminated by satanic breath," he put his hand on her head and she felt all his power permeated by a current of beneficent warmth. "Now I can leave you, my child. You're ready. Be brave and firm: the time of reward is at hand."

A bluish cloud enveloped the mage's figure and he disappeared. Taíssa drank the wine, ate the bread and felt stronger. Then she knelt in the same place where Supramati had appeared and where a bluish light still seemed to shine. Immersed in ardent prayers, she didn't feel the passage of time and only the sudden sound of the clock striking midnight brought her out of her reverie. A sudden anguish seized Taíssa. From all sides of the dimly lit room there was a strange noise, sounds of clawing, gasping breaths. When she decided to look around she shuddered with terror, from every dark corner creeping towards her were creepy beings, half-man, half-animal that she had never seen before. Their cadaverous faces, disfigured by all manner of passions, were hideous. Burning eyes bore into Taíssa, and claw-like hands reached out to her in an attempt to grab her. She turned back to the wall, where the image of a radiant cross had just been drawn, and leaned back, clutching the glowing crucifix, held to her chest by the mage. The disgusting filth receded. The stench that pervaded the underground made her chest tight and dizzy, yet Taíssa wasn't discouraged and prayed with all her fervour. After perhaps an hour, the door in front of her opened silently and Shelom appeared on the threshold, who stood motionless for about a minute, devoured the young woman with his eyes. Closing the door behind him, he approached and said in a mocking voice:

Let go of that cross, Taíssa. It prevents me from coming closer. I haven't come as an enemy; I love you as I have never loved a woman and you'll be mine, because this is my destiny and no one has ever managed to oppose it. I wouldn't want to resort to violence. You have my love at your fingertips. I offer you all earthly pleasures and riches. Share with me the throne of the world. And now, I repeat, let go of this cross that prevents me from clasping you to my heart. Mad with passion.

Taíssa answered nothing and falling to her knees and raising the cross as a shield, she continued to pray. Shelom was possessed. The blue radiation emitted by the cross caused unbearable pain throughout his body, but his animal passion was stronger than the pain. With increasing fury, he again demanded that Taíssa let go of the cross. As she remained silent, he pulled out a knife and prepared to rush at her to tear the hated symbol from her hands, at the risk of hurting her.

But the dagger suddenly flew to the ground, wrenched by an invisible force, and Shelom fell. Mad with rage, he sprang to his feet and began a repulsive scene. The monster threw himself at Taíssa, trying to grab her, and just as he thought he was about to overpower his victim, his hands touching the linen robe, an invisible obstacle appeared between them, pushing and pulling him to the ground. He turned round and convulsing, foaming at the mouth, he shouted terrible insults, calling for the help of the demons. they came, glowing yellow, red and green, but disappeared immediately. At last, totally exhausted by this unprecedented struggle, Shelom crawled to the exit, where his lackeys lifted him up, carried him to his chambers and he slept.

When she was alone, Taíssa thanked God, who had miraculously saved her from the hands of the devil, and sat down exhausted on the sofa. At the same moment a light shadow appeared before her, and a remote voice said:

Sleep without fear - you're being watched!

Filled with faith and gratitude, Taíssa settled down on the sofa and fell into a deep sleep. When she awoke, she saw the promised cup of wine and piece of bread on the table. Time passed slowly. Taíssa heard the clock ticking, but couldn't tell whether it was day or night. No one came, and no noise broke the prevailing silence. Suddenly, near the niche next to her, there was the creak of a spring and a dark figure in a cloak appeared. Uncovering herself, Taíssa recognised Iskhet.

"Hurry up! Take this cloak and follow me. I've come to set you free and I'm going to take you out of here by a secret way," she said hurriedly.

"Sister Maria, did you have the courage to come here, to the lion's mouth? If he finds you, you'll pay with your life."

"I don't fear death, and as the end of the world is near, I'll have to die anyway. Martyrdom will save my soul, and you'll pray for me, for you're immaculate and the fetid breath of the damned won't touch you. Quickly! Come on!"

She wrapped Taíssa in a dark cloak, covered her head with a hood, and when they were both near the niche, the door suddenly opened, and Shelom entered, accompanied by some people.

"Look, there are two mice instead of one!" he exclaimed. Suddenly, he stood next to the women and tore off the cloak of one of them. Taíssa ran to the wall where the glowing cross appeared again.

"Iskhet?" he let out a sarcastic laugh. "Well, I hadn't given up hope of finding you, my lovely wife, and I caught you here red-handed, just as you were about to kidnap my celestial dove! Ha ha ha ha! Isn't that jealousy, beautiful, Sabbath Rain? Anyway, your new faith has made you even more beautiful, and I swear by Satan it's worth taking you back to convert you to your old belief."

Taíssa shuddered, feeling a hellish anger echo in Shelom's voice and gleam in his eyes. What will happen to her, wretched woman who risked her life and freedom to save it? However, the old Iskhet wasn't intimidated at all. She was truly beautiful now and glowed with an entirely different beauty. The acquired purity and harmony transformed her features and her pale, thin face became spiritualised. She wore an ordinary robe, her hair was braided thickly, and she appeared taller and slimmer than before. With Shelom's speech. His large black eyes flashed, sizing up his terrible enemy with a look of contempt, he pressed the cross to his chest and said in a low voice:

"You're wrong, Shelom Iezodot! You'll never catch me, because you no longer have power over me and hell is no longer of any importance. At most you can take my life, for my soul belongs to God."

"Only life! However, my dear, there are many methods of taking a life, and among them. There are most unpleasant ones, such as being burned alive," laughed Shelom with a wicked laugh. "For the moment we'll put her in a safe place and see if hunger, thirst and other delights don't make her more sensible. Fortunately, there's no shortage of deterrents and they break people much stronger than you," he added with contempt, signalling for two men to take her away."

Iskhet stepped back quickly and raised the cross above his head.

"I'll go alone, don't touch me!" she said and approaching Taíssa, she kissed her and whispered in her ear:

"Be strong, Maria, we'll support you!"

Iskhet said goodbye and hurried off in the company of two Luciferians. Shelom and Taíssa were left alone.

This time the terrible sorcerer appeared armed with all his black science. Without approaching it, he surrounded it with small candelabras, on which in a short time herbs and powders began to burn and spread suffocating odours. At the same time, he began to utter invocations, and at his call, disgusting beings emerged from space, forming a semicircle, slowly but steadily approaching Taíssa. They screamed and writhed before the glowing cross, as if being whipped, but kept crawling forward. Taíssa's heart almost broke with fear, but she faced the fear bravely and her faith didn't weaken. Only when the fearsome faces of the demons drew near and the clawed hands were about to seize her, did she suddenly think of Supramati and a passionate appeal burst from her lips.

"Master, come and help me!"

At the same instant, a clear cloud arose from the ether, enveloping the young woman in a kind of transparent globule, and the infernal horde, thrown back as if by a mighty blast of events, gathered roaring behind Shelom. He waved his magic sword unnecessarily, drew signs and uttered powerful formulas. Sparks from his sword ricocheted off the incandescent globule, as if it were bronze, and some of them struck Shelom himself, causing burns and painful wounds. Such resistance, coupled with the defeat of his magical strength. It enraged him and wounded his self-respect. Roaring like a beast and foaming at the mouth, all bloody, he lunged desperately at the luminescent globule, but collided with the intangible barrier and crashed convulsively to the ground. When he got up a while later, pale as a corpse and shaking with his whole body, he made for the exit and, stopping at the door, turned back, shaking his clenched fists, shouting hoarsely:

Sordid creature, plaything of the accursed Hindu, you lose nothing by waiting! I'll have my revenge and devise a death that will make hell tremble!

Iskhet was also locked in an underground cell, but it was empty. A pile of straw served as her bed and in the middle of the room was a stone table, filled with plates of food, baskets and bottles of wine. Despite her hunger and thirst, the young woman didn't touch any of the food, convinced that it was all contaminated with dangerous drugs that could even kill her. Terrible hunger and thirst began to torment her at the sight of the prepared food and aromatic wine. But Iskhet resisted valiantly, desperately trying to find support in prayer. In the absence of a watch and due to the semi-darkness of the atmosphere, she couldn't realise how long she had been imprisoned, but, feeling weakened, she lay down and closed her eyes, trying to concentrate to continue the prayer, asking for death as a form of deliverance. Suddenly, she heard a slight noise and a familiar voice calling out to her.

"Sister Maria!"

Standing up quickly and dumb with surprise, she saw Nivara, the kind and courageous disciple of Supramati, standing before her with a basket in his hands, smiling.

"Here are the provisions, Sister Maria. Strengthen yourself and hide the leftovers. Have faith, hope and pray. We're thinking of you and soon you'll be free," she said affectionately, disappearing just as she had appeared.

Throughout the towns and villages, a veritable hunt for the faithful was instituted. Armed bands searched the streets and highways, rounding up those deemed "converts", taking them to prisons and then to Satan's sacrifice. Wherever shocking scenes took place, screams and groans hung in the air. People were tortured and killed in prisons and before bonfires to force the unfortunate to bring sacrifices to the devil. As the flesh is weak, only very strong spirits faced death calmly and fearlessly, resisting the tortures with the heroism of martyrs. Humanity seemed to have gone mad; the streets looked like battlefields, time seemed to turn back, and Shelom's executioners could have given lessons in cruelty to the executioners of Diocletian or Nero. Even archaic methods of torture resurfaced; men and women, maddened by so much suffering, howled under the lashes and iron tongs, cursing demons and crying out desperately for God and Christ. Some faltered and ended up bringing sacrifices to Satan, others stood their ground, and when, as evening fell, a huge bonfire was lit, they were dragged to it under the wild cheers and shouts of the bestified crowd. Among the not many who went quietly and with unwavering faith to the stake, there was always a priest, and when the damned, their eyes shining with exultation, fell on their knees and on all sides the fire began to crackle, the incognito priests offered them a large cup and made them take a sip of the incandescent liquid.

The clouds of smoke concealed from the spectators what was to follow. Only a strange fact, which nevertheless recurred daily, began to provoke disquiet and curiosity. Every time a fire was lit, a storm broke out, thunder rumbled, the wind spread the flames and columns of thick black smoke rose into the sky, becoming a kind of wall. The fire devoured everything and no one was able to find a single bone of any martyr.

For many days now, the temperature had been increasingly unpleasant. The air was heavy, thick and saturated with a caustic aroma that made breathing difficult. No more sunlight penetrated through the grey sky and something ominous hovered in the dim gloom.

What was not the terror of all, then, when the morning didn't dawn, the clocks showed noon, and yet the darkness hadn't only not vanished, but was deepening. A black vault seemed to have descended over the earth. Not a star could be seen in the firmament. The electric lamps that illuminated the darkness flickered strangely, reverberating red, yellow or purple colours. People left their jobs and abandoned their homes. Tantalised crowds gathered in the streets, staring perplexed at the gouache-coloured sky and breathing hard in the thick, heavy air. No one had ever seen anything like it: it didn't augur well. Was this not a dire warning of the catastrophe foretold by prophets and Christians? The certainty of approaching inevitable danger made everyone's heart race with despair. Thousands of voices roared like the waves of an angry sea, and the instinct of self-preservation told the people to seek shelter wherever possible. Some ran to the astronomical observatories, others to Shelom's palace. He, the son of Satan, would be able to avoid danger. Many others went to the satanic temples, which seemed even more terrifying in their blackness in the pale gloom. Meanwhile, a large proportion of men and women rushed towards the palace of the Hindu prince, and the bewildered crowd halted in perplexity before the residence of Supramati; all the gates were wide open.

When the bravest entered the interior of the palace, they saw that the magnificent palace was empty and everything was open. In the huge hall, illuminated by a startling bluish light, was a great black cross, and on it was Christ crucified with the crown of thorns on His head. Mute with bitterness and fear, the mob gazed upon Him whom they denied, whom they reviled, whose name they reviled, whose sacred precepts they repudiated. For this was what the great Hindu left them: the image of the Redeemer, the Son of God, who, crucified, prayed for his executioners! The prince and all the inhabitants of the palace had disappeared as well as the preachers, and the altars, on which the crucifixes shone and where the incense ascended in clouds, had disappeared everywhere. With cries, groans, and sobs, the crowd fell on its knees; lost eyes sought the help of the divine being; pale and troubled faces showed dread at the imminence of the terrible moment.

In satanic temples, strange and frightening scenes took place. The assembled multitudes brought sacrifices and invoked demons, getting in response mocking laughter. Hell was filled with horrified laughter in response to this blind and criminal humanity, which was fondled and seduced and finally given in sacrifice to the cosmic forces. Meanwhile, a new phenomenon occurred in nature. The deep darkness gave way to a dark violet light, which, like a shroud, clothed the doomed Earth, its lush vegetation, its grandiose buildings and the noisy crowds that ran disorderly everywhere.

Coming to their terrible lord for help and counsel, the Satanists crowded into Shelom's palace. In front of the square, the crowd shouted wildly, demanding that the son of Satan should restore the light and purify the atmosphere. Pale and sombre, standing at the open window, Shelom gazed gloomily at the violet sky, inhaling heavily the thick air saturated with an unfamiliar caustic aroma that swirled around his head. Deciding something quickly, he turned to the trembling, pale Madim.

"Order all the remaining prisoners, including Iskhet and Taíssa, be taken immediately to the stake and announce to the people that they must all go to the place of execution. I'm going to the main temple to make a sacrifice to the father and to ask for his help and advice."

Madim ran to fulfil the order and made his pronouncement to the people. Some of those present dispersed and some went to the place where a large bonfire had been started, others went to the main temple, where Shelom was to go, but the majority didn't move and continuing with their shouting and threats.

The news that the Hindu prince had disappeared and the palace was empty spread and caused national panic. If the great mage was gone, then danger was inevitable and terrible, they said. A thousand options and suppositions were discussed as to where the Hindu might have been hiding.

An hour later, a sad procession was making its way through the streets of the city. At the head of the condemned were Iskhet and Taíssa, with crosses on their chests. As the lights had gone out in some places and it was not possible to light them, the armed men accompanying the procession carried torches, and the light they radiated also took on a strange violet hue. Imparting a sombre appearance to all the illuminated objects. The condemned came to the execution calmly and bravely, singing a sacred hymn. In the square there was a mass of people, disorderly and worried. When they reached the huge bonfire, the condemned embraced each other and began to climb, one after the other, onto the platform. When it was the turn of Taíssa and Iskhet, Madim, accompanied by some men, made way for them and told them that the Lord had ordered them to take Taíssa to the temple. Without protesting, the two embraced each other effusively and Iskhet went into the fire. In the meantime, Madim tied up Taíssa and took her away. As the flames crackled and the clouds of smoke hid the condemned from the crowd, who genuflected and continued to chant prayers, there suddenly appeared in their midst a man dressed in white, holding a golden cup in his hand. It was Nivara.

"Brothers and sisters! - he said. To save you from a torturous death in the fire, our mentors send you a drink that will take your life. He approached Iskhet and held out the cup. "Take a sip, I will hold it," said Nivara.

"Yes, my brother. As I'm the most criminal here, I ask you to give me a fraternal kiss as proof that you don't despise me. Tell the master that I thank and bless him for the salvation of my soul and I beg him not to abandon me in space."

"I promise you in his name," Nivara replied, kissing the young woman, who picked up the cup and fell to the floor with a thud.

Passing quickly through all the condemned, they drank the liquid avidly and fell dead as did Iskhet. As was often the case during mass executions, a storm then broke out, thunder rolled deafeningly without lightning and only occasional gusts of wind blew. The smoke that arose was so thick that it seemed to extinguish the fire, and behind this kind of curtain a spaceship descended upon the place. In a few moments they took away the bodies of the victims and the ship, like a bird, took off towards the heights, and then disappeared.

In Lucifer's main temple, at the foot of the gigantic statue of the king of hell stood Shelom, surrounded by satanic priests and a frightened crowd seeking help and salvation from the dark sorcerer. Shelom was preparing for a great sacrifice and all around him exhaled the foul and suffocating smell of the resinous herbs burning in the candelabra. Shelom was completely naked; his hair was tied with a red ribbon containing cabalistic inscriptions.

In one hand he held the satanic trident and in the other a long, sharp dagger. Watching the preparations, he glanced impatiently from time to time towards the door through which Taíssa was to be introduced. Not even the mortal danger threatening the earth could quell his carnal passion for the young woman, and the mere memory of his vain attempts to possess her sent shivers down his spine. In his delirium, he tried to imagine what kind of torture he could devise to make the despicable creature suffer as much as possible.

Before he was sacrificed to Satan, his blood spilling over the steps of the altar. Black candles were distributed to all present, and a wild and dissonant chant was heard under the vault with the appearance of Madim carrying Thaissa, bound, naked, and without the cross on her chest. But long flowing hair covered her nakedness like a cloak, and her head was enveloped in a broad, clear aura. The young woman was calm, her fearless gaze fixed with indifference and contempt on the servant of Evil who devoured her with eyes burning with passion.

"For the last time I ask you, stubborn creature, if you will voluntarily worship Lucifer and bring him your innocence in sacrifice." Cried Shelom in a hoarse voice.

"No. My soul belongs to God, and with my body will come to pass whatever is His holy will. Kill me quickly, antichrist, so I can no longer see this rabble around you and so that my blood can purify this impure place," Taíssa answered bravely.

"You will be mine first!" Shelom replied with a nasty laugh and threw himself at her, throwing her to the ground and then grabbing her by the hair and dragging her over to the statue.

"Jesus Christ, save me!" shouted Taíssa, and at the same instant, Shelom, as if struck by a whip, leapt backwards, releasing his victim. An angry fury seized him. His face transfigured by convulsions, his eyes bloodshot and foaming at the mouth, he threw himself upon her again.

"Shut up and die, you monster of Heaven!" Shelom roared, burying his dagger up to the hilt in the chest of the young woman, who fell without letting out a groan.

From the wound from which Shelom drew his weapon, a fountain of ruby-coloured blood gushed forth, and the spectators watched in amazement as the liquid ignited in the air like fireworks and then covered the corpse with a burning veil. At the same time, under the vaults, an astonishing spectacle took place. Taíssa floated in the air, surrounded by transparent beings who, with jets of fire, cut the last threads that bound her to matter. Then the spirits of the elements suspended the young woman and, like a cloud pushed by the wind, the dazzling vision vanished with meteoric speed, as the temple was taken over by the harmonic sounds of the chanting of the spheres, causing the satanists present to totter and groan in pain. Shelom, lying on the floor on his knees, appeared to be suffocating. When the panic ceased, all saw that only a little ash remained on Taíssa's body, which soon dispersed into the air in invisible particles, and the basalt statue of Lucifer was cracked from top to bottom.

CHAPTER XX

In the Himalayan mountains, inside Supramati's palace, the activity was intense: they were preparing for the last general fraternal banquet on the doomed Earth.

From all the sanctuaries of the world, from the caves of the Holy Grail, from the mysterious tombs of the pyramid, the children of light were gathering to take their places in the spaceships that would transport them to the field of their future activity. The gigantic and enigmatic air fleet was already in the air. The young adepts, in white robes, plucked bunches of flowers from their exuberant gardens to adorn the doors and the tables arranged in great halls and decorated with objects of unknown style, archaic monuments of the world which had also already become extinct and which had come to this now dying earth, brought by the first legislators.

The cave, where Olga's body had once been deposited, was open again. Along the path leading to it, the children of the Magi, lined up and dressed in white robes, and from inside the grotto shone rays of blinding light. The spectacle inside was admirable. All the ancient magicians were gathered there without exception, together with the Grail brotherhood; on one side were the men, on the other the women, beautiful as celestial visions. In the centre was a wide oval tank, quite deep, of a silvery metal, filled with a strange mercury-like liquid that swirled and reverberated with the colours of the rainbow. Beside the repository, on a golden disc, stood Ebramar in sacred vestments, and beside him, in a semicircle, six magicians, who, like Ebramar, were crowned with five flames of blinding light and with resplendent insignia on their chests, conferred according to their high dignity. On the steps of the niche where Olga's body lay, stood Supramati dressed as a Grail knight, and under the step, as two guards of honour, Dakhir and Narayana. They removed the quilt covering the deceased and, despite the centuries that had passed, the body had the appearance of a sleeping woman. Only the marbled pallor and a strange expression on her beautiful face indicated that it was a corpse. All was profound silence. As soon as Ebramar raised his sword, there was a majestic chant, indescribably soft. A few moments later, the sound of a thunderous roar reached them all, as if angry waves were crashing against the rocks, and under the vaults, surrounded by transparent clusters of spirits of the elements, appeared an immense flame enveloped by an enveloping mist of silver. As if drawn by a higher force, the flame concentrated on the tip of Ebramar's sword.

At the same instant, Supramati loaded Olga's body and plunged it into the reservoir. The liquid that filled it effervesced, swirled into silvery foam, and then, with extraordinary rapidity, seemed to absorb itself into the inanimate body. Ebramar lowered his sword and the churning flame disappeared into the half-open lips of the corpse. With a sparkling gaze and raising his hands, the mage uttered in an authoritative voice:

"By the power vested in me as a magician of the fifth degree, I command you, body of flesh, to join this purified and renewing flame and return to a long and glorious life, which you, soul of Olga, have earned by your aspiration to truth."

As he spoke, the young woman's body shuddered, returning from its state of lethargy, then a broad golden glow formed around her limpid head, her large eyes opened and gazed absently at those present, but, at the sight of Supramati, they kindled in infinite love. He, meanwhile, suspended her from the reservoir, lifted her to her feet and walked away, seeing the risen one surrounded by women of the Grail Sisterhood. Nara was the first to kiss her, then helped her change her old garments into a robe of shimmering cloth, as if sprinkled with sparkling dust, hung a diamond cross from her neck, surmounted by a chalice, and placed a crown of luminescent flowers on her head. As the women around her walked away. Olga, who stood alone, moved and with a crestfallen look, was truly beautiful as a heavenly vision. Her spiritual face reflected shame and happiness, her loose hair covered her as if by a golden mantle, and on her bowed head shone her martyr's crown. When Ebramar approached her smiling affably, she knelt down and, taking her hand, raised it to her lips. Ebramar hastily raised it, kissed it, saluted and blessed; then he put his hand in Supramati's and said in a metallic, sonorous voice:

"By death she was deprived of you and by death she regained you. At the cost of long efforts, of painful trials, she has reached the degree of purity which will enable her to be and to remain united with you for a long time. I give you back your faithful companion."

Olga raised her head worriedly and looked at Supramati, who answered her with a look full of deep and burning love. And when he drew her to him and kissed her, Olga's face lit up with an expression of indescribable happiness.

"Now, Olga, look here at Airavana. He wants to kiss her too," said Supramati pointing to a handsome young man who approached them admiring them happily.

"Airavana! I left him when he was very little and now our little boy is a man!" xclaimed Olga, looking at him, overcome with maternal pride and happiness. She embraced her son affectionately, covering him with kisses.

The mages smilingly admired the moving scenes. Olga had noticed them, and with hands in prayer and moved by gratitude, she said:

"Wonderful mentors! What is the meaning of the sufferings endured, of the anguish of separation, of the life full of trials and mortification of the flesh, compared with this minute of superhuman happiness, of the limpid instant of love, when all the great significance of the triumph of the spirit over the flesh is clearly felt? Glory be to the Creator, whose blessing transforms the repellent and insignificant caterpillars into resplendent butterflies, capable of understanding and loving Him."

"Any task, my daughter, carries within it a reward, and there's no purer joy than the moment of awareness of the trials endured," replied Ebramar, approaching. "And now, I greet you once more and wish you a happy entry into our brotherhood as an official member, and give you a brotherly kiss."

After kissing Supramati as well, all the assembled members approached them in a line. With special affection they embraced Nara, Edith, Dakhir and Narayana.

After the greetings, they all left the cave and made their way to the palace, where a farewell meal was prepared, the last banquet in the dying homeland from which they would part forever. The faces of all were serious and thoughtful. The tragic weight of the past and the enormity of the work they would have to do in the future were stamped on everyone's faces. At the end of the modest lunch, all the mages went out to the huge square in front of the palace, where all the faithful saved by the missionaries were gathered and taken to the site to be organised for shipment under the control of the young adepts and mages of the lower grades. Pale as corpses, in white robes, they pressed uneasily against each other. In the front row was the young astronomer converted by Dakhir. The supreme mage entered the crowd and addressed them, explaining that strong faith had saved them from death, but that they must devote their remaining life to good and useful work.

In the new earth, where you'll be humble pioneers of progress, no navigator will shake your faith with fancies and sophistry, nor will he stop you in your pursuit of purification. And now, my children, say your last prayers on earth, and we will pray with you.

All fell to their knees and the adepts sang a hymn and read a prayer, which was repeated by the crowd who wept convulsively. Blessing the prostrate crowd, the mages departed, leaving only the adepts and the disciples to control the boarding of the ships. The travellers spread out into groups. From above, aerial columns began to descend, alternately, through which the travellers ascended. Some, so frightened that they couldn't walk, were carried and, immediately the ship was full, the embarkation attendant offered the passengers a glass of fortifying wine which caused them, almost immediately, to fall into a sleep that would last the whole voyage.

Olga and Supramati went to their old quarters. For the first time after the separation that was to last for centuries, they found themselves alone, and, stepping out onto the terrace overlooking the garden, they gazed thoughtfully at the magically beautiful landscape, despite the strange light that enveloped it: their souls were filled with serene harmony.

"And so we are united forever, my dear, and I read on your lips that you are completely happy," said Supramati, smiling and holding her close.

"Yes, Supramati, my happiness is complete from the moment I noticed in your eyes that you didn't regret that it was me, and not Nara, your partner. She's so better than me!"

"Nara belongs to Ebramar," Supramati replied, smiling and nodding, "she's his creation, since it was he who formed her soul. As a wise and good gardener, he worked for centuries to bring this flower to full bloom, imparting knowledge to her and raising her up to him, so it's only fair that he should be rewarded for it. Nara remains my faithful friend because she has done so much for me. She opened Ralf Morgan's blind eyes: it was through my love for her that I climbed the rungs of knowledge and love that made me follow her into the labyrinth of the occult sciences and, finally, the desire to become worthy of her gave me the strength and obstinacy needed in our difficult work. The same feeling of love that agitated in the core of her being impelled Nara to follow Ebramar, just as you, Olga, worked and suffered for the love of me.

All is held together and united by love, a golden thread of strength and warmth which attracts and eases the passage through the difficulties of trials, through the exhaustion due to spiritual labour, helping to ascend the steep and narrow stairway of perfect knowledge. Only God, in His infinite mercy, could endow His creatures with an immortal soul and with that gigantic force which already burns with divine flame in an insect or in a bird with fatherly love, making its tiny and imperfect heart beat. Who is endowed with love in its sublime and pure conception keeps a light bulb burning in the darkness and a heat bulb burning in the cold. Those who lack this sacred flame, those who don't know how to love, are renegades and their burden is doubly heavy: darkness clouds their path, they're alone, they wander without the hand of their guide, nothing but animosity or revolt emanates from their heart, and they condemn themselves to a harsh atonement. The great moment has come, Olga: we are spending our last hours on Earth, our ancient cradle. Soon we'll embark on the spaceship that will take us to a world where finally we'll lighten the burden of the body."

"I'll go with you wherever you go and there will be my home and happiness," answered Olga, resting her head on Supramati's shoulder. Will we be able to see the catastrophe?"

"Yes, from far away, through the optical glass of the ship."

They remained silent for a minute. Suddenly, Olga straightened up and asked with visible concern:

"Supramati, and what will be the end of my pets: the white elephant and his pifaupledon? You told me they drank the primal essence to keep them alive? Isn't it cruel to leave them here to their grim death?"

"Calm down," smiled Supramati. "Our faithful friends will follow us, only asleep and in a state where their weight won't be perceived. In a new place they'll wake up and come to greet their mistress and then," he laughed and said: "a few million years later they'll find the fossils of the unknown animal, representative of a completely extinct species. Now come on, my dear. You'll have to endure the last ordeal," he led her to the table next to the sofa and, taking a crystal glass, held it out to Olga. "Accept from my hands the cup of life, which will make you my companion until the end of my carnal life."

"Is it the elixir of life?" Olga asked and, at her husband's positive signal, took a sip.

As expected, Supramati settled Olga on the sofa, covering her with a silk blanket. Then, moving over to the railing, he drifted off into his thoughts. While Olga slept her last dream in the dying earth that gave her the last offering - a virtually immortal life - all over the palace the work was feverish. People with bronze faces hurriedly stuffed into strange sacks of phosphorescent and elastic material, precious archaic objects, used in the last fraternal feast of the magicians. All this luggage was placed in large windowless spaceships, intended for the transport of earthly archives, luggage, passengers, and having only a cabin in the bow for the mechanics and their assistants. When the last cargo was loaded, the workers prostrated themselves, kissed the ground and sang a sad and mournful song. Their strong bodies trembled in convulsions of pain at the moment of the final farewell. With gloom on their faces and a downcast look on their faces, they boarded the transport ships, the entrances were closed tightly and all the ships lined up to await the ships of the Magi.

A few hours later, in a large meadow in the park, all the sages in solemn robes gathered: The Hierophants of the pyramids, the Knights of the Grail, the Magi of the Himalayas, in short, all the sons of eternal light and wisdom. With concentrated thoughts, they all fell to their knees and sang a magnificent hymn that shook the atmosphere. At the same instant there was a strange sound, like the tolling of a powerful and harmonious bell, which shook every fibre of the organism. Suddenly, the dense darkness shook and split in two, giving way to the rays of the sun. Once more the majestic and triumphant sun appeared in all its splendour, covering the inspired faces of the genuflecting multitude with light, and its rays shone upon the white robes, the diamond veils, the silver panoply. A shout of admiration was heard, and the Supreme Hierophant exclaimed, raising his hands:

"Divine Star, bringer of warmth and life, merciful Rá, you have come to say farewell to your loyal servants!"

Happy and enraptured, all looked at that friend of rich and poor, who poured his beneficent rays inexhaustibly over the earth condemned to death, as if he were really saying goodbye to his children and with luminous rays, for the last time as a sign of farewell, illuminated the Areopagus of the wise. Then the sun paled, the darkness deepened still further, and the great generator of life disappeared forever from the earth. A deep silence lasted for about a minute. Finally, everyone got up and made their way to the ships. At the head of the procession were the senior Magi carrying crosses and chalices. On Ebramar's ship were his friends, disciples and all those who were close to him. The entrance was hermetically sealed, the apparatus was lit, providing the usual pure air with an enlivening aroma. In an extended room in the centre of the ship was a reservoir containing a silvery liquid, and from it emanated a bluish mist, which spread throughout the strange ship, giving the impression of a refreshing wind. They all dispersed to the pre-established cabins, but accepting Ebramar's invitation, Supramati with Olga and her two sons, Dakhir with his family and Narayana joined together in his cabin, which was more spacious. In the outside wall there was a rather large hole, closed by a thick convex glass of special composition that allowed them to see at great distances. At a kind of telescope, Ebramar and his friends fixed their gaze on the now distant planet that had once been their cradle. Black smoke continued to emanate from it, gradually taking the form of a broad film that stretched out and away into space.

"The final minute is coming. See how astral topics end up in the archives of the Universe," Ebramar said quietly, squeezing Nara's hand, who was weeping copiously, had leaned her head on his shoulder."

Everyone's eyes clouded over and their hearts clenched, as their gazes remained fixed on the dying little world, enveloped now by a bloodthirsty aura, like a flash, that gradually paled with distance. The spaceships continued their flight at dizzying speed, like a host of shooting stars. The mysterious silver fleet cut through the atmosphere, disappearing into infinity, carrying the past of one world and the future of another...

The end of the series is found in the novel "The Lawgivers".

ROCHESTER

Zibia Gasparetto's Greatest success stories

With more than 20 million titles sold, the author has contributed to the strengthening of spiritualist literature in the publishing market and to the popularization of spirituality. Learn more of the author's successes.

Romances Dictated by the Spirit Lucius

The Life Force

The Truth of each one

Life knows what it does

She trusted in life

Between Love and War

Esmeralda

Thorns of Time

Eternal Bonds

Nothing is by Chance

Nobody is Nobody's

God's Advocate

Tomorrow Belongs to God

Love Won

Unexpected Encounter

On the Edge of Destiny

The Sly One

The Morro of Illusions

Where is Teresa?

Through the Doors of the Heart

When Life chooses

When the Hour Comes

When it is necessary to return

Opening for Life

Not afraid to live

Only love can do it

We Are All Innocent

Everything has its price

It was all worth it

A real love

Overcoming the past

Other success stories by André Luiz Ruiz and Lucius

The Love Never Forgets You Trilogy

The Strength of Kindness

Under the Hands of Mercy

Saying Goodbye to Earth

At the End of the Last Hour

Sculpting Your Destiny

There are Flowers on the Stones

The Crags are made of Sand

Books of Eliana Machado Coelho and Schellida

Hearts without Destiny

The Shine of Truth

The Right to be Happy

The Return

In the Silence of Passions

Strength to Begin Again

The Certainty of Victory

The Conquest of Peace

Lessons Life Offers

Stronger than Ever

No Rules for Loving

A Diary in Time

A Reason to Live

Eliana Machado Coelho and Schellida, Romances that captivate, teach, move and
can change your life!

Romances of Arandi Gomes Texeira and The Count J.W. Rochester

Lancaster County

The Power of Love

The Trial

Cleopatra's Bracelet

The Reincarnation of a Queen

You Are Gods

Books of Marcelo Cezar and Marco Aurelio

Love is for the Strong

The Last Chance

Nothing is as it Seems

Forever With Me

Only God Knows

You Make Tomorrow

A Breath of Tenderness

Books of Vera Kryzhanovskaia and JW Rochester

The Revenge of the Jew

The Nun of the Marriages

The Sorcerer's Daughter

The Flower of the Swamp

The Divine Wrath

The Legend of the Castle of Montignoso

The Death of the Planet

The Night of Saint Bartholomew

The Revenge of the Jew

Blessed are the poor in spirit

Cobra Capella

Dolores

Trilogy of the Kingdom of Shadows

From Heaven to Earth

Episodes from the Life of Tiberius

Infernal Spell

Herculanum

On the Frontier

Naema, the Witch

In the Castle of Scotland (Trilogy 2)

New Era

The Elixir of Long Life

The Pharaoh Mernephtah

The Lawgivers

The Magicians

The Terrible Phantom

Paradise without Adam

Romance of a Queen

Czech Luminaries

Hidden Narratives

The Nun of the Marriages

Books of Elisa Masselli

There is always a reason

Nothing goes unanswered

Life is made of decisions

The Mission of each one

Something more is needed

The Past does not matter

Destiny in his hands

God was with him

When the past does not pass

Just beginning

Books of Vera Lúcia Marinzeck de Carvalhoç and Patricia

Violets in the Window
Living in the Spirit World
The Writer's House
Flight of the Seagull

Vera Lúcia Marinzeck de Carvalho and Antônio Carlos

Love your Enemies
Slave Bernardino
the Rock of Lovers
Rosa, the third fatality
Captives and Freed

Books of Mónica de Castro y Leonel

In spite of everything

Love is not to be trifled with

Face to Face with the Truth

Of My Whole Being

I wish

The Price of Being Different

Twins

Giselle, The Inquisitor's Mistress

Greta

Till Life Do You Part

Impulses of the Heart

Jurema of the Jungle

The Actress

The Force of Destiny

Memories that the Wind Brings

Secrets of the Soul

Feeling in One's Own Skin

World Spiritist Institute

www.ingramcontent.com/pod-product-compliance
Lightning Source LLC
LaVergne TN
LVHW041739060526
838201LV00046B/863